D0389366

REGENT'S PARK

Skating in the Regent's Park. Winter fashion for 1838 and 1839. One of a series of fashion plates issued by Messrs B. Read of Bloomsbury Square. Sussex Place and the Colosseum can be seen in the background as well as the islands on the lake and a refreshment tent

REGENT'S PARK

A Study of the Development of the Area from 1086 to the Present Day

by

ANN SAUNDERS

(Ann Cox-Johnson)

AUGUSTUS M. KELLEY PUBLISHERS

New York

Published in the United States of America
by Augustus M. Kelley Publishers
New York 1969
69-11238

Printed in Great Britain
by Clarke Doble & Brendon Limited Plymouth

CONTENTS

LIST OF ILLUSTRATIONS

PLATES

IN TEXT

Photographs were supplied by courtesy of the following: page 18, a private collector; page 36, The Trustees of the Public Record Office; 71 (above) and 125 (above), the Trustees of the British Museum; 126 (above) and (below), the Greater London Council; all the rest are from the Ashbridge and Local History Collections belonging to the Westminster City Council, whose help the author most gratefully acknowledges.

INTRODUCTION

> This enclosure [Regent's Park], with the new street leading to it from Carlton House, will give a sort of glory to the Regent's government, which will be more felt by remote posterity than the victories of Trafalgar and Waterloo, glorious as these are.[1]

Henry Crabb Robinson made this entry in his diary on 15 February 1818 and the claim is so bold that we are forced to pause and reconsider this familiar corner of London. As we do so, we realise what a curious development it is, quite unlike anything else in the capital. Although it is a residential area, half its 550 acres are left as parkland, freely opened for the enjoyment of all who care to walk there. The terraces which surround it are made up of tall, narrow houses, their interiors identical with those in any other eighteenth-century town dwelling, but their façades are iced with stucco and designed to look like palaces. The plan of the Park is essentially a pair of eccentric circles instead of the gridiron pattern of streets on which London had developed throughout the eighteenth century. Its creation by John Nash marks the end of a great tradition in English architecture and the beginning of something quite new.

But Regent's Park had a history which can be traced back through seven centuries before Nash and his patron, the Prince Regent, laid it out at the beginning of the nineteenth century as the first of the improvements they had planned for London. Originally, it was a tiny part of the Middlesex Forest—'a great forest with wooded glades and lairs of wild beasts, deer both red and fallow, wild bulls and boars.'[2] Then its acres were parcelled out between the manors of Tyburn and Rugemere, now parts of St Marylebone and St Pancras; the lion's share lay in Tyburn which the Abbess of Barking held direct from the Crown. For nearly 500 years after the Norman Conquest, the local pigs fed on its acorns, and throughout these years, the village of Tyburn existed as something quite separate from London Town three miles away, its main link with the city being the provision of water for the citizens from the stream, the Tyburn, which gave its name to the manor and village.

At the Dissolution of the Monasteries, Henry VIII acquired the manor and enclosed a hunting park in the north-east, which he called Marylebone Park. It was used as such until the Civil War when it was mortgaged by Charles I. In 1649 it was sequestered with the rest of the Crown lands and was speedily disparked by the men who purchased it. When Charles II regained his throne, the Park remained as farmland, supplying the growing capital with dairy produce. During the eighteenth century, Marylebone changed from a country village a bare hour's walk from London to a newly built estate on the outskirts of the city so that, when the farming leases ran out in 1811, Marylebone Park was ripe for development. Within two decades, it had become the Regent's Park, London's new West End, and the way was cleared for the city to continue its expansion northwards.

The story of the Park and its environs is worth studying in its relationship to national history as well as the growth of London. If proximity to the capital meant that Marylebone, as village, parish or borough, existed to serve London's needs, whether they were for water, farm produce or building land, then the Park's association with the Crown meant that in times of change its fate was often a microcosm of events in the whole kingdom. It was the Dissolution of the Monasteries that created the Park and the turmoil of the Civil War that destroyed it, felling its trees and turning the forest into farmland. Its prolonged continuance as such was due to the inadequate administration of the Crown lands; its emergence as the Regent's Park development was due as much to the administrative reforms of a civil servant, John Fordyce, as to the imaginative patronage of the Prince Regent or the architectural genius of John Nash. Though the history of the Park loses most of its excitement once Nash's work was complete, its later history reflects faithfully some of the changes in social conditions since 1830, and its redevelopment since the Second World War has been dramatic.

The story of Regent's Park is simply the story of one small area of land, near to the capital and belonging to the Crown. It is only a detail in the history of England and, like most details, cannot be understood properly unless it is related to the history of the whole kingdom, but it is a story worth telling because of its dual association and because a detail can sometimes be grasped when the entire account is too vast to be comprehended. The dilemmas and struggles of a single man, the uses to which a particular field has been put, can be understood directly and so give a new reality to the whole by their own urgency. Local history has a double purpose, to illumine national history by making it more comprehensible and immediate, and to give a deeper meaning and interest to familiar surroundings by linking the present with the past, the particular with the whole.

CHAPTER 1

THE FORMATION OF MARYLEBONE PARK

THE MANOR OF TYBURN

On the northern slopes of the Thames valley, three miles westward from St Paul's Cathedral, lies the parish of St Marylebone.[1] It covers 1,500 acres and is shaped like a parallelogram with a mile of Oxford Street for its base and two miles of the Edgware Road for its western side; its northern and eastern boundaries, though less well defined, are roughly parallel with the first pair. The ground, undulating slightly, rises slowly to the north, and beyond are the heights of Hampstead, Highgate and Harrow.

Geologically, the parish is divided in half along a line west to east, virtually where the Marylebone Road runs today; to the north the subsoil is heavy London clay but southwards the clay is covered by a layer of gravel known as the Taplow Terrace. In early times this meant that, while the northern half was heavily wooded, hard to drain and deficient in springs of water near to the surface, the southern half was covered by light vegetation more easily cleared with primitive tools, could be drained readily, and was provided with springs of fresh water. The southern half was therefore well suited to settlement and cultivation, while the northern was scarcely habitable until there were tools strong enough to hack down the trees and a piped water supply to make up for natural deficiencies.

Marylebone is again divided, this time from north to south, by the Tyburn stream[2] which runs down from Hampstead, meanders through the parish, and at last, splitting into two separate streamlets, joins the Thames at Westminster and Vauxhall. Both banks of the stream and all the lands eastward formed the manor of Tyburn; westward as far as the Edgware Road lay the manor of Lilleston or Lisson. The stream was wholly in Tyburn to which it gave its name; it did not form a boundary between the manors.

The first village of Tyburn grew up in the valley where the stream crossed Oxford Street. Since Oxford Street and Watling Street (Edgware Road) were the main Roman roads from London to the west and north-west, the little village was well linked to the capital. Both village and manor belonged to the Abbey of Barking, a house of nuns in Essex founded about AD 666 by St Erkenwald, Bishop of London, for his sister, St Ethelburga, who was the first abbess. The convent was destroyed by the Danes but refounded by King Edgar, and it was there that William of Normandy stayed soon after the Conquest. During his sojourn, he issued a charter[3] granting to the abbess 'his peace and love and all her rights within and without burh, as fully as any abbess in that monastery of St Mary had them in the time of King Edward'. Tyburn, though not mentioned by name, was included, for Domesday Book, compiled in 1086, describes the manor as belonging to the convent. From the entry we can deduce that the original local community consisted of eight families, or about forty people farming perhaps 600 acres.[4]

If it is reasonable to assume that the arable land lay on flat ground close to the village and that the pasture was further away, then ploughed fields probably extended over what is now Cavendish Square and cattle grazed on the sites of Wigmore Street and Portman Square, whilst the village pigs rootled northwards under the oaks and beeches that became Marylebone Park. Although the Domesday Survey for Middlesex omits all mention of churches, archaeological evidence indicates that a church, which we know from later records to have been dedicated to St John, stood from very early times near the east bank of the stream on a site where the Dolcis shoe shop and the Stratford Court Hotel now stand. The churchyard was beside it, for quantities of bones have been exhumed there at intervals.[5]

The Abbess of Barking was certainly a non-resident owner of the manor, and by the middle of the twelfth century the whole manor of Tyburn had been leased to the de Sanford family for an annual rent of thirty shillings, which the convent continued to receive until the Dissolution of the Monasteries.[6] The de Sanfords were influential people and took an interest in the property although they did not reside there. Gilbert de Sanford, who was cupbearer to Queen Eleanor at her coronation, granted land in 1237 to the citizens of London on which to build a water conduit to supply the city.[7] His daughter Alice married Robert de Vere, Earl of Oxford, and having inherited the manor when her father died in about 1250, built a manor house with a garden and home farm round it some time before 1279.[8]

During the years that followed, the village centre shifted northwards from the church to the manor house until in 1400 a new church, dedicated to Our Lady, was built opposite the manor with the consent of the Bishop of London. The villagers told the bishop that the old church 'was in too lonely a place' and that 'on account of the snares and plunderings of robbers, the books, vestments, images, bells, and other ornaments cannot be preserved as they should be, nor divine service celebrated as is fitting'.[9] There is no reason to disbelieve the villagers' statement—in 1375, William Danyell confessed to four robberies with violence 'at dusk by Tyburn',[10] and the gallows had been set up at the crossing of the Edgware Road and Oxford Street in 1388—but their desire for a peaceful life was surely reinforced by the steady opening-up of the lands to the north as woodland became pasture or arable land. It seems more likely that the church was moved primarily to suit the convenience of the parishioners, than that it was rebuilt to protect the plate and bells, and that the whole village followed these valuables. The rededication and the proximity of the church to the stream gave a new name—

Marybourne or Marybone—to the village, meaning Mary's church by the burn.[11]

But long before the church was rebuilt Alice de Vere had died, and in 1312 the manor became the property of her grandson, John de Warrenne, Earl of Surrey and Sussex. He died without issue in 1345 and his estates passed to his nephew, Richard, Earl of Arundel, and from him to his son, another Richard, and eventually in 1415 Tyburn was divided between the second Richard's three daughters, Elizabeth, Duchess of Norfolk, Jean, Countess of Abergavenny, and Margaret, wife to Sir Roland Lenthall. The descendants of these three ladies continued to assert their claims to the land,[12] but before the end of the century Marylebone had a new resident lord of the manor, a senior member of Henry VII's new civil service called Thomas Hobson.

Hobson was a man of obscure birth[13] but considerable administrative ability. He was one of the seven auditors of the Exchequer; until 1707 he was auditor to the Duchy of Cornwall and thereafter to the Duchy of Lancaster. On the death of the Lady Margaret, Countess of Richmond and mother of Henry VII, he was made auditor of her estate and was rewarded with the keepership of Burne Park in Lincolnshire.[14] In short, he was a trusted senior official, holding positions of influence and financial advantage. He also turned his talents to acquiring a fine estate for himself, for when they became available he bought up portions of the manor of Marybone.

During the 1490s, Sir Reginald Bray, Chancellor of the Exchequer and Hobson's superior, exchanged various lands, some in Tyburn among them, with George Neville, heir to the Earl and Countess of Abergavenny, and bought other property in the London area from Thomas Styllington, Bishop of Bath and Wells.[15] He paid Styllington £133 6s 8d and on 4 June 1499 he sold all that was in Marybone to Thomas Hobson for 400 marks or £266 13s 4d—a nice profit. By this and other smaller purchases, Hobson had acquired the greater part of the manor before his death on 6 September 1511.

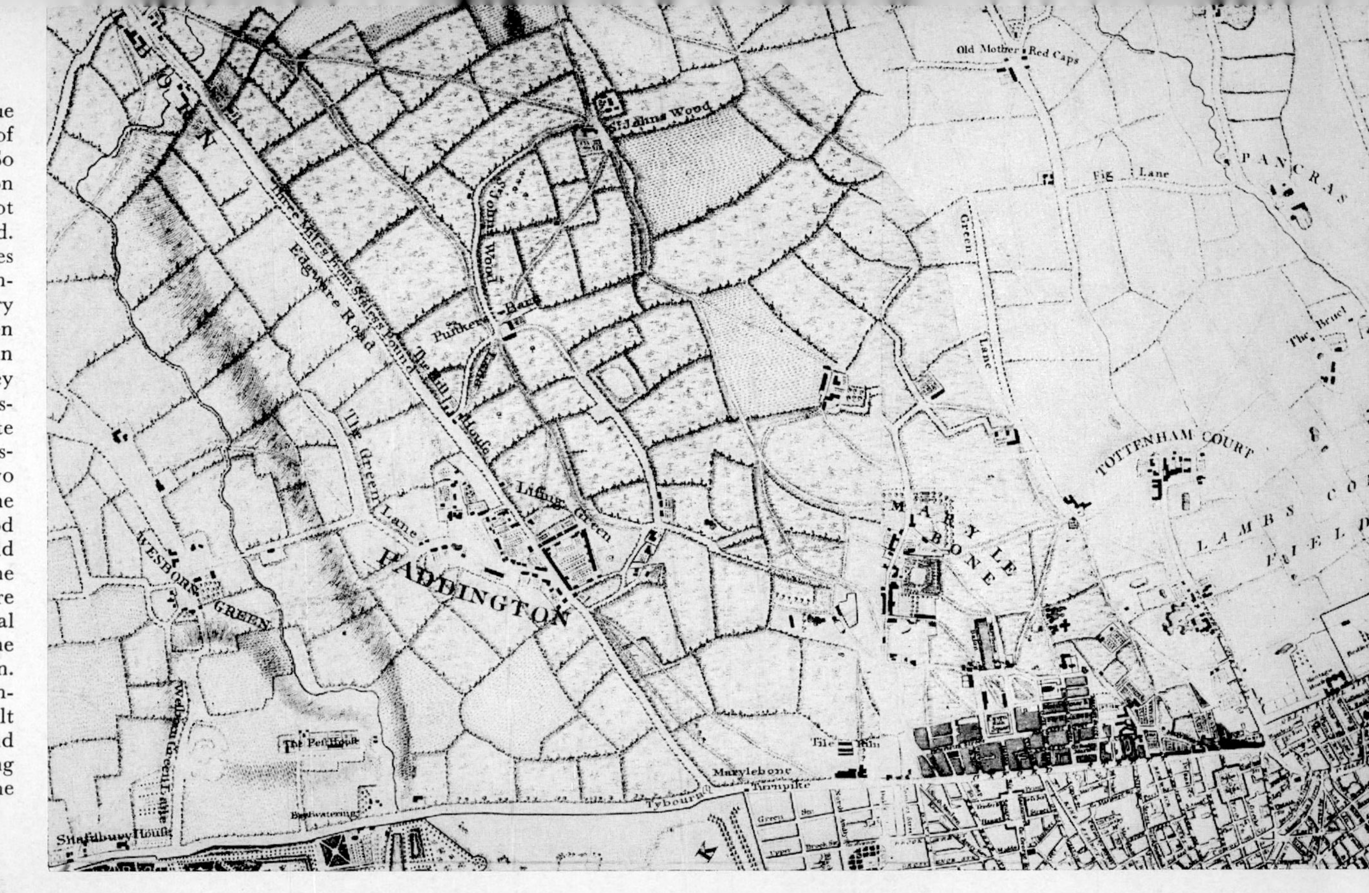

Page 17: John Rocque issued his map of London in 1746. So detailed a survey on such a scale had not before been attempted. The field boundaries were, however, inserted in an arbitrary manner as can be seen if compared with an exact local survey such as Crew's (Illustration, p 36). Note the prevalence of pasture land—the two farms at Marylebone and St John's Wood have a single cornfield each. Marylebone Park's boundaries are unmarked. The formal walks of Marylebone Gardens can be seen. Three sides of Cavendish Square are built up and the Portland estate is developing northwards across the fields

Page 18: The Manor House, St Marylebone. Water colour by J. Ellwood. There was a manor house on this site by 1279 but the building shown here was probably begun by the elder Thomas Hobson about 1500 and enlarged by later owners, the Forsetts and the Austens. In 1703, it became a school for young gentlemen under the headmasterships of Mr De la Place and the Rev Dr J. Fountayne, his son-in-law; the latter can be seen in the painting, surrounded by his boys who are playing a variety of games. The school was closed and the manor house demolished in 1791; a garage now covers the site

In his will,[16] he bequeathed his soul to God and asked that his body should be buried in St Botulph's Aldersgate, to which he left £2 9s 8d. He bequeathed 6s 8d to the 'high aulter of Marybone' and then, having completed his spiritual benefactions, he turned to temporal matters. The manor of Marybone with 'all the messuages, lands, medowes and pasture lying in Marybone, Lilleston, Westbourne, Charyng, and Eye [Hyde]' was to belong to his wife Joan for her lifetime, thereafter passing to their son Richard; she was adjured to 'sell noo woods but that she shall spend reasonably w^t^out any wast' and to do any feudal service 'the which must be made' to the earls of Surrey, Derby and Abergavenny for the land which had been bought from each. If Richard died without a child, then his executors were to sell the manor,

> the which hath cost me in purchase and in building about a thousand pounds and bistowe the money as shall advise them . . . If Elizabeth my daughter be married and have yssue then I will that hir husband and she have the said manor better chepe by vi^c^ pounds than any man will geve for them.

Hobson's high valuation of his estate suggests that he may have rebuilt the manor house, for the building shown in eighteenth-century water-colours is not medieval but a gabled red-brick dwelling. Hobson was clearly the most important man in the parish—the first real lord of the manor that Marylebone had ever had.

On his death, the wardship of his son Richard was granted to John Blenerhaysett, who owned land nearby in Lilleston. The boy was already fourteen, and died in 1522 aged only twenty-four leaving a son, two-year-old Thomas, and a young wife, Petronilla, who was pregnant again.[17] Little Thomas became the ward of William Hollys[18] and the child Petronilla was carrying proved to be a girl, Margaret, so there was no other claim to young Thomas' lands. The village continued its quiet existence, the manor house stood surrounded by its gardens, orchards and dovecote; the home farm was in the hands of Richard Jacquett and the village windmill was managed by Thomas Holte. The first signs of industry began with the clay and gravel workings which had been opened just to the north of the manor house, on the borders of land that was soon to become Marylebone Park; these William Hollys reserved for himself.[19] The gravel was used for roads and the clay for brick-making; both concerns continued to be active until the nineteenth century. Thomas grew older and, deciding to become a merchant, went over to Brittany, probably as apprentice to Edward Cockerell, citizen and grocer of London and son-in-law to Thomas Huttoft, the Customer of Southampton.

MARYLEBONE PARK

Suddenly, the Dissolution of the Monasteries changed the whole history of the parish. Almost overnight, the hamlet of Marylebone became the gateway to the nearest royal hunting preserve to London and the manor house was transformed into a king's resting-place.

We are not concerned with the religious or political effects of the king's actions, all-important though they were, but we must remember that his appropriation of the lands of the monasteries resulted in the biggest transference of real estate ever to have taken place in this country except at the time of the Norman Conquest. Inspectors travelled all over England compiling the record of church revenues known as *Valor Ecclesiasticus*, and in 1536 the Court of the Augmentations of the Revenues of the Crown was set up to deal with this enormous increase in royal wealth.[20] The files of the court are arranged under the names of those who bought church lands from the king, for he neither kept them nor gave them away, and the bulk of some of the files is considerable.

The only church revenue at Tyburn was the thirty shillings a year due to the Abbess of Barking, and this Henry appropriated,[21] but he coveted the land itself as well. Since the abbey held the land in chief from the Crown, the claim was not unreasonable, but he needed to buy up Thomas Hobson's interest in it. The king was growing old. He no longer wished to ride long distances before he could enjoy his hunting. He had his parks at Hampton and Nonsuch, and there was Hyde Park near Whitehall but another to the north, within easy reach of Whitehall by horse or litter, was desirable. There was a fine forest of trees beyond Marylebone village, so the king decided to acquire the whole manor of Tyburn and to empark as much of it as pleased him.

The first surviving indication of the king's intentions is a survey with valuations made in June 1538 by Geoffrey Chamber, Surveyor and Receiver-General, of the land which the king wished to possess.[22] The manor house with its orchards, gardens and surrounding meadows—Welmedow, Swanmedow and Dofehousemedow—were worth £5 1s 8d a year; all the valuations given were annual. The home farm, where Richard Jacquett's lease was to run till Thomas came of age, was worth £10 6s 8d, and Thomas Holte's windmill[23] was valued at £1. The area which the king selected for his hunting park covered a total of 554 acres. It was a curious shape, almost circular, and there seems to be no good reason for this rough regularity, which bears no relation to any of the known manoral boundaries nor to any observable local physical feature. Indeed it bisected the manor of Tyburn, cutting off a fragment to the north at what is now Barrow Hill. Perhaps a map was made on which Geoffrey Chamber, or even the king himself, drew a rough circle and declared it to be Marylebone Park. An entry in Cromwell's accounts for 6 July 1539 for the payment of 6s 8d to the keepers of Marylebone Park 'by my Lord's command' suggests that the king may have inspected his new possession personally, and possibly the boundaries were determined then.[24] We do not know; we can only conjecture.

On the eastern side of the park there were 315 acres of pasture and woodland that had belonged to Hobson and had been worked by his tenants, Thomas Osborne, Richard Styles, Richard

Jacquett and his son Thomas. The woods were valued at twenty pence the acre and the pasture at fourteen pence, excepting for twelve acres near the Tyburn which were worth five shillings apiece and were presumably very fertile. To the west, 252 acres altogether were taken from the Prior of St John of Jerusalem, from William Portman, from the Master and Fellows of Eton College, and from the Masters and Prebends of Rugemere, Tottenham Court and St Giles. There were apparently no buildings worth mentioning in the park and the land enclosed was either woodland or pasture. The whole area was valued at £92 12s 3d a year, of which land worth £70 15s 2d was to be emparked, while the manor house and home farm were intended to provide accommodation and provender for the king when he wished to hunt, and for whomsoever he might appoint as Keeper of the Park. The land taken from Hobson was worth an annual £40 0s 7d and owing on it were £3 6s 8d due to the Duke of Norfolk and £1 10s to the Abbess of Barking. The debt to the abbess could be conveniently ignored, and the duke's interests were bought out for £40.[25] Since the land in Rugemere was held from St Paul's and Henry did not wish to offend the cathedral clergy, the master and preband and their tenant were given proper compensation and a private Act was passed to secure it for them.[26] Thomas Bennett, the Prebendary, was given the rectory of Throwleigh in Kent, and the farmer, John Palmer, was given land nearby at Belsize in Hampstead. Eton was paid £40 6s[27] and accounts were settled with William Portman and the Prior of St John, though the terms are uncertain as only a fragment of the document remains.[28] Thomas Leighe was paid £35 'to the use of the Master and brethren of Burton Lazar for ten acres of pasture, parcel of the late hospital of St Giles . . . enclosed in Marylebone Park.'[29]

We know nothing of Thomas Hobson's reaction to the king's assumption of his lands. Had he objected, there was nothing he could have done about it. He was by this time about eighteen years old and both he and his guardian must have known what was happening. On 17 April 1539, Henry Huttoft, the Customer of Southampton who was father-in-law to Edward Cockerell and whose grand-daughter Thomas later married, wrote to the Secretary of State, Thomas Cromwell, to say that he would send for young Thomas to return from Brittany with speed and 'doubted not he would agree' to the king's demands.[30]

The compensation offered for Marylebone was good. Thomas sold the whole manor to the king and received in return several houses in Southampton and the manor of Colbury nearby, as well as considerable property on the Isle of Wight where he was granted Ningwood, Shalcombe, Wellow and Wilmingham and the grange at Hamsted. All these lands had belonged to Quarr Abbey or Christchurch Priory. The transactions passed through the Court of Augmentations;[31] Hobson was paid £203 15s 10d for his Marylebone interests and bought £261 11s 11d worth of land. He settled in the Isle of Wight, married Barbara Huttoft, begot a family, changed his name to Hopson and throve, dying at last in 1559.

The king granted the manor of Tyburn to Sir Anthony Denny, a Privy Councillor and Keeper of Westminster Palace, making him Keeper of Marylebone Park as well.[32] Denny probably stayed at the manor house from time to time and he may well have enlarged or at least redecorated it. A drawing made by Michael Angelo Rooker about 1780 shows some fine carved panelling and balustrading of an earlier date, fit to decorate a palace.[33] No records of expenditure survive, however, and it is extremely doubtful whether Henry ever stayed there himself. Denny certainly let part or all of it, for on 13 January 1544 Lady Wentworth, wife of Sir Nicholas, Governor of Calais, wrote asking for a room for herself and stabling for her horse at Maribourne Place, adding that she hoped to become 'sole tenant to good Mr Denny'.[34]

From its inception, the Park was well looked after. A ring mound was thrown up round the boundary to keep deer in and poachers out and lodges were built for the gamekeepers. Thomas

Bridges and Thomas Mervyn were appointed in 1540 at salaries of 4d a day, or £3 0s 10d. a year.[35] In 1541 they were replaced by John Free and Andrew Wedon, and in 1546 a vermin-catcher Richard Sawforde, was appointed at the same wage. About 1550 John Free was succeeded by Thomas Savage, who was also granted the office of Yeoman of the Crown for life.

Henry VIII died on 28 January 1547, unaware—or determined not to believe—that death could treat him like any other man, until Sir Anthony—'good Mr Denny'—warned the monarch of his approaching end and advised him to make his peace with God. Denny was rewarded for his courage with a pair of gloves, £300 and a place on Edward VI's council of advisors. He outlived his master by two years and the manor reverted to the Crown.

Edward inherited his father's love of hunting and had a fence set up on top of the ring mound, the better to guard his deer.[36] The accounts for this work are the first record of royal expenditure on the estate. Thirteen loads of railing and paling were brought from Westminster and a carpenter and his man spent eighteen days erecting the fence. The pair were paid 1s 8d a day and used 3,000 elevenpenny nails and 'two hundred of doble tennepenny nailes'. Some work must have been carried out earlier, for we find the entry:

> Item for fyve score loade of sandie gravell from Knyghtsbrydge to Marybone pke, for to overspred the brydge and waies that were made laste yere wt. clay gravell wch yf yt had not bene nowe donne would have coste vi tymes the charge that yt dothe noew at xd. pr. casting & carying every lode.

A trench was dug to keep the Tyburn away from a house, probably belonging to a gamekeeper, and a 'greate grate of tymbre worke'—possibly a sluice-gate to dam the water in time of drought—was repaired. In the autumn of 1552 more courses and trenches were dug 'for the conveyinge the water into two ponds which yf it hadd nott ben don wode have byn the dethe of many dere.'[37] These ponds must have been on the west side of the Park where the Tyburn runs; making them was an expensive business for they were lined with brick at a cost of £15 15s. In all, some £20 11s was spent. Speed's and Saxton's maps, drawn some fifty years later, show the palings clearly; the Park was private property, on which a poacher or a man searching for firewood must venture at his peril.

A much larger sum than £20 11s was spent on entertainments in the Park during the summer of 1551 when an embassy from Henri II of France, headed by the Maréschal de Saint André, arrived in England to present the Order of St Michael to the young king. Most elaborate revels and hunting parties were arranged and on the account rolls of Sir Thomas Carwardine, Master of the Tentes and Revells, there is an entry for £433 6s 8d spent on 'banketyne howses, standings and other charges att Hidde and Marybone pks against the Marchall Saint Andrewes comyng thether.'[38]

Edward died during a summer storm on the night of 6 July 1553 and, after the pitiful interlude of Lady Jane Grey's reign, was succeeded by his sister, Mary Tudor. On 8 November she confirmed a grant of lands to Sir Henry Sydney made on the previous 23 May by her brother; one of the properties was the manor and manor house of Tyburn.[39] The Park was exempted from the grant, which was for thirty-five years at a rent of £16 11s 8d. Sydney was only a year older than Edward VI and the two youths were friends. The Duke of Northumberland, Lady Jane Grey's father-in-law, married his daughter Mary to Henry Sydney, but the young man supported the duke for one day only and then gave his allegiance to Mary Tudor, for which, as a reward, he was confirmed in his lands which included Marylebone.

On 13 January 1554 the queen granted Thomas Savage a Keepership of the Park for life in place of John Free, who had died. The wages remained at 4d a day but permission was added to keep twelve cows, one bull, four geldings and two foals.[40] A lodge must have been built in the Park, probably on the southern

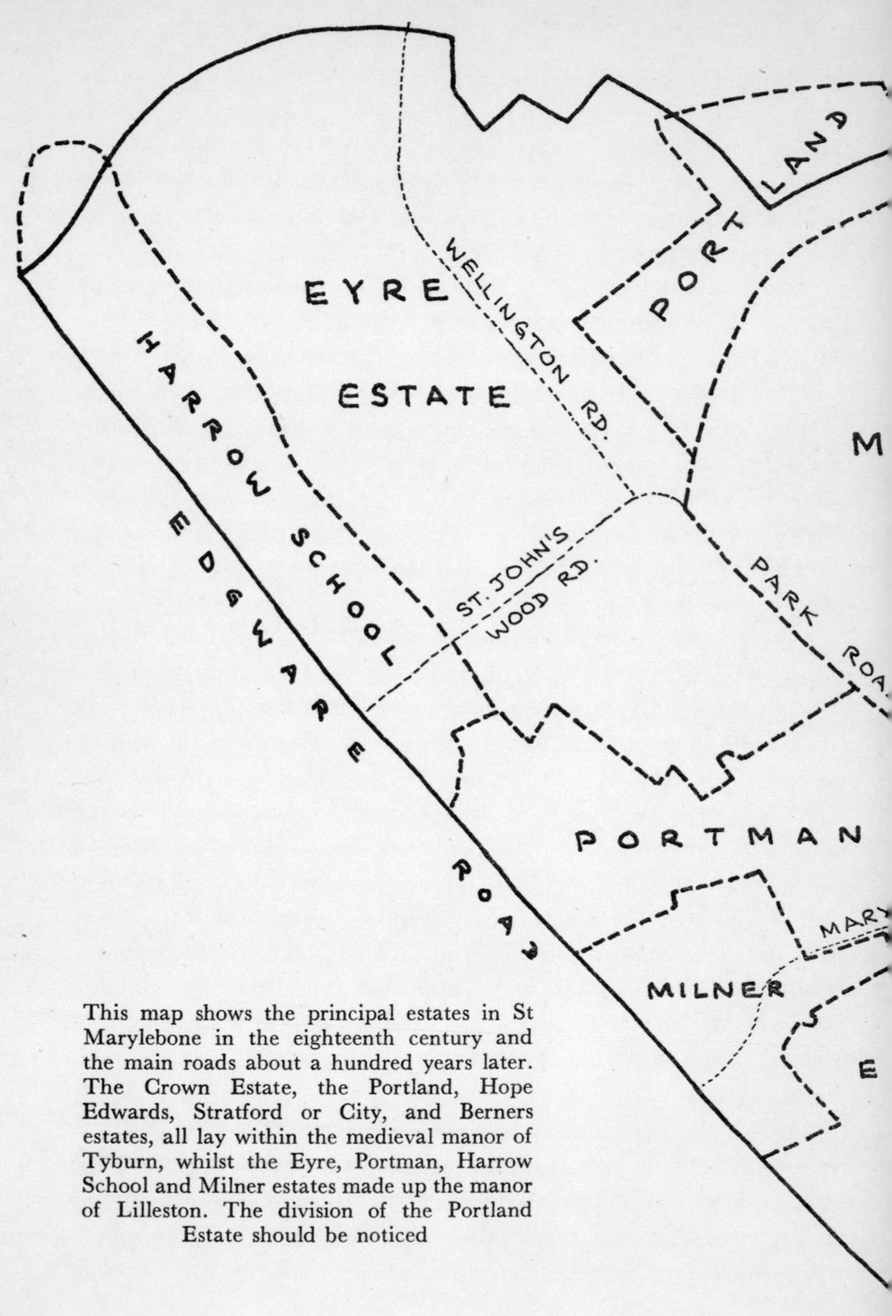

This map shows the principal estates in St Marylebone in the eighteenth century and the main roads about a hundred years later. The Crown Estate, the Portland, Hope Edwards, Stratford or City, and Berners estates, all lay within the medieval manor of Tyburn, whilst the Eyre, Portman, Harrow School and Milner estates made up the manor of Lilleston. The division of the Portland Estate should be noticed

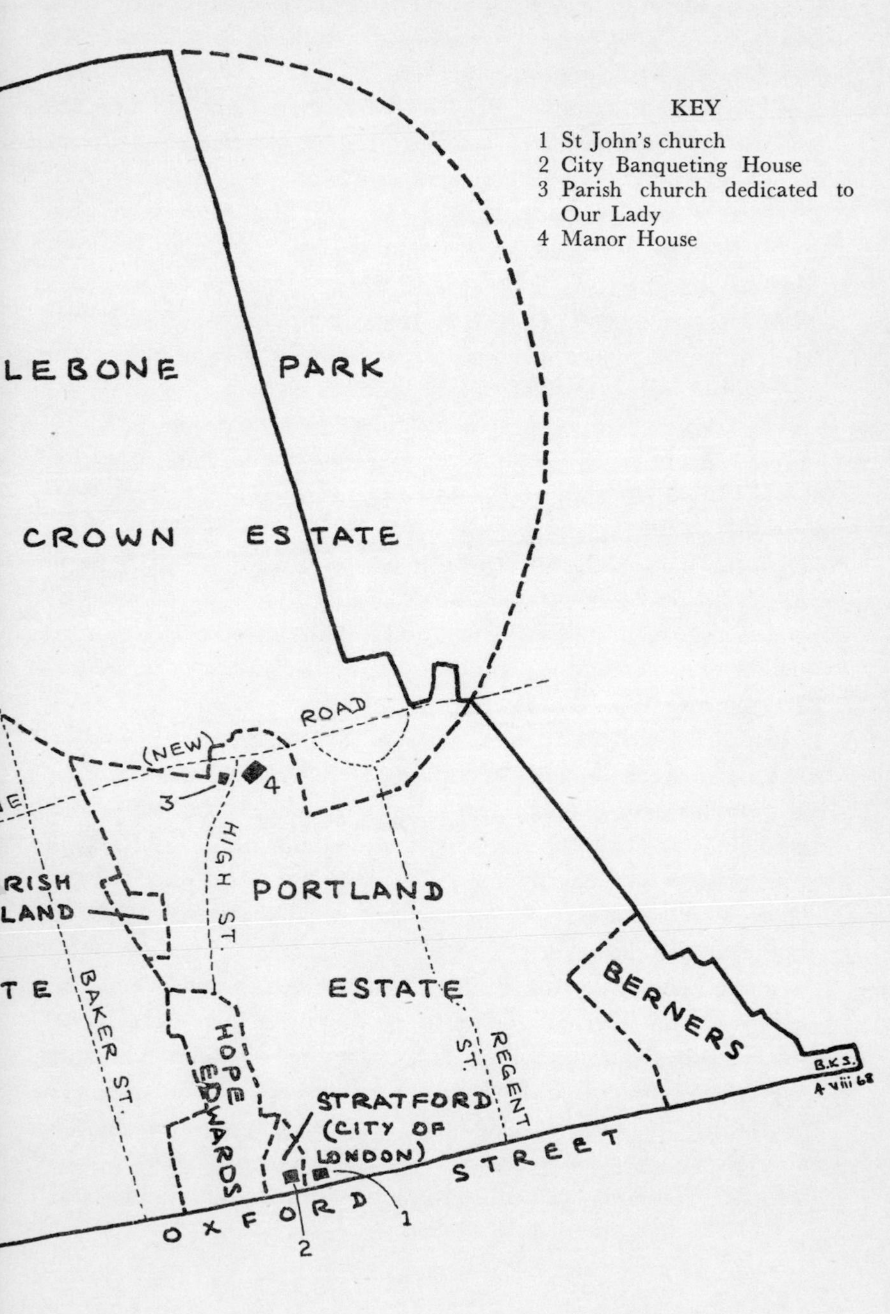
KEY
1 St John's church
2 City Banqueting House
3 Parish church dedicated to Our Lady
4 Manor House
LEBONE
PARK
CROWN
ESTATE
(NEW)
ROAD
3
4
RISH
LAND
HIGH ST.
PORTLAND
TE
ESTATE
BAKER ST.
HOPE
EDWARDS
STRATFORD
(CITY OF
LONDON)
REGENT ST.
BERNERS
OXFORD
STREET
1
2
B.K.S.
4 viii 68

boundary near to Marylebone village, which by this time had become a sizeable hamlet of sixty-six households with some 400 inhabitants. Three months later on 20 April, Andrew Wedon, park keeper and yeoman, was included in the general pardon issued to all who had been accused and cleared of complicity in Sir Thomas Wyatt's rebellion against the queen.[41] In the indictment of Wyatt's supporter, Sir Nicholas Throckmorton, it was stated that he marched on London by way of Brentford and Marylebone Park. If Wedon had opened the gates to give any rebel an easier road, he might easily have been suspected of treason. Throckmorton was acquitted and Wedon's name cleared; he retained his post until his death in 1560.

The keepers seem to have been a turbulent pair, for in the same month Savage was in trouble for assaulting Arthur Stourton, the Royal Gamemaster and Keeper of Westminster Palace.[42] On the morning of 16 April 1554 Stourton, with three servants, rode across the Park to Barrow Hill to fetch brushwood for the Palace and on his return met Savage; he told him that a new stand was needed for the hunting parties and questioned the location of the old one. Wedon joined Savage and they all walked to the gate that led into Marylebone village, where Stourton noticed that the crossbar was broken. Savage said it was no business of his and Stourton replied 'It is partly negligence in you to suffer the Queen's gate spoiled', and asked why Savage did not report the damage. Savage growled out 'I know your mind; you would have your own men to be keepers' and Stourton told him to report to the palace. This he did not do but sent Wedon and another man in his place.

A week later Stourton returned to the Park and this time he and his servant carried crossbows. As they went towards Barrow Hill, Savage came out of his lodge carrying a bill or pike and said 'Mr Stourton, whither walk you? It is past good manners to come by the keeper's lodge and not to say "good morning" '. Stourton said he would do as he liked, to which Savage replied that he would knock the crossbow out of his hands and lay him on the ground, adding 'other naughty words' so that Stourton called him a villain and said he was not afraid though his arrows were still in his quiver. Savage told him not to ride through the Park any more but Stourton said it was his duty and he would come as was needed, at which the gamekeeper shouted: 'If thou come here tomorrow, thou shalt well prove I will keep promise', and he called Stourton a villain and a boy. John Simpson, a labourer who was sitting in a thicket nearby, heard Savage say he would pull Stourton's ears. Then Savage went into his lodge and Stourton rode on to Barrow Hill and collected the brushwood.

When Stourton returned next day with his brother-in-law and several servants, Savage came out of his lodge with his bow at the ready and shouted 'By God's Blood, are ye come? God's Blood, have at thee!' One of the servants called out 'Hold thy hand in the Queen's name! Here is no body that comes to do thee any hurt!', but Savage loosed two arrows, one of which lodged in somebody's coat and the other narrowly missed Stourton's leg. A boy who was with Stourton ran in and cut at the bow string, missed, was shot at, and then managed to sever it, whilst another servant, Burbridge, hit Savage on the head so that he fell down yelling he was slain. They picked him up, saying to him 'some English words' whereupon he offered them all a good breakfast, but Stourton told him to put on his jerkin and come and answer to the Queen for such behaviour. The whole party set out, but when they reached St James's Palace, Savage took refuge in the chapel, eventually bringing an action in the Star Chamber against Stourton for assault. Most unfortunately, Savage's evidence and the verdict are missing but probably the pair were bound over to keep the peace, for they both retained their offices. One would like to know more—not only the verdict, but why John Simpson was sitting in the thicket and what the 'English words' were that they exchanged.

Later in 1554, the very existence of the Park was threatened by the queen's policy of economic retrenchment, for the Treasury was empty at Edward's death in spite of all the wealth of the Church that had been poured into it. On 16 September, Mary, who had just been married to Philip of Spain, decided with her Privy Council 'to desolve the Parkes of Maribone and Hyde and having bestowed the dere and pale of the same to their Maiestie's use, upon a due surveye of the groundes of the saide Parkes so to distribute the parcelles thereof to the inhabitantes dwelling thereaboutes, as may be mooste to their Highnes' advauncement and commoditie of their loving subiectes'.[43] Nothing came of this particular suggested economy; the survey was never made nor were the parks sold.

On 17 November 1558, the poor queen died, abandoned by her husband and knowing she must be succeeded by a sister whose mother had supplanted her own and whose faith would mean a second disestablishment of the Catholic Church. Elizabeth was proclaimed queen and gave to the royal parks the care that might have been expected from a child of Henry VIII. On 17 December 1560, Thomas Savage was confirmed in his office of Keeper of the Park and all the buildings therein. Wedon had died earlier that year on 12 March and the two offices were now united in one man. The wages remained unchanged but Savage was granted pasture for more animals, thirty cartloads of hay in winter and twenty cartloads of fallen brushwood. It must have been quite a comfortable smallholding. He was the last working Keeper of the Park, for when he died in 1563 or 1564 he was succeeded by Sir Edward Cary of Berkhamstead,[44] a groom of the Privy Chamber and Master of the Jewel Office; Cary received a salary of 8d a day but the real work was done by a gamekeeper called John Haynes. The Keepership remained with Sir Edward's family through four generations.

During 1567, an immense amount of work was undertaken in and around the Park.[45] John Fothergill, the Woodward for Middlesex, was allotted £66 13s 4d by Nicholas Holbourne, the Deputy Receiver for the county. This sum he increased to £70 19s 10d by the sale of timber, the bark going to a tanner in Clerkenwell at 4d a trunk. This suggests that some of the trees were oaks, since it is oak bark that is used for tanning. The money was spent 'in the repayringe & amendinge of the lodges, cowrses, parrocke [park] pales, posts, and rayles,' and the work went on till October 1568. The fence was repaired and painted with pitch by John Stowe the paler, whilst Thomas Stafforde, the sawyer, and Thomas Parke, the carpenter, repaired the bridge over the Tyburn with 900 'planck and joysts'. The necessary timber was felled in St John's Wood, which had recently been let to Sir Thomas Wade, the Governor of the Tower of London. Robert Westfelde, the smith, made new locks and hinges for the ordinary gates and 'two plate locks with their halves for the two great gates'; these would have been the main gates out into Marylebone town. Robert Carter reglazed the windows of the lodge where John Haynes and his assistants lived, and the buildings were retiled. The river banks were neatened and a new quickset hedge made along them. The carpenters were paid by the day, 11d or 1s, the sawyer at 1s 8d the hundred planks, and the ditchers at 1s the rod.

The Park must have been a well-kept place when the work was completed with the fencing in good order and the gates working properly. A survey made in 1591 by William Necton, of the manor of Tottenhall [Tottenham Court] shows the stout edge-to-edge fence that surrounded the Park and a pair of deer within the enclosure.[46] Two ways into the Park are marked, very much where Park Square and Gloucester Gate enter it now, and a lane runs almost along the line of Albany Street. Four closes of pasture land are marked as held by Sergeant Haynes, the gamekeeper. He was not employed, nor were the fences erected, for nothing, for there were regular cases at the Middlesex Sessions of men arrested by him and his fellow wardens for poaching the deer. The land around the Park was dangerous too, for there were bodies found and men robbed in the lonely fields to the west of the Park and in the alleyways off Marylebone High Street.[47]

Sir Robert Naunton in his *Fragmenta Regalia* tells of a duel between the Earl of Essex and Sir Charles Blount that took place near the Park; the story is best given in his own words.[48]

> Sir Charles Blunt had the good fortune to run one day very wel at Tilt, and the Queene was therewith so well pleased that she sent him in token of her favor a Queene at Chesse in hold [gold?], richly enamelled, which his servants had the next day fastened unto his arme with a crymson Ribband, which my Lord of Essex, as he passed through the Privy Chamber, espying with his cloake cast under his Arme, the better to command it to the view, enquired what it was, and for what cause there fixed. Sir Foulk Grevile tould him that it was the Queene's favour, which the day before and next after the Tilting, she had sent him; whereat my Lord of Essex in a kind of emulation and as though he would have limited her favour said now I perceive every foole must have a favour: This bitter and publique affront came to Sir Charles Blunt's eare, at which he sent him the chalenge which was accepted by my Lord and they met neare Marybone Park, where my Lord was hurt in the Thigh and disarmed: the Queene missing of the men was very curious to learne the truth but at last it was whispered out, she sware by God's death it was fit some one or other should take him downe and teach him better manners, otherwise there would be no rule with him.

The encounter took place during 1587; thereafter the young men were firm friends.

The queen herself made good use of the Park. A new standing was erected to watch the hunting in 1582 when the Duke of Anjou came to pay court to her,[49] and even at the very end of her reign, when she was no longer able to join in the sport herself, she used the Park to provide entertainment for guests such as the Russian ambassadors who came to England in 1601.[50] They rode through London to Marylebone on 3 February, hunted there and, after spending the night at the manor house, returned to court next day. The manor house, with all the lands southwards to Oxford Street, had been leased to Edward Forsett,[51] a Justice of the Peace for Middlesex, who must have been proud to celebrate the acquisition of his new estate by entertaining the queen's guests on her behalf.

Two years later, Elizabeth was dead and her place was taken by James I who, however much he may have differed from the last Tudor sovereign, was also a keen huntsman. Sir Henry Cary, later Viscount Falkland, was granted on 26 July 1604 the reversion of the Keepership after his father, Sir Edward, and in the summer of 1608 the fence with its fifteen gates was repaired and four new bridges were built over the Tyburn under the supervision of Thomas Norton, Surveyor of the King's Highways.[52] Nineteen loads of timber worth £17 were felled, though we do not know whether it was used on the site or sold to pay for the work. A further £80 was laid out in 1610 on repairs to the lodges and fences and again in 1612, £23 15s 6d was spent on building six new bridges, whilst William Stacey, underkeeper, was paid £100 for his expenses in keeping the deer there.[53]

The landowners around the Park were men of substance and importance. St John's Wood to the north, which was also Crown land, was let to Sir William Wade, Governor of the Tower of London, and to the south Edward Forsett held a thirty years' lease of Tyburn, running from July 1598 at a rent of £16 11s 8d. In 1611 the king sold him the freehold for £829 3s 4d; the Park was excluded from the sale, though Forsett was granted a right of way across it to the fragment of the manor at Barrow Hill. Forsett had been a Fellow of Trinity College, Cambridge, from 1574 to 1581, and had thereafter held a post in the Office of Works and been MP for Wells from 1606 to 1611, but on the purchase of the estate he settled in Marylebone and devoted himself to local affairs, living in the manor house and becoming a Justice of the Peace in 1612.[54] As such, he was responsible for dealing with poachers in the Park, on to which his windows looked. On 28 June 1612, he sat in judgment on Sampson Burton, Clement Tailor and Richard Pleasington for 'stealing of deere forth of His Majestie's Park at Marribon'. Recognizances of £50 and £100 were taken from the men and they were bound over to appear at the next sessions, though the case does not seem to have been brought.[55]

The Keepership of the Park remained with the Cary family, John Cary receiving the reversion from his uncle, Viscount Falkland, on 7 March 1624. That winter, the deer suffered in severe rains and three brace of bucks were taken from Hyde Park to Marylebone. Charles I succeeded his father on 25 March 1625 and granted the Keepership to Sir Robert Carr should he outlive the Carys, but before that could happen national and local events were twisted out of all recognition by the quarrel between king and parliament, and Charles had little time for hunting or for caring for his parks. Civil war became a reality in 1642, and in May 1642 the citizens of London turned out to dig trenches and throw up earthworks in Hyde Park against attack from the king's forces which were at Oxford. Marylebone Park was left undisturbed since there was no reason to defend it, but in the following winter, which was bitterly and unusually cold, the trees and the brushwood must have suffered depredations for 'in regard of the extraordinary want of fuel, the House of Commons ordered to be cut down the underwood within sixty miles of London in the King's and Queen's parks, and those belonging to any bishops, prebends, deans or chapters; a select committee being appointed to distribute it among the poor.'[56]

By 1645, the king was becoming desperately short of funds and any royal possession on which money could be raised was used as a security. Land is always one of the best securities and in May Marylebone Park was pledged to Sir George Strode and John Wandesford, the Royalist Ordnance Commissioners, in return for supplies of gunpowder at twelve pence the pound with 'Musquette Match and Pikes'.[57] The Park was to 'be for their Securitie for what is or shall remayne due unto them upon their said Imploym^{t}'.

Strode and Wandesford were ardent and efficient supporters of the king. George Strode was the son of William Strode of Shepton Mallet in Somerset.[58] He was born in 1583, came up to

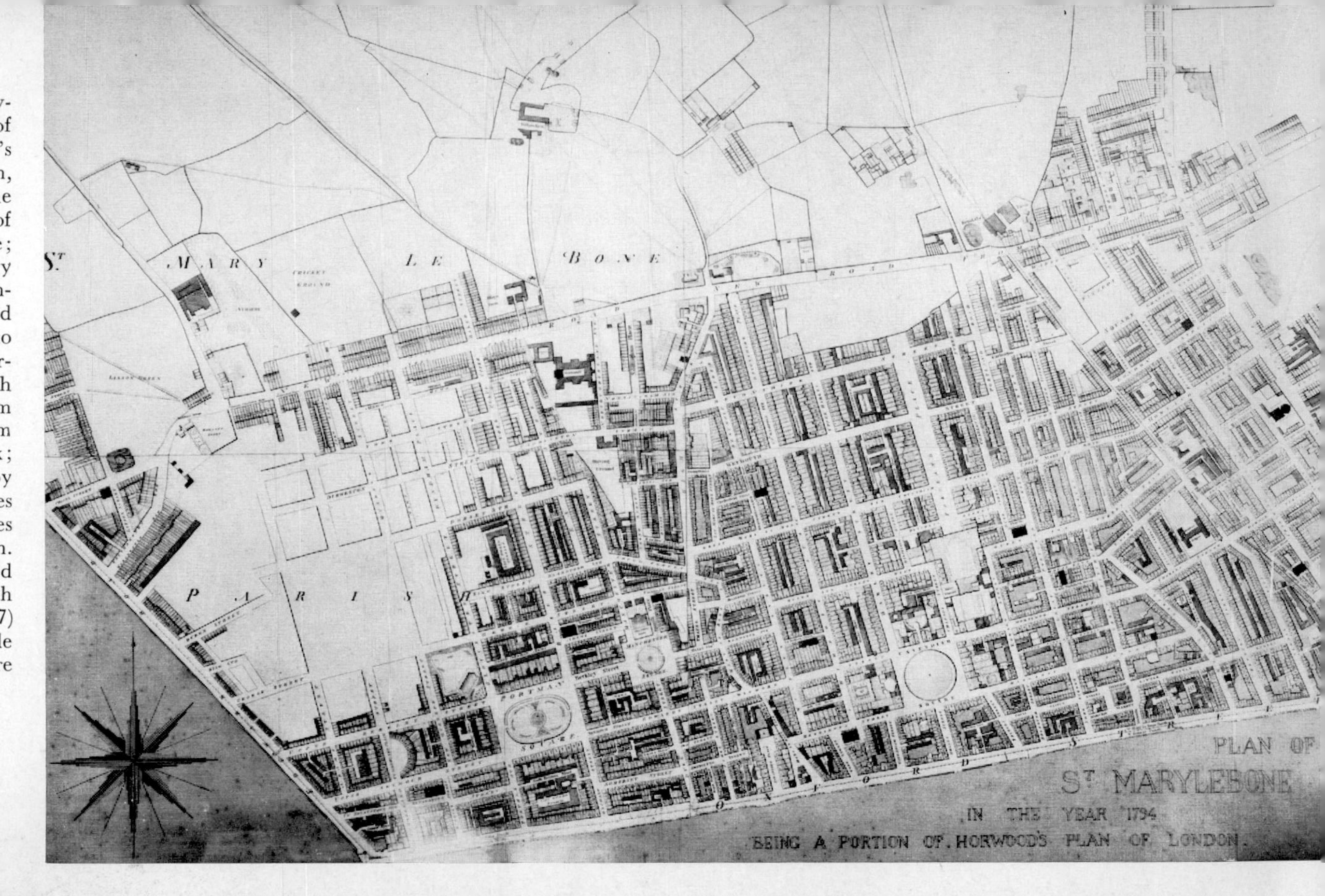

Page 35: The Marylebone portion of Richard Horwood's great map of London, issued 1792-9. The eastern boundary of the Park is visible; southwards every house is shown individually. Horwood dedicated the map to the Phoenix Assurance Company which had advanced him £500 to enable him to complete the work; it was much used by insurance companies to locate properties under their protection. The map should be compared with Rocque's survey (p 17) where the north side of Cavendish Square was still unbuilt

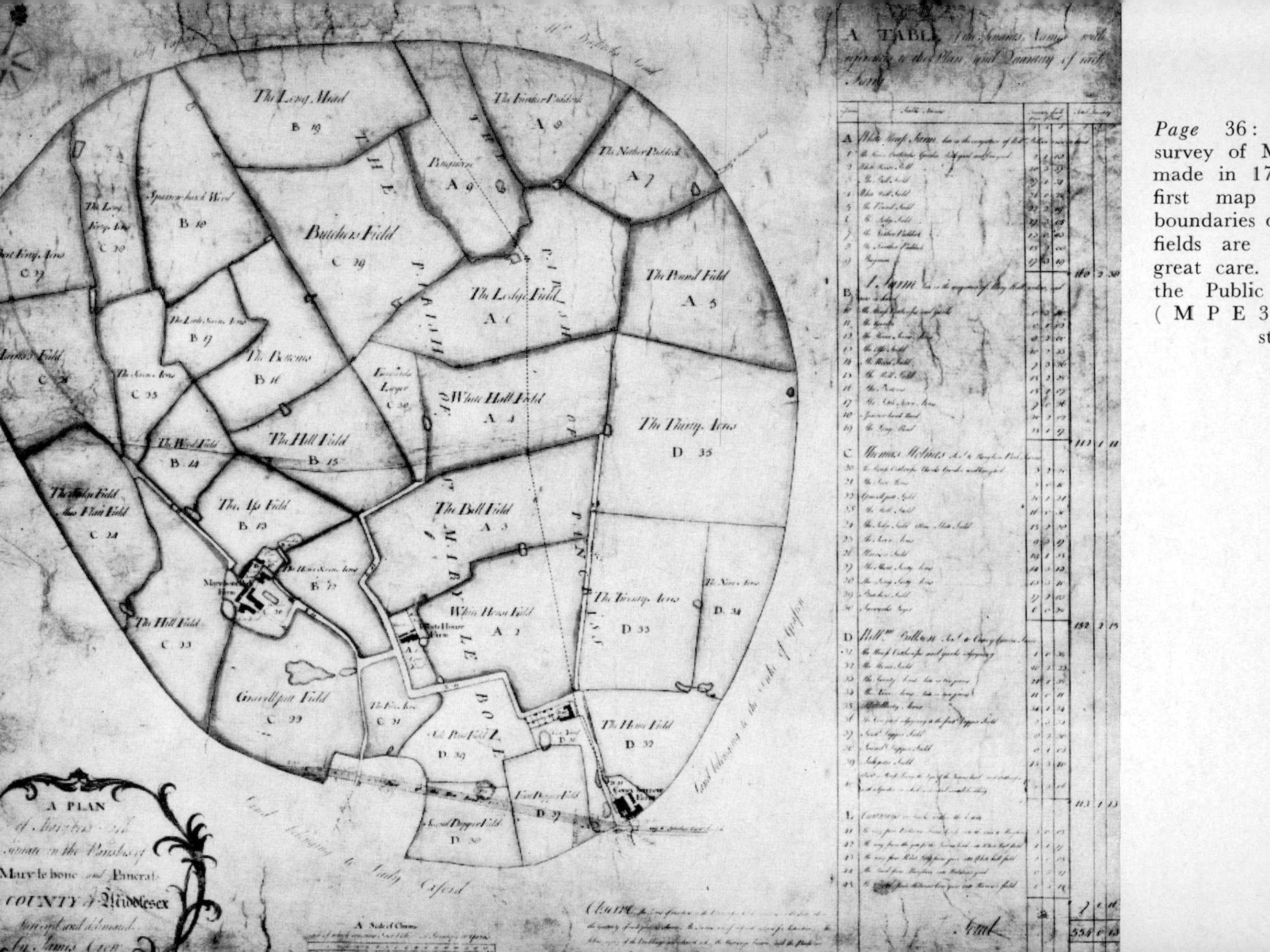

Page 36: James Crew's survey of Marylebone Park made in 1753. This is the first map to show the boundaries of the Park. The fields are drawn in with great care. The original in the Public Record Office (M P E 315) is worn and stained

London, engaged in trade and became an Examiner in Chancery. In 1615 he married Rebecca Crisp, the daughter and co-heiress of Nicholas Crisp, an important London alderman. During the next twenty years of their marriage, they had twelve children; Sir John Suckling the poet was godfather to their eldest son Thomas, and the Earl of Bristol was sponsor to their third boy, John. The marriage brought useful connections in commerce; Strode had money in the East India Company and Turkey Company expeditions, and in the early 1630s bought a fine estate called Squerries in Kent. His wife brought him political alliances too; his first cousin was Sir Nicholas Crisp,—'my little old faithful farmer', as the king called him—and his brothers-in-law were the staunchly Royalist aldermen, Sir Abraham Reynardson and Sir Thomas Cullum. Strode himself was knighted by the king in July 1641, but in the following April he was impeached by Parliament as part-author of a petition desiring that in Kent 'the militia might not be otherwise exercised than the known law permitted'—that is, it should not be used against the king. He broke his bail, joined the king and commanded the artillery at Edgehill although he was nearly sixty. He was severely wounded but recovered to take up his duties with the Ordnance at Oxford.

In the battle, Strode had the support of John Wandesford, a member of the Yorkshire family and brother to Christopher Wandesford, Lord Deputy to Strafford in Ireland. Born in 1593, John entered Gray's Inn in 1613 and was called to the Bar on 30 May 1617 'at the espetiall request of the Right Honourable Sir Francis Bacon'. From 1629 to 1638 he was British consul in Aleppo, and then returned to England to sit in the Short Parliament of 1640 as member for Hythe. He joined the king's standard at York in April 1642 and followed him to Shrewsbury where he was put in charge of the artillery.[59] After the action at Edgehill, he and Strode applied their administrative abilities and private fortunes to maintaining the supplies of ammunition. They contracted with private manufacturers—powdermakers such as

William Baber and gunsmiths such as Henry Hornor—and made themselves personally responsible for payment of the bills.

They paid dearly for their support of the king. All Strode's fortune in stock was confiscated by Parliament and his estate at Squerries was sequestered. He had to send to his wife's family in London for credit: 'Cozen, monies doth grow scarce with us, having lyen here long with wyfe and children (although not so many as God sent me); my meanes is kept and taken from mee, and my rents detayned'.[60] Lady Strode died in October 1645 and was buried in Oxford; Sir George went abroad where 'in the declination of my age, I was enforced to eat my bread in foreign parts'.[61] He beguiled his exile by translating *A Discourse of Holy Love* from the Spanish of Cristofero da Fonseca. Wandesford remained in charge of the magazine at Oxford till the summer of 1646, and then he too left for the Continent where he remained until 1660. Strode decided to return to England in 1649 to prevent his entire remaining estate being forfeited and was allowed to compound for it at a half. He paid the fine by February 1652 and thereafter lived very quietly, publishing his translation during that year. Wandesford was still in exile and neither man was in a position to claim Marylebone Park.

THE DESTRUCTION OF THE PARK

The king was executed on a cold January afternoon in 1649 outside his palace of Whitehall, and Cromwell succeeded to the problems as well as the privileges of authority. A change of ruler did nothing to fill the Treasury; he was as penniless as Charles had been and his New Model Army was clamouring for pay. The lands of those who had followed the king had already been confiscated and applied to the needs of the Parliamentary forces, and there was only one source of revenue left—the royal estates themselves. Within a few days of the king's death an Act was passed legalising the sale of all his lands. The income from them was considerable but Cromwell's financial straits were such that nothing less than a realisation of the entire capital, which amounted to some ten million pounds, could suffice his needs. Before the lands could be sold, it was necessary to know exactly where they were, so a committee was set up under Colonel William Webb and surveyors were sent out to each county to compile a new Domesday of all the estates held by the dead king and his family.[62] The reports were made and returned within the year, which demonstrates both the urgency with which Cromwell needed money and the efficiency of his administration. The surveyors were required to report on the acreage of each estate, on the nature of the land and the buildings upon it, if any, and to give a valuation. The reports were made with varying degrees of efficiency—on the margin of one, Webb, the Surveyor-General, wrote 'Welcome Hodge-Podge I understand you not'—but far more of them were clear, competent pieces of work so that it is possible to draw a good picture of most of the Crown lands.

Marylebone Park was assessed and surveyed with the rest and the various claims upon it were disregarded. Money might be owing on it to Sir George Strode and John Wandesford and the Park might be their surety, but that money had been spent on arms and ammunition for King Charles and the Commonwealth had no reason to pay the dead monarch's war debts. Similarly, John Cary asked to be allowed compensation for his loss of the Keepership, pleading that he had never borne arms for the king and had only attended upon him at Oxford, but he could produce no evidence good enough to convince the Committee for Compounding that he had a right to the Keepership, and since no one had the time to go through the warrants for the late king's reign, even if they could have been found, the claim was dismissed.

The survey for Marylebone Park is missing but the text was copied on to the Roll of Particulars when the land was offered for sale and gives many details about the Park and the buildings within it.[63] The area was given as 534 acres and in it were 124 deer valued at £130, and 16,297 trees—oak, ash, elm, whitethorn and maple—2,805 of which were reserved for the Navy.

They were valued at £1,774 8s. The Keepership had been granted to Sir John Ipsley, since John Cary could not make good his claim to it, and the gamekeepers were Roger Gibbs and his sons, Francis and John. The surveyors observed critically that the Gibbs family had, on Ipsley's orders, hunted and killed three brace of deer on 11 July in the previous year. There were four dwellings, the Great and Little Lodges in which John and Francis Gibbs lived near to Marylebone Town Gate, the Old Lodge on the east side of the Park in St Pancras, and a small building in Lodge Field in the middle of the Park beside which was the standing, made of three bays of oak, from which Queen Elizabeth and her successors had watched the hunting. This was valued separately at £3 6s 8d. The Great, Little and Old Lodges were of brick and each had barns and stables and orchards about it, so each gamekeeper must have had his own smallholding.

The survey was made in December 1649 by Ralph Baldwin, and an additional survey of rights of way across the Park from Marylebone Town Gate to Barrow Hill was made in July 1650.[64] Meanwhile, the horses of the artillery train on its way to Ireland were put to graze in the Park in June 1649 and the felling of trees for the Navy began in that October. The crane at Whitehall was repaired to handle the timber which was to be boated down from Scotland Yard 'to the Yards to build the Frigates'. These yards were at Shadwell and Wapping and the timber would have been loaded onto carts and drawn by horses to Whitehall or Scotland Yard for embarkation. By March 1650, 171 of the 2,805 trees earmarked for the Navy had been felled. The deer went too; in June 1649 Alan Ratcliffe and Thomas Simons, labourers of St Pancras, climbed over the palings 'and there with bowes and arrows unlawfully killed a buck worth twenty shillings against the public peace'[65] but in January 1651 a hundred of the best remaining animals were driven away into St James's Park and we hear no more of the deer thereafter.

The sale of Crown lands was by sealed tender, the highest bid being accepted and the money to be paid in two equal instalments with a two-months' interval between payments. All woodlands were settled on the cavalry, and Marylebone Park was to pay the arrears due to three troops of cavalry in the regiment of Colonel Thomas Harrison, one of those who had signed the death warrant of the late king. The land was sold on 23 September to three of Harrison's own officers, Captain John Spencer, Lieutenant Edmund Tapp and Lieutenant William Gough, for £13,215 6s 8d.[66] This represented eighteen years' purchase at an annual valuation of £628 4s, plus £130 for the deer, £1,774 8s for the trees other than those for the Navy, and £3 6s 8d for the oaken stand.

It is worth pausing to compare this valuation with the £70 15s 2d at which Henry VIII's surveyor assessed the Park, or the £829 3s 4d that Forsett had paid for the freehold of the rest of the manor in 1611. The king had given valuable surety to Strode and Wandesford for his debts, could they but have kept it.

In the village of Marylebone, the Forsetts remained in possession of the manor and compounded for their estate with £400. St John's Wood was sold in 1650 to William Clarke of the Inner Temple for £3,645 1s 8d.[67] There is a great discrepancy between this price and that of the Park, but Clarke was Cromwell's personal secretary and the government was already in his debt. Hyde Park on the far side of Oxford Street was sold, too, but continued to be the favourite Sunday resort for all Londoners. Even the Lord Protector himself was seen driving there, and the defences that had been thrown up so hastily in 1642 were levelled again.

Marylebone Park was altogether changed. The tree-felling for the Navy continued without a pause, save between April and June of 1651 when there was 'no present necessity'[68] but in the late summer of that year it had begun again. The purchasers of the Park also began to cut down the trees for, like all those who had bought up royal, church or sequestered lands, they knew that such contracts might be declared null and void if the monarchy were to be restored, and it behoved them to recover their outlay with a good profit on it as soon as they could. Spencer had probably acted as Harrison's agent from the beginning, for within a very short time 232 acres of the Park were made over to the colonel. An entry on the Close Rolls for 1653 for the sale of four fields[69]—Tenne Acres, Thirtie Acres, South Lawne and the Great Course—was probably only ratification of a previous agreement, for in the autumn of 1651 Robert Cotymor, the Clerk to the Admiralty, was having to deal with the complaints of Mr Walter, Harrison's agent, that 'men driving carts laden with timber out of Marylebone Park, go over his grass, brake down his pales, and do other damage'.[70] No price is mentioned in the Close Roll entry, so Harrison may have put up the purchase money in the first place. As the four fields named had a total area of 120 acres, it would seem that he acquired another 112 by some other transaction. Tapp retained 100 acres which he let to Edward Baker for £100 a year, and Gough, in association with Captain John Barker, held 120 more.

In order to realise the maximum amount of money as quickly as possible, the Park was let out in smallholdings, the tenants paying an additional premium for the right to fell the timber. William Tubb took a lease of 120 acres from Gough and Barker at a rent of £160 and paid an additional £420 for the trees.[71] The names of the fields—North Woode, Sparrowhawke Woode, Spring Lawne, Lodge Lawne, Deerehouse Lawne, and Dupper Field—indicate that some at least were well wooded. Tubb died in 1657 and his widow married William Thompson, who thereby took over the lease. Other tenants were John Stanton, William Byer and Nicholas Cotterell, and the rent roll amounted to £667 9s 10d—almost £40 more than the parliamentary surveyor's valuation.

Apart from the land held by Harrison, Tapp and Gough, William Clarke,[72] who had become secretary to Major-General Monck after his appointment with Cromwell, had a house and sixty acres worth £120, probably as a reward for his services.

Since the only buildings in the Park were the lodges, the house may have been the Great Lodge which Clarke may have rebuilt or enlarged. Another fifty-six acres, valued at £84, were in the hands of Symonds, Nicholson and other soldiers from Harrison's regiment who had held on to their pay debentures and claimed land with them rather than accept money.

All these occupants of the Park must have applied themselves to tree-felling and the sale of timber. In December 1652 Edward Mundy, a timber merchant from Woodbridge in Suffolk, was writing to the Admiralty to say he had delivered £177 worth of trees from Marylebone Park to Chatham and should he get any more? He was told to buy all he could. By the time Charles II returned to his throne in 1660, few of the 16,297 trees which were flourishing fifteen years earlier, could have been left standing. The tenants ploughed up the roots and used the land for dairy farming.

Once the king came into his own again, all those who had supported or suffered for his cause sent in their petitions for compensation. The resettlement of land claims was probably the most difficult problem that the king and his parliament had to face. Marylebone Park was a comparatively easy case. The chief landholder, Harrison, was executed as a regicide and, as far as we know, the claims of Tapp, Gough and Barker were ignored. They had almost certainly recouped what they had laid out on the purchase. William Clarke, who had been knighted even as his master, General Monck, had been created Duke of Albemarle, petitioned to be allowed to keep his house and was granted a lease for his lifetime. Sir George Strode and John Wandesford put in their claim to the Park which was inspected by the surveyor-general, Sir Charles Harbord, and he recommended that they should receive the rents from the tenants until such time as the debt due to them was cleared. John Cary asked for the Keepership again and a grant of all the remaining timber, but received instead the Mastership of the Hunthounds and Privy Bloodhounds, which carried a salary of £400 and later £500 a year.

He continued to receive his due of 8d a day as Keeper of Marylebone Park till 1677; the payments probably ceased only with his death. Mrs Clara Bolton, the widow of a loyal linen-draper, Theophilus Bolton, who had undergone much for his Royalist sympathies, also asked for a tenancy of the Park but was compensated with a pension of £200 a year.[73]

Strode and Wandesford possessed themselves of the rents with some difficulty and only after bringing an action of the Exchequer Court against the tenants.[74] Their petition states that trees to the value of £3,000 had been cut down; the 1650 survey had valued the trees as worth £1,774 8s. It was agreed that there was £2,316 11s 9d owing to them from their service with the Ordnance at Oxford, but in 1662 Sir Nicholas, acting for his father who was now an old man, and Wandesford asked for an enquiry since they felt the accounts had been misrepresented and that there was at least another £4,000 due to them. Meanwhile, fresh leases were made out to William Thompson, Edward Baker, Matthew Barrett, William Bardine who had married John Stanton's widow, John Wells who had purchased William Byer's lease, and Widow Amy Saunders who had taken over William Cotterell's land in St Pancras. Sir George died in June 1663 and his tombstone in St James's, Clerkenwell, referred to the wounds he had received at Edgehill.[75] Wandesford, who had become Member of Parliament for Richmond in Yorkshire, died in the following year, and his brother William took over his interests. The enquiry into their accounts had not been held but by 1664 the original £2,318 11s 9d owing to them had been recovered from the rents. In May of that year, Sir Henry Bennett, later Lord Arlington, who had served Charles II when in exile, petitioned the king for a lease of the Park; this was granted and the tenants were ordered to pay their rents to the Crown for the time being. Nicholas Strode and William Wandesford refused to give up the Park and a suit was brought against them in May 1666. They presented a bill for £12,516 8s 1d, but since it contained such items as £8,666 13s 4d for loss of profits on a monopoly for gunpowder-making, it was disallowed. A further suit was brought in July before the claim was relinquished, and then it was probably settled out of court, for Arlington wrote later that he had had to pay Sir Nicholas Strode £2,020. Arlington was granted a thirty-one-year lease in November 1666 at a rent of £36 14s 6d. This sum, so very much below the true value of the estate, was an acknowledgment of and a reward for the earl's services during the king's exile and after his restoration. The surveyor-general inspected the Park at the time and declared that it was worth £750 a year, and that such a lease should have carried a fine of £6,000 and a rent of £200.[76]

The new arrangements brought hardship to several people such as the powdermaker Henry Baber, whose mills had been requisitioned, and Henry Hornor, by then a very old man, who had given his services as a gunsmith to Strode and Wandesford. They and Margaret Symmes, the widow of another powder-maker, had been given pensions out of the income from the Park, but these Arlington ceased to pay. All the sufferers petitioned the king but there is no evidence to show that they received any redress.[77]

In June 1668, Arlington's lease was extended until 1728 at the same low rent and the estate was declared disparked and disfranchised. This was merely a formal recognition that the Park had become farmland. Arlington was also granted St John's Wood on an indefinite lease for £13 9s a year, which he promptly sold to the Countess of Chesterfield for £7,050.[78] These grants, so favourable to the earl but so detrimental to the interests of the Crown, indicate the esteem in which Arlington was held by the king who, in 1672, married Henry, his nine-year-old son by Lady Castlemaine, to Isabella, Arlington's four-year-old daughter. That event, however marked the apogee of the earl's power. As a Catholic, it was believed he exerted a dangerous influence over the king and his advocacy of war with the Netherlands was abhorred. In 1674 he was impeached, and although he defended himself so well that he was acquitted his power declined. His place at court was taken by Sir Thomas Osborne, later Earl of Danby, and in 1678 a lease on a great number of royal manors and woodlands was made out to Charles Osborne and John Knight.[79]

Charles Osborne was the earl's brother and the grant was probably in connection with the marriage of Danby's daughter Bridget to the Earl of Plymouth, another of Charles' illegitimate children. The terms of the lease were curious; it was to run for ninety-nine years provided the queen, Catherine of Braganza, should live so long. Marylebone Park was included at a rent of £3 18s 4d, though the premises were to be Arlington's until the end of his lease. When he died on 28 July 1685, six months after his royal master, the remainder of the lease passed to his brother, Lord Ossulston, who petitioned in 1689 for a twenty years' extension. The surveyor-general, noting that a fine of £1,000 should be paid, marked the petition 'Respited till His Maties returne'[80] and there the matter remained, for by that time William III was king. Now it was Danby who had arranged William's marriage to Princess Mary on which his claim to the Crown of England depended, and it was Danby who had invited the couple to take over the throne from Mary's father, James II. An extension of Ossulston's lease would have prejudiced Danby's interests so Ossulston petitioned in vain. Danby progressed through the peerage, eventually becoming Duke of Leeds, and in 1695 all the lands that had been leased to Osborne and Knight were put in trust for him for thirty-one years from the death of Queen Catherine, now a widow and living in Portugal. She did not die until 1705 and the duke lived until 1712, so the Park was in the charge of trustees until 1736. It had slipped from the royal hands that had created it and returned to more plebian keeping; the new owners set to work to see what could be made from such valuable farmland so near to the capital.

CHAPTER 2

PASTORAL INTERLUDE

While the Crown lease of Marylebone Park changed hands as a political reward, both the city of London and the village of Marylebone were altering and growing. Buildings spread out along the Thames until London and Westminster became one, natural expansion was accelerated by the emergency of the Great Fire, and a new aristocratic quarter sprang up westwards in Mayfair.

Marylebone was growing too—sixty-six households on the Hearth Tax Return for 1664, seventy-eight on the next roll ten years later, and eighty-four in the first rate book for 1684.[1] The church still stood at the end of the High Street, unchanged since it was built in 1400, but in 1659 Marylebone Gardens, a bowling green with a garden and refreshment rooms, had opened behind the manor house. The entrance was through the 'Rose of Normandy' public house and Pepys went there on 7 May 1668; he wrote in his diary:

> Then we abroad to Marrowbone and there walked in the garden; the first time I ever was there and a pretty place it is, and here we eat and drank, and stayed till nine at night, and so home by moonlight.

The Forsetts were still living in the manor house, for Squire Robert's name heads the list of ratepayers and the Hearth Tax Return tells us that the house was large enough to have eighteen hearths. His daughter Arabella married Thomas Austen and the estate passed to her husband's family on the squire's death in 1688.

Meanwhile in the Park Matthew Barrett had moved out to farm in Lisson Green, John Wells had taken land southwards, and the six smallholdings had been combined into three or four. Of the original leaseholders, the only one remaining in 1674 was Edward Baker who held the main farm to the west of the Park. The farmhouse was a substantial dwelling with ten hearths and may well have been the one leased to Sir William Clarke who had died at sea on 2 July 1666, mortally wounded in the naval battle against the Dutch off Harwich. Since the lease was for his lifetime only, his death would have left the house untenanted and his 120 acres untended, and it would have been natural for Baker, the senior farmer in the Park, to have taken over both house and fields. This farm came to be the largest in the parish, being called by the names of its tenants—Daggett's Farm, Willan's Farm—and finally Marylebone Farm.

The rest of the Park was divided, sometimes into two, sometimes into three farms. Their size varied from year to year depending on what a man—or his widow—could afford. After a good season extra fields would be rented, in a bad one fewer. Two farmhouses lay on the southern boundary close to Marylebone town and sometimes the land to the north-east was let off as a fourth farm, though this only happened sporadically. Baker's neighbour to the east was William Bilson, whose descendants worked the land there until 1752. The pattern of farming shifted, even within such a small area, almost continuously, but by studying the rate books and vestry minutes and supplementing them with such maps, rentals, water-colours and agricultural surveys as we can find for the area, we can build up a picture of what was happening.

In 1708 the village and manor of Marylebone were sold by the Austens to John Holles, Duke of Newcastle, for £17,500. The estate was mapped by a surveyor, Samuel Pratt, but the duke was content simply to possess the land. When, however, it passed to his daughter and heiress Henrietta, wife of Edward Harley, Earl of Oxford and Mortimer, the young couple decided to develop it as a residential estate. The last east of Hyde Park and northwards from Piccadilly to Oxford Street had been successfully built up by Lord Scarborough and Lord Grosvenor, the fields of the Russells' estate in Bloomsbury were already covered with a little town, and the Harleys decided to emulate their neighbours and share in the profits. A plan with a table of distances, showing how conveniently the estate was sited for communication with Westminster and the Law Courts, was drawn by John Prince in 1719 and the chequerboard of streets and squares began to spread north. The layout was virtually identical with those of the Scarborough and Grosvenor properties and was to be repeated on the Bedford and Foundling estates. The first house went up in Cavendish Square in 1720 and from then onwards the farm fields shrank as the clay was dug up and fired into bricks on the spot. Sand was taken from the fields beside Cavendish Square to mix the mortar for Lord Bingley's house and brick-earth was bought at £30 for 400 square yards from Cotterell's Close in the north-west of the Park from Daniel Harrison who was keeping cows there.[2]

Meanwhile Edward Baker had died and was succeeded by his son Thomas, who lived until 1710. His widow Elizabeth carried on for another year and then surrendered the farm to George Daggett, while the fields on Barrow Hill were taken over by John Mist. Daggett was a notable—even a notorious—local character; the farm was still called by his name nearly twenty years after his death in 1728. He was constantly receiving firm but polite letters from William Thomas, the Earl of Oxford's surveyor. Either his rent was overdue so that proceedings had to be threatened against him, or he was diverting the Tyburn for the better supplying of his own cows, or he was shooting night-soil in unseemly places. He was also denying right of way over his land to John Mist of Barrow Hill Farm so that the latter could neither carry dung northwards nor hay southwards across the Park.[3] In March 1725 he forced a party of carters to turn back so that they had to go all round the Park with their load.

The matter was patched up, but when Daggett died the Land Revenue Office extracted a guarantee of right of way from William Francis, the next tenant, for which he was paid £9 8s yearly as trespass money.

Francis' neighbours to the east were Thomas Hall and William Bilson. Hall held the central strip of the Park, known as White House Farm, and Bilson worked the north-eastern sector in St Pancras called Coneybarrow or Coneyburrow Farm; the name suggests that rabbits abounded there at the time. Later this farm became Richard Kendall's, and finally Thomas Rhodes'.

Arlington's lease of the Park was due to expire in 1728 and the Duke of Leeds' in 1736. In 1724, the duke's trustees sold the remainder to a certain Samuel Grey who petitioned for, and was granted, an extension till 1755 at the rent which Arlington had paid—£36 14s 6d. Grey sold the lease for £1,200 to three eminent money-scriveners of Lothbury—Thomas Gibson, John Jacob, and Robert Jacomb—on 20 March 1727; their ownership was confirmed and a reversionary lease granted in 1730 for a fine of £800. The surveyor-general inspected the Park and reported that the rent from the three farms amounted to £1,217 5s 6d. The figures show that the Crown's income from the estate was lower than it should reasonably have been; low rents and fines are rarely the most profitable form of management.

The three bankers were men of considerable standing and substance who understood well the value of the lease. Gibson was MP for Marlborough from 1722 to 1734 and for Yarmouth from 1736 to 1744 and Jacomb was MP for Thetford and Deputy Paymaster of the Forces. Jacomb died first, bequeathing his interest in the Park to his wife Lucy, 'not doubting in her prudence and affection', and left his share in the joint business to his partners. Gibson and Jacob purchased a five-and-a-half-years' extension in 1735 for £800 and another seven years was acquired in 1742 for £1,000, so the lease ran till 1773. Jacob died in January 1737, leaving the partnership to Gibson and everything else to his son-in-law, Peter Hinde, in trust for his grandsons, Jacob and Robert; the Hindes were an old Marylebone family for the name appears in the earliest rate books. Gibson, the surviving partner, died on 21 September 1744 leaving his widow Martha as residuary legatee but bequeathing the business and all interest in land to his new partner, Richard Sutton.

In 1745 John Rocque published his great map of London and its environs which gives us a general visual survey of the Park and its surroundings as buildings spread northwards towards it from Oxford Street. The palings that had fenced it off from the outside world were gone; now that it was no longer the purlieu of kings, a boundary would only have been an impediment to farmers whose lands lay both within and without the Crown estate. Most of the area appears to have been grassland, and this is confirmed by the *Journal* of Pehr Kalm,[4] a Swedish botanist who visited England on his way to America in 1748. On 24 June he recorded that in Marylebone Park there was hay- and dairy-farming while market-gardening went on in Lisson Green. The land to the north, as far as Hampstead and beyond, was grassland; 'the meadow here is all their food and sustenance'. The fields were cut and the hay stacked in May, the work being done by itinerant Irishmen. A second harvest was reaped in July, followed by a third in September if it were a good year, and then the cattle were turned into the fields until February when the grass was left to grow again. This extensive cultivation of hay was stimulated by Marylebone's proximity to London.

> As there is an unknown number of horses kept in the stables, it is not wonderful that hay is very dear there, especially at some times of the year, of which these farmers situated near to London are well able and know how to avail themselves.

All vehicles, whether passenger or freight, were drawn by horses, but a nobleman could not put his steed out to grass in the centre of the city, nor could a drayman have a field there in which to quarter his beasts. The animals had to be stabled, and were fed on hay, grain and mash which the farmers around London produced for them.

Marylebone and St John's Wood supplied the capital with dairy produce as well and in 1745 this trade was affected by a terrible murrain or rinderpest which attacked animals all over the country. The disease came in from the Low Countries, started in Essex and spread alarmingly so that hundreds of thousands of beasts died.[5] Although inspectors were sent round to see that infected animals were destroyed, the scourge was not brought under control till 1757, by which time farmers all over England had been ruined in spite of the forty shillings' compensation paid for each dead cow. There were two such tragedies in Marylebone Park, both the sufferers being widows who were trying to carry on their husbands' farms. Mrs Jane Francis at the main farm failed, and so did Mrs Mary Hall, whose creditors had to settle for 2s 4½d in the pound. Thomas Holmes took over Mrs Francis' farm at a reduced rent and Mrs Hall's land was let out first to a Mr Walker and then to Thomas Allaley. William Bilson was only able to take up £300 worth of land instead of £700 as he usually did; Bernard Gardiner took over the remainder for £250 and by 1752 was renting all that had been Bilson's. Trouble was not confined to the Park; numbers of poor labourers such as Agmonition Innocent, and John Viall who had six children, had to be excused their rates, and so had Anne Berry who farmed where Portman Square now is and who suffered 'great losses by the death of cows'. It was cheaper for the vestry to forgo the rates than to have some poor wretch and all his family fall a charge on the parish.

Inevitably the income from the Park declined.[6] In 1730, it had been £1,222 12s 6d, and in 1743 £1,599 15s 8d, but in 1745-6 it fell to £661 2s 5d, there being no proper entry at all for 1745. In 1747-8 it was £682 3s 10d, and the three years 1749-51 together yielded only £1,304 12s 9½d. Richard Sutton, Thomas Gibson's successor and one of the main leaseholders, went bankrupt in 1748, and among his debts was £3,500 owing to the

Page 53: (above) Marylebone Park, 1801. This oil painting, now in the Tate Gallery, by the Academician James Ward, shows cattle grazing, possibly by the banks of the Tyburn, in which case they must have belonged to Farmer Willan; (below) Willan's Farm, a water-colour by William Sherlock painted c 1800. The farmhouse could have been built in the seventeenth century and might possibly have been the house of Sir William Clarke, who acquired land in the Park when Cromwell's Secretary, continued to hold it after the Restoration, and was killed in 1666 fighting against the Dutch in the sea-battle off Harwich

Page 54: (above) The 'Jew's Harp' tea gardens. Water-colour by an anonymous artist, c 1800; (below) Willan's Farm, a water-colour by Robert Marris, c 1800. Willan's Farm consisted of an extensive group of buildings, three of which are shown here. The water in the foreground is a mystery. Presumably the buildings are viewed across Gravel Pit Field but 1800 is early for such an extensive wet working. The boat is a large one for casual fishing and the men could be using gravel pans. Possibly the artist exaggerated what he saw and made a lake from a small gravel working ladies of the Jacomb family, for which the Park lease had been used as surety.[7] Bankruptcy proceedings dragged on until 1753, which prevented any new lease being taken out, but at last Lucy Jacomb, Robert's widow, and Peter Hinde were able to obtain an extension to 1784 for a fine of £1,900. At the same time a properly mapped survey was made by James Crew of the whole Park on a scale of twenty inches to the mile—large enough to show details of the buildings and give field names [Illustration, page 36].[8] The total area is given as 554 acres 13 perches, divided between four farms occupied by three tenants.

To the south-west was Marylebone Park Farm, covering nearly 153 acres, whose tenant was Thomas Holmes. The farmhouse was a substantial building facing two parallel lines of cow byres with a small pond beyond them. To the south was Gravell Pit Field with a large wet-working; the right to work gravel had been added to the lease and would have been let off to a contractor. Along the western boundary was Hill Field, where the ground still rises a little, and beyond it the Sedge or Flatt Field whose name speaks for itself. The footpath to Barrow Hill is marked and the Tyburn is shown as a field boundary. To the north-west 112 acres had been farmed by Mary Hall but were in hand when the survey was made; the farmhouse was a small building with a garden around it next to Holmes' larger dwelling. Its eight fields included Wood Field, where no trees are marked, and Sparrowhawke Wood, a name that had not changed since Cromwell's day. Beyond these fields were two others rented by Holmes—Butcher's Field and Farwards Layer, called after the midden there; during the next few years the whole of Hall's farm was added to Holmes'.

The east of the Park was divided between White House Farm, which presumably took its name from the colour of the building, and Coneyburrow Farm, both of which had belonged to William Bilson. White House Farm is noted as being in hand but the rate books indicate that it was being worked by Gardiner. It consisted of a farmhouse, a few byres, and eight fields; one of them, Lodge

Field, was called after the hunting lodge which must have stood there, though there is no indication of a building. The boundary between Marylebone and St Pancras ran through the farm from north to south; a lane led out of Nether Paddock and beyond was the Eton estate. The farmhouse disappeared as such a few years after the map was drawn but, judging from ground plans, the building was converted into the 'Jew's Harp' public house. To Coneyburrow Farm, which was almost entirely in St Pancras, belonged seven fields including Salt Petre Field and the two Dupper Fields. Salt Petre Field was a large midden; when manure is exposed to atmospheric nitrogen, it becomes saltpetre. The curiously named Dupper Fields formed a rough crescent with their southern boundaries and in one of them there was a small gravel pit. The farmhouse was one of a compact group of buildings in the south-eastern corner of the Park, almost on the site of Holy Trinity Church opposite Great Portland Street Underground station today. There were several outhouses and a cow yard, and just beyond them the 'Queen's Head and Artichoke' public house, a ramshackle tavern of considerable antiquity which could even have been one of the original hunting lodges. Around it were a few small cottages and from it a broad cart-track ran due north to Thirty Acres Field. We have already mentioned this track, which is marked on Necton's survey of Tottenham Court, and we shall meet it again as Albany Street.

A line was added to the map across the southern boundary to represent the New Road, which was laid out in 1757 across the fields from Islington to Paddington, as London's first bypass. The road then marked the northern limit of development both of London and Marylebone, but south of it the gap between the Harleys' new estate and the old village was shrinking. The cluster of buildings at the end of the High Street grew until the hamlet became a small town. In 1742 the old church which had served the parish for nearly three and a half centuries was pulled down and a new one built. A year earlier, Lord Harley had died, just as the library built behind the manor to house his collection was completed. The countess sold the manuscripts to the newly founded British Museum and dispersed the books; the library housed a school for young ladies, until in 1811 it was turned into Tilbury's storage warehouse—the first to be opened in London. The manor house became a school for young gentlemen, and the estate later passed to Margaret, the Harleys' daughter and heiress, who was Duchess of Portland. Her husband continued and intensified her parents' building plans while west and east the Portmans and Russells developed their estates. Straight new rows of dignified flat-fronted houses edged their way northwards across the fields, and when Peter Hinde acquired Little Conduit Field at the south end of the High Street and built on it Hinde Street and Thayer Street in the 1750s, the straggling village enlaced itself with the precisely planned streets of the Portland estate. The development was greatly to the advantage of Marylebone Gardens, then in their heyday, and the resort became so popular that in 1754 Dr Arne was appointed resident composer and music master.

Peter Hinde died in 1764 and another extension of the Park lease was purchased by Lucy Jacomb and Peter's son, Jacob, for £2,400. A fresh disposition was made of the property, for Mrs Jacomb was granted an undivided fifteen twenty-fourths while the remaining nine twenty-fourths went to Hinde. She paid £1,500 of the fine and £22 9s of the rent; he paid £900 and £13 15s 6d. The division was probably due to memories of the bankruptcy, and a less close association between the families than had existed between the original leaseholders. Henceforth there were always two separate Crown leases for the estate.

Meanwhile a new family had moved into the Park. John Willan's name first appears in the rate book for 1746 replacing John Mist's for the farm at Barrow Hill. In 1756 he took over some of Mrs Hall's land off the High Street and in 1760 he became tenant of Marylebone Park Farm in place of Thomas Holmes. His neighbours to the east were Bernard Gardiner and his wife, until Gardiner's death in 1769. Mrs Gardiner carried on alone until 1776, when Richard Kendall and Thomas Allaley took over the land which they continued to farm until 1808. White House Farm ceased to exist, for its buildings were taken over by Willan and the fields were annexed to Coneyburrow Farm, as the whole eastern half of the Park came to be called. The distinction between the two farms remained in fact, for Kendall farmed the land that had been White House Farm in the centre of the Park, and the easternmost strip was let to Allaley. Willan died in 1787 and was succeeded by his son Thomas, who became the holder of the largest farm in Middlesex. A map drawn in 1799 by John Jones, the vestry clerk, shows that Willan had taken over part of St John's Wood Farm and was in control of a good 500 acres.[9] In 1806 he appealed against his rating assessment and the valuation on Marylebone Park Farm was reduced by £40 to £2,345; in 1811, he was paying £1,946 rent for it. He was probably a hard man in his dealings and there is a painting of him, executed by Ben Marshall in 1818, which shows him bestriding a well-groomed chestnut horse in an open landscape. He wears a bottle-green coat and a low-crowned top-hat; he sits his horse erect and confidently, holding the reins in one hand only. His hair is turning grey but the face is still young, the mouth and chin very determined.[10]

At the turn of the century, the Marylebone area was still important for providing London with its hay, as Kalm had observed fifty years before, and with dairy produce. Contemporary agricultural reports[11] speak of local herds of 550 and 1,000 cows; farmhands received 12s a week in summer when working from 5 am to 7 pm, and 9s in winter when the day lasted from 7 am till 4 pm. An hour was allowed for dinner and for breakfast. Women were paid 6s and 4s according to the season. Another local industry was brick-earth, which fetched between £100 to £350 the acre. A depth of one foot over an acre yielded a million bricks, and brick-earth generally went four feet deep. We may remember that in the 1720s £30 had been paid for 400 square yards.

The Park leases were jointly renewed in 1772 by Mrs Jacomb's son, William, and by Jacob Hinde. Jacomb paid a fine of £940 and was said to receive an income of £773 18s 6d; Hinde paid £540 and had an income of £464 7s. In 1780 Jacomb purchased for £1,000 another eight years' extension to 1811 but Hinde had become insane so no renewal was made on his lease which was due to expire in 1803. This was the last time that the farming leases were extended. In 1789 Jacomb died and the remainder of his lease was sold at auction to the Duke of Portland, who thereby controlled all the old manor of Tyburn from Oxford Street northwards to Barrow Hill, from the High Street and the Park boundary eastwards to Clipstone Street and St Pancras.

It has been estimated that London's population was about 676,750 in 1750 and the first census of 1801 gives a figure of 900,000. The individual families which made up the increase had to be housed. If we compare Rocque's map of 1745 [page 17] with Horwood's map of 1794 [page 35], we can see how completely built up the southern half of Marylebone had become, and we must remember that the rest of London was expanding similarly. The houses crowded along the New Road and pressed on the Park which, so long as it remained farmland, was an effective check to northerly development. Once the leases fell in, however, there would be a unique opportunity for building a new estate. The auction particulars said as much:[12]

> The ESTATE lies exceedingly compact occupying the most valuable plot of land in Marybone, immediately adjoining Portland Row, Charlotte Street, Portland Place, and Upper Harley Street, possessing the invaluable advantage of continuing the above Street parallelly and in right Lines to the Road; also, on the opposite Side of the Road, an extensive Plot of Ground uncommonly well calculated for laying out a noble Square, and spacious leading Street, from which local Situation, Neighbourhood, and beautiful Prospects, is not to be equalled in the Environs of London.

The duke and his active and able surveyor, John White, realised the possibilities of development and must have confidently

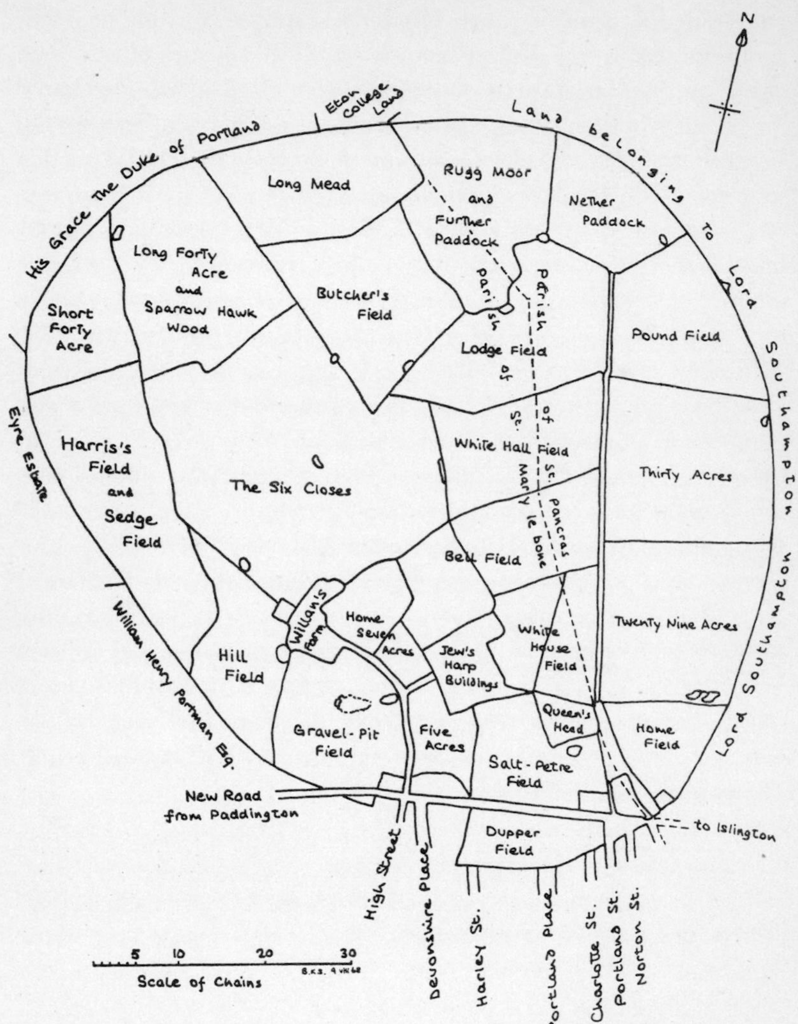

Marylebone Park as surveyed by Thomas Marsh in 1789. The eastern half of the Park was Willan's Farm; Rugg Moor, Lodge Field, White Hall Field, Bell Field, White House Field, Salt Petre Field and the 'Queen's Head and Artichoke' buildings made up Kendall's farm and Rhodes, formerly Allaley's, contained Nether Paddock, Pound Field, Thirty Acres, Twenty Nine Acres and the Home Field. Gravel Pit Field, to the south of the Park, is shown on page 54; Willan's Farm, the 'Jew's Harp', and the 'Queen's Head and Artichoke' are on pages 53, 54, and 71 anticipated controlling, or at least participating in, the resulting profits. It was most desirable from the duke's point of view that he should be able to maintain the link between the two halves of his estate. At first, local politics seemed to play into his hands. Marylebone Church was small and shabby, too lowly an edifice for a wealthy parish, and the churchyard was overfull. The vestry had been vainly seeking a new site since 1770. The duke offered them land free of charge at Barrow Hill, provided they obtained an Act of Parliament permitting a road to be built across the Park to it, and provided the Crown would give him two slips of land, which White calculated at two acres, at the end of Harley Street and on the southern boundary of the Park. The request was put forward in 1793 and was referred by the Treasury to the surveyor-general. For a century and a half, that officer had complaisantly renewed the leases of Messrs Gibson, Jacob, Jacomb, and Hinde, or as many of them as were alive, but a new surveyor-general had been appointed in that very year. His name was John Fordyce and he was not a complaisant gentleman at all; we shall say more of him in the next chapter.

Fordyce remeasured the ground for which the duke had asked and found that it covered nearly six acres instead of two. He realized that the road, following the line of the footpath which Cromwell's surveyor had measured and which Daggett had blockaded, would cut diagonally across the Park, thereby blocking the natural line of development of all the streets to the south. The link between the two halves of the duke's estate would effectively control all future Crown development. Fordyce opposed the plan, explaining to the Treasury that a burial road cut almost at random across the Park could not but lower the future value of the land; he advised that a general plan should be made for the improvement of the whole estate. To this end, he proposed that a surveyor should examine and correct Crew's map of 1753 and that the result should be engraved and circulated to leading architects who might submit their designs. The best scheme would be rewarded with £1,000. The Treasury agreed and the duke's request was rejected in spite of a personal appeal to the Prime Minister.

The survey was made by George Richardson, advised by Joseph Pearl, a ninety-year-old labourer who had worked in the Park all his life, and by John White. The map was prepared carefully; since all the old boundary marks had disappeared, holes were dug to determine where the fence posts had been, for the Tudor carpenters had left their mark below ground even though the work above ground had vanished. The chainsmen were paid 12s a week and all through the summer they worked, examining, digging, measuring, surveying. In July, Richardson wrote for an advance of ten guineas to pay the men's wages. The survey was sent to the engraver, William Faden, in August 1794. It was twice the scale of Crew's plan, and showed every building, however small, that was standing at the time.

Ten years later, Fordyce had a rental made of the tenants in the Park.[13] From this, from the survey, the rate books, the auction particulars of 1789, John Jones' map of 1799 and numerous surviving water-colours, we can form a picture of the vanished community. Let us pause in our history of events and try to picture the Park as it was at the turn of the century, during its last years as Marylebone Park, before it became Regent's Park.

* * *

At the turn of the century, Marylebone Park was simply a part of the countryside surrounding London. Neither fence nor visible boundary separated the Crown estate from the surrounding farmlands. Willan's land extended westwards into St John's Wood and northwards over Barrow Hill, almost doubling the 298 acres he rented in the Park for £475 a year. His farm was a pretty, well-kept place. Contemporary paintings record a near-idyllic pastoral landscape. Thomas Cooley's wash drawings show long, low cow byres, little cottages and stout fencing—in need of repair but still strong enough to serve their purpose. A water-colour by William Sherlock [Illustration, page 53] depicts the old four-square farmhouse and its yard with carts and farm implements, cows reclining to chew the cud and small clouds scurrying across a very blue sky. James Ward's oil painting, now in the National Gallery, shows a proud white bull and several cows standing in the Tyburn as the sun sets behind them.

Richardson's survey and a plan made by Thomas Marsh in 1789 indicate that a number of fields had been combined. Long Forty Acres and Sparrowhawk Wood had been thrown into one and so had Harris's Field and Sedge Field. Around the main farms were cottages; the 1804 rental names their tenants. This rental was illustrated with detailed plans made by John White and his son which give an approximate ground-plan for each building. Most of the cottages were let to labourers but a few were rented by gentlefolk as weekend or summer residences. Even in the eighteenth century, there were those who wanted to escape from the noise and bustle of London. The Reverend Dr Fountaine had one for twelve guineas a year. He had been headmaster of the School for Young Gentlemen in the old manor house, but the home of the Hobsons and the Forsetts had been pulled down in 1791 and Beaumont Street and Devonshire Mews built over it. According to J. T. Smith's *Book for a Rainy Day*, the occupants of these cottages were extremely jealous of their privacy and one old gentleman went so far as to put up a notice: 'Steel Traps and Spring Guns ALL OVER these grounds. N.B. Dogs trespassing will be shot.'

Attached to Willan's farm was a building that had been White House Farm but was now the 'Jew's Harp' tavern. Opening about 1745, just as poor Mrs Hall relinquished the farm, it had replaced Marylebone Gardens as a popular rendezvous when they were closed down and built over in 1778. The 'Jew's Harp' was one of the prettiest inns near London [Illustration, page 54] with a long room on the first floor, reached by an external staircase, where dinners and dances could be held. Outside was a semi-circular rose-arbour divided into bays with a wooden soldier at the entrance to each. Tea and other refreshments were served;

the proprietor, advertising in the *Morning Chronicle* in 1785, announced that he had 'a stock of the Best Wines, Spirituous Liquers, Cyder, Perry, Fine Ales, &c.' There were skittle alleys, rose gardens, and a pond with willows around it; the premises were rented by Messrs Poole and Brown for £80 a year.

Near to the 'Jew's Harp' stood several labourers' cottages. Robert Barton, Willan's overseer, had one rent-free with a good-sized garden and there was one larger dwelling with an octagonal tower that may have been a pigeon loft, rented by a Mr Barling for six guineas a year. There were also two small factories, one of which produced japan lacquer and copal varnish, used to protect the paintwork of coaches against minor scratches. It was run from 1777 to 1798 by Allen Wall, and from then until 1805 by John Strahan. The other, owned by John Tye, manufactured hair-powder between 1785 and 1792.

To the south lay Gravel Pit Field. A water-colour by Robert Marris of about 1800 shows Willan's Farm seen across an extensive lake.[14] The water in the foreground is mysterious, for 1800 would be an early date for such an extensive wet-working of gravel. There is, however, a boat on the water too large for casual fishing and the man in it could be using a gravel pan. These pits were first mentioned in 1538 and the right to dig clay and gravel had been sought by every tenant since. There must have been digging going on in the field and we can only suppose that the artist allowed himself a little licence to make a lake of a small working. [Illustration, page 54.]

A couple of acres had been granted in 1757 to the Turnpike Trustees when the New Road was made; it ran across the southern boundary of the Park dividing the Dupper Field from Kendall's Farm to which it belonged. The houses fronting on the thoroughfare built high walls round their properties but the view from their upper windows was open across the fields. No 20 Devonshire Place looked towards the 'Jew's Harp' and the cluster of cottages round it, as we can see from another of Marris' water-colours. On the north side of the New Road in the Park itself, where no one would have expected polite buildings to be, neighboured as they were by farms and taverns, were two fine houses, one of them belonging to John White and the other to a Miss Lucy Pearce. White built his house, no doubt to his own design, in 1791, a fine solid building in a corner of Salt Petre Field with a good garden round it.[15] Miss Pearce's was in Gravel Pit Field and was bought by the Duke of Hamilton in 1807. In another corner of Salt Petre Field was a market garden, originally run by a Mr Stuart but by 1804 in the possession of Messrs Eliot and Hastings. Owing to some oversight, the lease had been extended to run till 1812, a year longer than any other.

South of the New Road in Dupper Field a small piece of ground was let to Samuel Dash of 17 Upper Harley Street 'for Leave to erect an Arch under ground'.[16] The arch was rediscovered in 1961 when the western sector of Park Crescent was being rebuilt. It was an enormous ice house, forty-two foot deep and thirty feet in diameter, lined with brick. The vault was covered over when Park Crescent was built and forgotten for 150 years until a bulldozer uncovered the entrance. Within a few hours it was filled in with rubble and disappeared again.

In the eastern half of the Park, Thomas Rhodes had succeeded to Allaley's farm in 1804. Richard Kendall had the fields in the centre which had been White House Farm; the Coneyburrow Farm buildings, with a few extensions, served for both men. Rhodes paid £840 a year in rent, Kendall £827. The boundary between Marylebone and St Pancras ran from north to south across Kendall's farm and boundary marks were affixed to the farmhouse, to the cow house, to the wall of a public house, the 'Queen's Head and Artichoke,' and to posts in the hedges in White Hall Field, Lodge Field and Rugg Moor Field.[17] Rhodes' farm lay in St Pancras and he rented a slip of land for a garden from the Southampton estate which bordered the Park on that side.

The 'Queen's Head and Artichoke' was a tavern of considerable antiquity. It was said to have been the property of Queen

Elizabeth's gardener who called it after his royal mistress. The tale had no good foundation but it is worth remembering that the queen's cook, Daniel Clarke, had the lease of Tottenham Court manor and the inn building was certainly old.[18] It appears in Crew's survey of 1753 and, though the rate books give no details whereby to trace its earlier history, it is just possible that it may have been one of the sixteenth-century hunting lodges [Illustration, page 71].

Around it were several buildings, some of them of an unusual character. There was a wheelwright's yard, run by Messrs Bell & Craddock, which would have been kept busy repairing the heavy farm carts; there were also the workshops of an architect and sculptor. James Wyatt, royal architect to George III, rented a large carpenter's yard for £50 a year from 1784 to 1812. Wyatt lived at 39 Queen Anne Street East, a house built to his own design in 1778, and a bare ten minutes' walk from the yard. During the quarter of a century that he lived in Marylebone Wyatt was responsible for many country houses and also, in London, for the Pantheon, an assembly rooms in Oxford Street, and for additions to 20 Portman Square, originally the home of the celebrated bluestocking, Elizabeth Montagu, now the Courtauld Institute. It is possible that the woodwork—the doors, lintels, window-frames, staircases and balustrades—for at least some of his commissions in London and the home counties was made in the Park.

In an adjacent group of buildings, John Charles Felix Rossi had an artificial stone manufactory. Rossi, who was of Italian parentage, while a student at the Royal Academy Schools, won a gold medal for sculpture and a travelling scholarship with which he spent three years in Rome. When he returned to England, he worked for a time at Coade's Artificial Stone Manufactory at Lambeth, as did many other sculptors of the period, and then in 1798 he set up on his own in the Park, remaining there till 1810. During most of this time he was living in Lisson Grove, about fifteen minutes' walk away. The rental describes the premises as 'A Cottage, Artificial Stone Manufactory and Stable &c . . . £52 0s 0d'. The manufactory would have included a modelling room, a slow-fired kiln since the larger pieces required two to three days' firing, and a drying shed. Rossi made the angels for the cupola of Marylebone parish church, though it is unlikely that the work was carried out in the Park for his bill of £300 15s was not paid by the vestry until October 1814, well after the manufactory had been closed. It is worth noting that Rossi cast a bronze bust of Wyatt, whose working premises were next to his own, and he received at least three large commissions from Wyatt—a statue of Sir Edward Coke for Stoke Poges, plaques representing the signs of the zodiac for the Radcliffe Observatory at Oxford, and a marble St Anthony of Padua for Fonthill Abbey, which Wyatt designed for the eccentric William Beckford.

In a corner of Salt Petre Field, beside a terrace of five little houses called Portland Row, where Park Square now stands, stood the strangest building ever erected in the Park. It was a temporary art gallery built to house the collection of Joseph, Count Truchsess-Zeyl-Wurzach, Grand Dean of the Cathedral of Strasbourg and Canon of the Metropolitan Chapter of Cologne.[19] The gentleman was usually referred to in England as Count Truchsess. The count had made his collection between 1783 and 1796 chiefly of German and Flemish works, with a few by French, Spanish and Italian masters, but he was then forced to move it from his home in Wurzach to Vienna because of the wars with Napoleon. It remained in Vienna, open and accessible to all those who wished to admire or study the paintings, until 1802 when the count found himself in financial difficulties. He decided to bring the collection, which he valued at £60,000, to England and sell it there, since the highest prices were obtained at the London art auctions. The money for transport was put up by the banking house of Fries & Co in Vienna, the pictures were packed into thirty-eight crates, shipped to England and £4,000 customs duty was paid on them.

The count hoped that they would be purchased for the nation but 'considering the rigid economy which the British Senate observes in the application of the public money in support of the fine arts and sciences, the grant of sixty thousand guineas for the purchase of the gallery was not to be expected.'[20] The count therefore rented a plot of land with 220 ft of frontage on the New Road from Richard Kendall for £50 for eighteen months from 3 March 1803, thereafter for a rent of £50 per month. On it he proceeded to build a temporary gallery in which to display the collection. The architect was George Edwards of 13 Upper Titchfield Street, a former clerk or pupil of John White; the cost was about £8,000. No picture has been found of the gallery but the count had hopes of a more permanent building and plans were drawn up which show a most ingenious and modern structure, all on one floor with a pitched glass roof to admit the daylight. The building on the New Road may well have been on the same plan, but was made chiefly of wood.

An American, Benjamin Silliman, who toured England in 1805, noted in his journal for 5 July that he had been to see the collection housed in 'eight large rooms lighted from above and so connected that every successive room seems a capital discovery as one is impressed with the idea that every new apartment is the last.'[21] There were refreshment rooms too, a refinement not to be found in any other gallery of the time nor for many years afterwards. The price of admission was one shilling. The collection, now known as the Truchsessian Gallery, was described at great length in *The Picture of London*, published by Richard Phillips in December 1803; it received more space than the Royal Academy. The 966 pictures by 635 artists shown included works by, or attributed to, Durer, Rembrandt, Leonardo da Vinci, Holbein, Cranach, Aert van der Neer, Murillo, Poussin, and Watteau. The gallery issued its own catalogue, 135 pages long, with short biographical sketches of the artists represented; the layout and cross-referencing were excellent.

London, however, gave the count's gallery a poor reception. Joseph Farington noted in his diary for 21 August 1803 :

> Lawrence had been this morning to see the Exhibition of Count Truchesis [sic] pictures near the New Road, Marybone. He gave a most unfavourable account of them—saying that there was scarcely an original picture of a great master among them. . . There are 1,000 pictures & Lawrence does not think the whole are worth £2,000. The Count values them at £60,000.

Since the nation would not buy the pictures, the count proposed that gentlefolk should take up subscription shares to purchase the collection for Great Britain. There was an enthusiastic letter about it in *The Gentleman's Magazine* for October 1803, but little response. An account had been opened with Messrs Coutts in August 1803 on the count's arrival in England, but only nineteen subscriptions were paid in, amounting to £77 14s.[22] Thomas Coutts paid in ten guineas, his daughters, the Countess of Guildford, Lady Burdett, and the Marchioness of Bute, gave two guineas each, and his partners subscribed too. Sir William Hamilton, who had admired the collection in Vienna, Lady Hamilton and Lord Nelson gave two guineas each, the Marquess of Lansdowne gave ten and Lord Carysfort gave twelve, but no one else was interested.

In January 1805 the count issued a *Plan of Subscription* asking for 75,000 guineas. The gallery was to be built in Lincoln's Inn Fields; subscribers were to be entitled to free entry and so were donors of important pictures, once the gallery was established; artists were to be admitted freely and to be allowed to study and copy. The pamphlet was a most sensible document, well written and well informed, but still there was no response. The count was by now in difficulties with his Viennese backers and the gallery closed early in 1806. In March, April and May of that year the contents were dispersed at three auction sales. There are marked copies in the Victoria and Albert Museum of the catalogues for the first two of them,[23] so we know that none of the prices were high—£315 for Guercino's 'Susannah and the Elders', and £126 for Rembrandt's 'Children entertaining their parents with a Serenade', were among the highest, while a 'Crucifixion' by Cranach fetched only three guineas and the majority of other lots changed hands on the same level. The March sale brought in £3,152 15s 6d and that in April £5,255 in all, so we may assume that the count regained what he had expended in bringing the collection to England and in building the gallery, but that he had lost the capital he had invested in the pictures.

The prices seem very low and it would appear that the judgment of other experts confirmed Lawrence's suspicions. It must, however, be realised that in so large a collection some of the works were liable to be copies or fakes. The count only sold two-thirds of the whole collection; he retained the really valuable works and dispensed with the more worthless items to pay his heavy out-of-pocket commitments and to keep his creditors quiet. When he died in 1813, the Art Gallery and Museum at Darmstadt[24] bought eighty-one of his paintings, where they still hold an honoured place.

Once the pictures were sold, the gallery soon vanished. Messrs Skinner, Dyke & Co, who had conducted the auction of the paintings on the premises in the New Road, sold off the materials, furniture and fittings on 1 June 1806; finally the gallery disappeared from the rate books, for it was completely demolished.

This, then, was the Park at the beginning of the nineteenth century—open farmlands as far as the eye could see northwards from Marylebone High Street, with only a few buildings, most of them ordinary enough, a few of them unusual, on its southern boundary. It was this rural landscape that was to be replaced by the most successful venture in town-planning ever to be undertaken and completed in London.

Page 71: (above) Hampstead and Highgate from Devonshire Street, a wash drawing by Samuel Hieronymous Grimm, 1793 (British Museum Additional ms 15542, f 136). The Dupper Field, where Park Crescent now stands, can be seen in the foreground. The line of the New Road (now the Marylebone Road), along which a coach is driving, is marked out by a fence. To the right in the background is a group of buildings, among which is the 'Jew's Harp'; (below) the 'Queen's Head and Artichoke' public house, c 1800. The origin of the name is uncertain but it may be a tribute to Daniel Clarke, cook to Queen Elizabeth and to James I, who held the lease of Tottenham Court manor. The old house was partly demolished and then completely destroyed by an accidental fire in 1811; a successor was built on the corner of Albany Street, where it still stands today. The landlord was the first man to take up a lease on the new estate

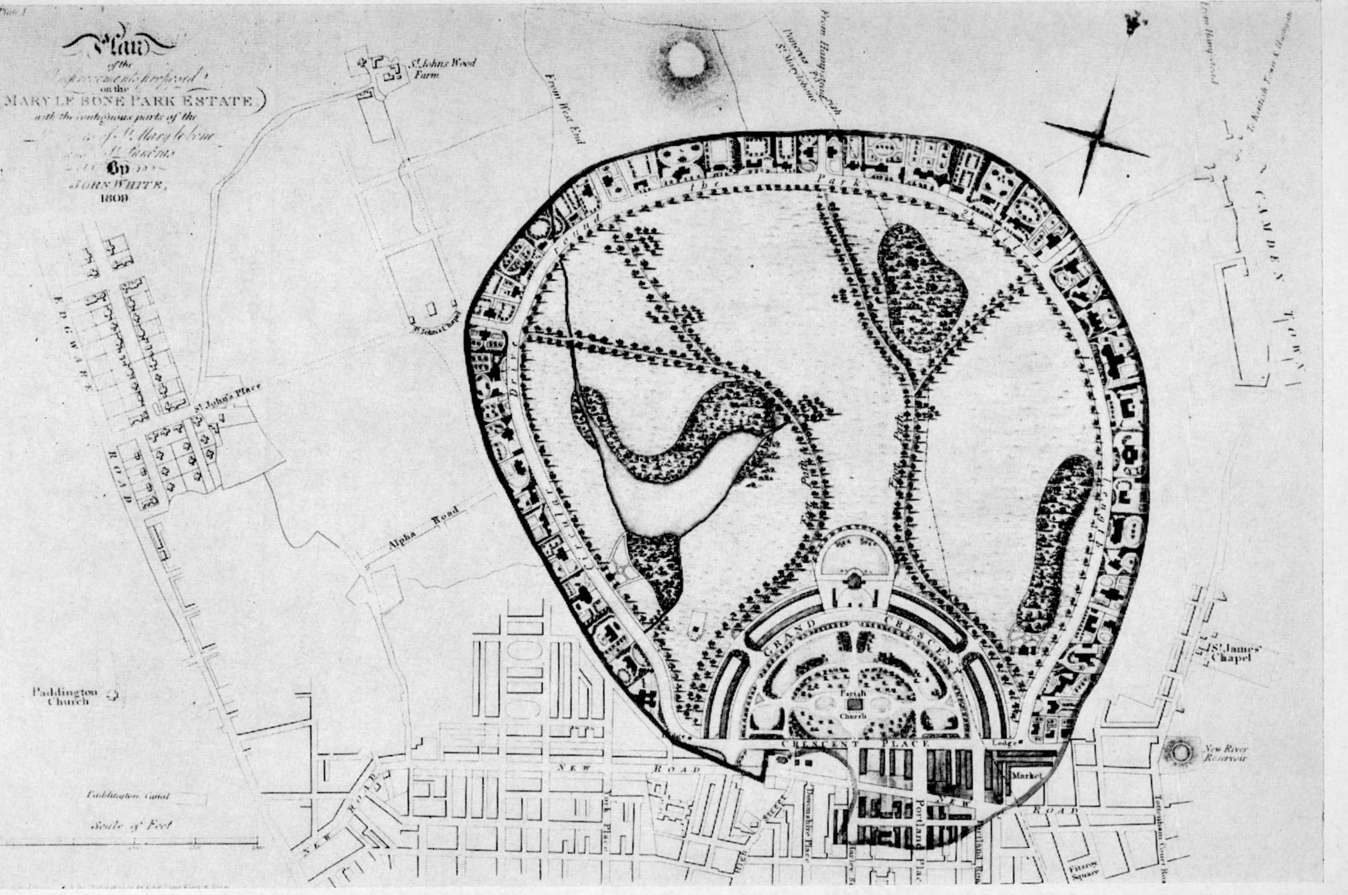

Page 72: John White's plan for the development of Marylebone Park, 1809. Nash borrowed, without acknowledgement, White's ideas of a curving lake and a splendid crescent

CHAPTER 3

THE NEW CROWN ESTATE

The creation of the Regent's Park was the work of three men—a civil servant, John Fordyce, an architect, John Nash, and the Prince Regent, later George IV. In the first instance, its development was the result of an administrative reorganisation, and if we are to understand the background to its planning and building we must go back to the seventeenth century and briefly survey the management of the Crown estates, the revenue from which had been steadily decreasing. Charles I sold a good deal and, though his son was declared to be restored to full possession of all his lands the Crown lost much through concealment at the Restoration, while Charles II was bound to reward those who had suffered for him or promoted his return. The total revenue from land was about £218,000 in 1660 but by 1663 it had dwindled to £100,000 largely because of grants made by the king. William III found that he, too, needed to reward those responsible for the Glorious Revolution which had set him on the throne, so that by the end of his reign the net revenue from the Crown estates was estimated at £6,000.[1] Since the more the Crown disposed of its lands for the enjoyment of private individuals, the more heavily it depended on public taxation, there was proper reason for complaint, and on the accession of Queen Anne the Crown Lands Act was passed, restraining the sale of the royal estates and restricting leases to thirty-one years. The income from the property was to be devoted to 'the better support of the sovereign's household and to the honour and dignity of the Crown'; similar Acts were passed in 1714 and 1727 on the accessions of George I and George II. When George III came to the throne, another Act was passed, surrendering the revenues to Parliament for the king's lifetime in return for an income from the civil list. The revenues were first paid into the General or Aggregate Fund but in 1787 were transferred to the Consolidated Fund.

The debates that preceded the setting up of the Consolidated Fund revealed that no one had any real idea of the extent of the estates, so three commissioners, Charles Middleton, later Lord Barham, John Call and Arthur Holdsworth were appointed to survey the woods, forests and land revenues of the Crown. Their first report, issued on 25 January 1787, confined itself to a schedule of such Crown lands as were leased out under old arrangements and would therefore be capable of improvement once the leases fell in. Marylebone Park was, of course, included. The commissioners decided to raise the rents, Jacob Hinde's from £16 10s 7d to £57 13s 11$\frac{3}{4}$d, and William Jacomb's from £27 10s 9$\frac{1}{2}$d to £96 3s 4d. Hinde's land was valued at £478 2s 6d a year, the leases ending in January 1803; Jacomb's was worth £796 7s 6d and the lease ran till January 1811.[2] The most cursory inspection of these figures shows that the rent which the Crown received from the Park bore no resemblance to the true annual value, and that the fines did not compensate for the difference between £153 17s 3$\frac{3}{4}$d and £1,274 10s. It is probable that other Crown properties were returning a similarly inadequate yield.

The second report was a mere twenty pages signed by Middleton and Call only, but the third, which appeared on 3 June 1788, was a fuller, more detailed work, 115 pages long with forty-one appendixes. It showed how ill the archives of the royal estates had been kept. The commissioners had written to John Pitt, the late surveyor-general, for an 'exact list of all the Woods, Forests, Parks, and Chaces under his Charge, with such plans or descriptive Surveys of them, as he might have in his Possession', but he replied:

> That not having received from his Predecessors any Maps, Surveys, or other Accounts of His Majesty's Woods and Forests,

> except a few old Surveys of Woods and Coppices which had been formerly inclosed, he could not give any Official Information as to the Particulars of each Forest: but he had some Books and Papers, which he had purchased at Public Sales, containing Ancient Manuscripts and Particulars relative to the Forests and Wood Grounds. . . Of these, he offered us the Inspection; and his Son, Mr William Morton Pitt, hath since, with the utmost readiness, sent them for our Perusal.

So long as the Crown depended on its land revenues, the archives were carefully kept, but once the income from the property became a negligible part of the whole, then the records were neglected. The most significant thing about the third report, however, was that a new commissioner had been appointed to make up the triumvirate. His name was John Fordyce, and he was a formidable gentleman.

Fordyce, of whom we have already spoken, was born in 1735, the son of Thomas Fordyce of Ayton in North Berwickshire, who had been factor for the York Building Company when it was dealing with estates forfeited during the 1745 Rising. A factor in Scotland is often a person of greater authority and higher social standing than an agent would be in England. Thomas married the daughter of Sir Adam Whitefoord of Blanquhan in Ayrshire and had six children. His eldest son, John, succeeded to his father's estate when he was twenty, and four years later was a merchant councillor in Edinburgh. In 1761 he stood, unsuccessfully, for Parliament and in 1766 succeeded his uncle, Sir Allan Whitefoord, in the post of Receiver-General of Land Revenues for Scotland.[3] In the following year, he married Catharine Maxwell, daughter of Sir William Maxwell of Monteith, and her sister Jane was wedded to the Duke of Gordon from the Fordyce's house in Edinburgh. These genealogical details are worth recording for they show that Fordyce was not an ordinary civil servant nor was he dependent on any man, but a landed proprietor in his own right, connected by marriage with one of the greatest landowners in the whole country. He was still more than this.

He was a man of objective vision, energetic in all things, able to express himself clearly and succinctly on paper, and ready to tend the Crown estates as well as he cared for his own land in North Berwickshire.[4]

The fourth to the sixteenth reports appeared rapidly, dealing with the royal forests one by one. The seventeenth, and final report contained suggestions for the future management of Crown lands. It proposed that the estates should be retained by the Crown and controlled by a board of commissioners under Treasury supervision. The government agreed but as an interim measure, in 1793, entrusted matters to a new surveyor-general who, very properly, was none other than Fordyce himself. At the same time, an Act was passed authorising the granting of ninety-nine-year building leases, a measure that was to have an important effect fifteen years later.

The first project to be submitted to Fordyce after his appointment was the Duke of Portland's request for a turnpike road through Marylebone Park. Fordyce, however, understood the value of 500 acres of undeveloped land on the northern boundary of the expanding metropolis. He knew how much money the Bedfords and the Grosvenors and the Portlands had made from their estates, and he realised that this was the Crown's first golden opportunity to do likewise. He reported to the Treasury that the duke's road

> would cut obliquely through all such Streets Westward of Nottingham Place, as should be extended over this Estate. This circumstance, as well as that of the proposed Road being made a passage to a Burying Ground for so large and populous a District, might perhaps, be found to lessen the value of the Ground for building to such a degree as no price or value that could be expected to be given to the Crown, for the Land desired, would be found sufficient to compensate.[5]

Fordyce, as we have seen, asked for a new survey of the Park and for a competition to be held to find the best plan for its development. From that moment, the future of Marylebone

Park was assured; Londoners owe as much to John Fordyce, whose name is forgotten, as they do to John Nash or the Prince Regent.

The survey was made, engraved and circulated among leading architects, a reward of £1,000 being offered for the best scheme, but the architects were not interested. No compensation was offered to unsuccessful competitors and the labour involved was too great to be expended on so slight a chance of success. Three entries only were received and they were all from the same person, John White, who knew Marylebone as well as any living man and whose own house stood in the Park. He was anxious that the Park should remain rural, open to all who chose to walk there. He encircled it with villas standing in their own grounds with access to a circular drive two and a half miles long [Illustration, page 72]. To the south, another road, almost parallel to the new road, provided the axis for a grand crescent with a new parish church in the middle. The centre of the Park he left free of buildings but crossed by two wooded winding drives, and to the west he planned a curiously shaped lake. It was a good design with a number of exciting ideas, some of which Nash borrowed without acknowledgment, though the drive and crescent bear no proper relation to the roads on the Portland estate, which is curious since White was the duke's surveyor. The plan was published shortly after his death in 1813 by his son who accompanied it with an explanatory essay and a criticism of Nash's design which was by then becoming a reality.[6]

In April 1809 Fordyce published his fourth triennial report, in which he said:

> Distance is best computed by time; and if means could be found to lessen the time of going from Marybone to the Houses of Parliament, the value of the ground for building would be thereby proportionately increased.
>
> The best, and probably upon the whole, the most advantageous way of doing that, would be by opening a great street from Charing-Cross towards a central part of Marylebone Park.

The whole germ of west London's future development was contained in those paragraphs; Regent Street and Trafalgar Square were both there. Fordyce had realised that the main deterrent to suitable development of the estate was its remoteness from Westminster and the mean streets lying between it and the Court, the Houses of Parliament, and the Law Courts. He recommended that the new street should not be less then seventy feet wide, observed that a number of existing buildings would need to be demolished, and offered an additional reward of £200 for the best suggested line for the street. He advised on the water supply and on sewage disposal, suggested the formation of local markets, the laying of a grand drive round the Park, and the building

> of some great Public Edifice, in which, as has often been proposed, statues or monuments may be placed in honour of persons who have distinguished themselves in the service of the Country . . . and as no reason can exist against its being a place of Public Worship, it may serve as one, and probably the most splendid of the Churches . . . It is to be hoped from the known talents of some of the persons who have agreed to give their attentions to this great National object, that this opportunity will not be lost, and that something will be produced that will do credit not only to themselves but to the Country.

Fordyce probably knew to whom the scheme would be entrusted. It says much for his, and his masters', strength of spirit that such an undertaking could be planned when the country was in the throes of the Napoleonic wars. Two months later, on 1 July 1809, John Fordyce died at his house in Whitehall and it was left to others to give reality to his dream of an improved and expanded capital that was also a national adornment.

On his death, the Departments of Woods and Forests and of Land Revenues were united under a board of three commissioners responsible for all decisions, subject to Treasury control. They were Sylvester Douglas, Lord Glenbervie, William Dacres Adams, and Henry Dawkins. Glenbervie, a dull, worthy, slightly unwise man, who had started life as a doctor before turning to the law and becoming King's Counsel, was the most important of the three. He had married the daughter of the Prime Minister, Lord North, had entered politics and held posts as a lord of the Treasury and as paymaster-general, but the appointment as commissioner came after a change of government and never pleased him.

Under the commissioners, dealing with the day-to-day work, were two hard-working permanent secretaries, one for woods and forests and the other for land revenues; they were Alexander Milne and James Pillar.[7] They were assisted by a clerical staff, two surveyors, Thomas Leverton and Thomas Chawner, and two architects, John Nash and James Morgan.

John Nash is the true hero of our story. He was a strange, or at least very unusual, man. His appearance is best described in his own words: a 'thick, squat, dwarf figure, with round head, snub nose and little eyes.'[8] He was born in 1752, trained as an architect under Sir Robert Taylor, inherited a legacy from an uncle, set up on his own, went bankrupt and retired to Wales to recuperate. In spite of this unpropitious beginning, Nash was an architect of genius with a flair for the broad effect and little patience with rules and regulations. He was also a shrewd business man, willing to take a risk, careless of details of pounds, shillings and pence, delighting in large-scale, many-sided projects that called upon his capabilities for persuasion, intrigue and financial manoeuvring, and above all, a manager of men.

His greatest opportunity and achievement was the creation of the Regent's Park and the resulting metropolitan improvements. Though he was nearly sixty when the work began and over seventy before it was completed, Nash was more than equal to the undertaking. He had spent his maturity in designing country houses, chiefly in Wales, and had a friendly relationship with a group of landowners there which included Richard Payne Knight and Sir Uvedale Price. These two gentlemen had evolved a theory of the Picturesque and had applied it to the buildings on their own estates. They believed in the supremacy of the natural, the romantic, the picturesque over all other types of beauty, and they believed that buildings should be related to the landscape in which they stood. The greatest practical exponent of their theories was the landscape gardener, Humphrey Repton, who endeavoured, not to regulate nature, but to release the latent possibilities in the grounds of the country estates where he was employed. He and Nash worked in partnership between 1795 and 1802, and from him Nash learnt a great deal. It seems likely that he was also indebted to Repton for his introduction to the Prince of Wales, later Prince Regent and George IV, for whom he designed a conservatory in 1798.

The prince's greatest interest and amusement was architecture, and he was always planning, building or altering one or another—or several—of his residences, whether it was Carlton House, the Pavilion at Brighton where Nash first worked for him, Windsor Castle, or finally Buckingham Palace. Nash was someone after the prince's own heart. Both as a man and an architect, he was ready for anything. He could conjure up a dream-palace with a scribble of a pencil, his quick brain could make the financing seem the simplest thing in the world, and he was ready to urge the vision on to reality with hard talking, erratic spurts of work, and sheer personality. Soon he was doing work for the Carlton House set, offering to stand for Parliament as the prince's man even though it should cost him £3,000,[9] and possibly serving his patron in a more intimate capacity, for in 1798 he married a pretty young woman some twenty-one years younger than himself, called Mary Anne Bradley who was, people whispered, the prince's mistress.[10] Be that as it may, from the time of his marriage Nash and his royal master were allies, and the architect had a fortune at his disposal impossible to reconcile with professional earnings, and which could not have come from the lady's father, who was a coal-dealer.

The unparalleled opportunity offered by the development of Marylebone Park aroused both the prince's imagination and Nash's architectural and financial interest. It was a chance that would never come again, for already the Portman and Southampton estates to the west and east of the Park were being laid out with poor, mean, artisans' dwellings. The chance was there, not only to develop the new estate but to reorganise all the west of London with a new street that could be made into a royal mile, a processional highway rivalling the arcaded Rue de Rivoli that Napoleon was creating in Paris. As Sir John Summerson says: 'Once and only once, has a great plan for London, affecting the capital as a whole, been projected and carried to completion.'[11] Fordyce's foresight had preserved the Park for planned development; now the prince's influence put Nash in a position where he could exercise his genius.

Such evidence as survives indicates that plans were made well in advance. Nash and Morgan were appointed joint architects to the Department of Woods and Forests as early as 22 August 1806. Their joint salaries amounted to £200 a year—too little to have persuaded Nash to undertake the drudgery unless there was to be a more substantial reward. Fordyce in his last report of 1809 implied that the project would be entrusted to worthy hands but it was not until October 1810, only four months before the end of the duke's lease, that the commissioners formally renounced the idea of a public competition and instructed their surveyors, Leverton and Chawner, and their architects, Nash and Morgan, to draw up plans for the new estate and new street. The Park was to become a residential area with provision for a barracks and a new parish church, since the vestry were still searching for a site. The plans were not submitted until July 1811, but in March Nash was talking openly at a dinner party given by the banker, Sir Thomas Bernard, of what he intended to do,[12] and the prince was declaring that the splendours of Napoleon's Paris would be eclipsed by what he planned for London.[13] With such influence behind him, the selection of Nash's design was inevitable, but it was in fact incomparably better than Leverton and Chawner's, or White's. Of the three plans, only White's bore a scale; Nash was inclined to ignore such details, and the hearts of the two surveyors were scarcely in the work since they were probably being employed chiefly to check Nash's figures.

The design by Leverton and Chawner was decidedly dull. They proposed an extension of the gridiron of streets that covered the Portland estate, with a church in the middle, a barracks to the west, some large villas with private grounds to the north, markets on the east and the whole encircled by a broad drive [Illustration, page 89]. A small crescent at the end of Portland Place, corresponding to the boundary of Dupper Field, was the only curve. They ignored the necessity for a new street and suggested that Harley Street should be the main communication with the Park. Their accompanying report was sensible and painstaking, specifying the type of earth in every field, but it was neither inspiring nor particularly profitable.[14] They calculated that an initial expenditure of £10,100 on roads and fences would produce an annual income of £23,000 from ground-rents.

Nash's plan was very different. The accompanying report was long and exciting, and promised a large income—£59,429 for an outlay of £12,115 with a capital valuation of £187,724 when the ninety-nine-year leaseholds terminated. Nash began with a description of his charge, and of Marylebone Park and its surroundings. Fortunately, he observed, the best property in Marylebone lay between Baker Street and Great Portland Street, and the Park was directly north of that area. He spoke of the recent rapid expansion of the town and noted that the preferred parts of London were those near to the parks—Hyde Park, St James's Park, Green Park—but that once an area was built up, then 'a good neighbourhood becomes the substitute for open fields and gardens.'[15] He then stated the principles behind his plan.

> That Mary-le-bone Park shall be made to contribute to the healthfulness, beauty, and advantage, of that quarter of the Metropolis: that the Houses and Buildings to be erected shall be of that useful description, and permanent construction, and shall possess such local advantages, as shall be likely to assure a great augmentation of Revenue to the Crown at the expira-

> tion of the Leases; that the attraction of open Space, free air and the scenery of Nature, with the means and invitation of exercise on horseback, on foot and in Carriages, shall be preserved or created in Mary-le-bone Park, as allurements or motives for the wealthy part of the Public to establish themselves there : and that the advantages which the circumstances of the situation itself present shall be improved and advanced; and that markets, and conveniences essential to the comforts of Life shall be placed in situations, and under such circumstances, as may induce Tradesmen to settle there.

Nash next described his plan. The Park was to be an exclusive self-contained residential area, approached only from Baker Street, Devonshire Place, and Portland Place to the south and with no proper means of entrance from the poorer estates on either side. For the centre he planned a double circus partially girdled by a curly lake, very similar to that on White's plan. The barracks for the Lifeguards and the Artillery was to the north, well away from the main residential area, and a drive fifty feet wide ran round the remaining two-thirds of the Park. This drive Nash encircled with terraces facing inwards, each house with an assured view, and the interior he left as open parkland with fifty-six villas so sited that each should appear to possess the whole Park and yet be invisible to the others. One was larger than the rest and faced on to an ornamental basin of water. Though it was neither described in the report nor named on the plan, it was to be a small palace or, as John White remarked, was 'ill-naturedly said to be intended as a cangette for His Royal Highness', and we can hardly doubt that the guingette was meant to shelter the prince's leisure moments.[16] To the east, Nash planned a service area with small houses for tradesmen and three markets for meat, hay, and vegetables; this and the barracks he separated from the Park proper by a canal, which also served to diversify the scenery and to provide cheap transport for merchandise and troops. This canal was a commercial enterprise on which Nash was engaged; it acted further as a bulwark against the less salubrious estates to the west and east, whilst the land northwards, as far as Hampstead and Highgate, was free of buildings and Nash assumed that it would long remain so. To the south, at the end of Portland Place, was a huge circus with the parish church in the middle and the new road re-aligned to accommodate the church.

The plan was essentially Nash's own creation—Morgan did not even sign it—but it is possible to recognise four sources from which he borrowed ideas. We have already mentioned Nash's association with Repton, the practical exponent of the picturesque, and the siting of the villas certainly owed much to Repton's dictum that what mattered was the *apparent* extent of the landscape surrounding a dwelling. Secondly, Nash must have seen an anonymous, unexecuted plan published in 1794 for the development of the Eyre estate in St John's Wood which included an elaborate double circus and pairs of semi-detached villas—the first appearance of a now-familiar arrangement.[17] The third source was John White's design, from which Nash borrowed the shape of the lake and suggestions for the drive. Finally—though it has not been proved that Nash ever saw them—there were published in 1804 two magnificent volumes of plans by Claude-Nicolas Ledoux for the building of the salt manufacturing town of Chaux in France, near to the Franco-Swiss border.[18] Some of the buildings are similar to the villas built in the Park but, what is more important, Ledoux describes his view of how social factors must govern architecture, and it is just possible that his ideas were in Nash's mind when he transformed Marylebone Park into a complete little town.

Nash linked his Elysium to the busy world of Westminster by means of the new street which became Regent Street. Arcaded like the Rue de Rivoli, it was superbly sited. Nash took advantage of Portland Place—'the most magnificent street in London' he called it—and used it as the first quarter mile. To avoid Foley House, he gave it a half-turn eastwards and then continued it southwards along the line of Edward Street and Bolsover Street. The junction with Oxford Street was masked with a circus and the street then cleared its way through the built-up area to Piccadilly, roughly following the line of Swallow Street. It cut off the aristocratic area around Hanover Square from the slums and alleys of Soho, curved to cross Piccadilly, where another circus was formed, and then opened up a vista towards the prince's residence, Carlton House. The street provided a triumphal royal processional mile from the south to the north of the capital. Its creation meant the demolition of a good deal of property, but chiefly of the meaner sort, much of which already belonged to the Crown, so the amount due in compensation could be limited. The separation of Soho from Hanover Square was deliberate; Nash later explained that he had hugged the good streets as a sailor might hug the coast.[19] He assured the commissioners it would end traffic entanglements and, as John Prince had done nearly a century before,[20] he added a table of distances to show how conveniently the Park might be reached by the new street. He also recommended that a new sewer, already needed to drain the mushroom growth of buildings in Marylebone, should deal with waste matter from the Park too and should follow the line of the new street. He estimated it would cost £54,000 to construct, and since John Rennie the engineer had recently planned a new sewer for the north of London costing £70,000, this seemed reasonable.

Nash's report had an air of inevitability. On reading it, the commissioners were convinced that an enormous profit was to be made for the outlay of a mere £12,115. They reported staidly to the Treasury:

> We submitted, on the whole, that the measure he had suggested appeared to us to embrace such a comprehensive, yet, generally speaking, rationable and practicable scheme of public Improvement, exclusive of the great increase of the Land Revenue to be expected from it, as would call for mature consideration,

but they were in fact carried away by Nash's confident forecasts. They knew that behind him was a Royal Personage, ready to lend his title to the Regent's Park. It must have seemed as if Fate had ordained that the Park should be a source of vast profit to the

Crown at very little trouble to all concerned. The profit was made, but only after very bitter pains; had Fordyce lived, he, being a landowner himself, might perhaps have realised how much hard work would be needed.

Among the records of the Crown Estate Office are two panoramas of the Park as Nash envisaged it. They were made about 1810 and on them are notes and remarks in French; probably they were the work of Augustus Charles Pugin, who for some years was Nash's assistant.[21] These panoramas bear little resemblance to the Park as it was built; broad highways open on to vistas punctuated by Greek temples and sumptuous palaces; villas stand, not in their own grounds, but surrounded by whole parks; hills, never known in the London area, swell up; valleys, that have nothing to do with the Thames or Tyburn basins, undulate [Illustration, page 90]. Glanced at casually, the panoramas seem nothing more than clever advertising, but in fact they contain the key to Nash's concept of what the Park was to be. He had brought the picturesque to town and had created the first garden city. The Park was to be an entirety in itself, intended primarily for 'the wealthy part of the Public' but with proper accommodation provided for every class in society, from the prince himself down to the humblest tradesmen.

The new Crown estate was different from everything else in London. Nash ignored the accepted gridiron arrangement of streets and squares and took advantage of the roughly circular shape of the Park on which he based his whole concept, the fundamental pattern of which is two eccentric circles. His component parts were all old and well-tried—the crescents which graced Bath, the terraces which dignified Edinburgh, ground-plans virtually identical with every other tall house in London—but he placed them in a new rural setting. He showed that it was possible to combine urban architecture with a country landscape, to achieve in fact an ideal *rus in urbe*. Nash accepted the terraces which were the hall-mark of Georgian London, with their rooms one behind the other, one storey on top of another, so that their inmates lived as birds in cages,[22] but he changed their setting, covered their bricks with stucco and adorned them so that they looked like fairy-tale palaces.[23] He set his terraces round a park —250 acres, nearly half the total area was left free of buildings— and throughout it he scattered villas, delightful country houses, English in everything but their appearance, for they, too, were iced with stucco and as imaginatively decorative as any Italian palazzo.

Any map later than 1820—Greenwood's is a good example— shows that the Regent's Park is unlike all the rest of the capital. Instead of the straight, sedate streets and squares of Marylebone and Bloomsbury or the warrenlike maze of Seven Dials, there are open spaces; the square has widened into a whole park, and the houses, though they are no bigger and little different from those on the neighbouring estates, enjoy far greater amenities than their counterparts in other areas of London. Where Repton had perfected the landscape around a single country house, Nash landscaped a whole small town, and in doing so created a new architectural and social ideal on which architects and town planners have drawn ever since. His ideas reappeared in altered, less aristocratic, guises; Victoria Park, the work of James Pennethorne, Mrs Nash's adopted son and Nash's own pupil, was a poor man's imitation of the Regent's Park,[24] and, though Nash might not have recognised them as such, Bedford Park and the Hampstead Garden Suburb are direct, if second generation, descendants. The eighteenth-century theory of houses laid out round a square, related to each other in an orderly manner, with a formal garden common to all in the middle, gave way to a wilder, more individual more picturesque ideal, with each dwelling enjoying an apparently exclusive stretch of parkland.[25] Nash combined the orderliness of Georgian London with the openness, the wildness, of the countryside. He mated the town with the country, the palace with the ordinary dwelling-house, and made a new London of an old park.

CHAPTER 4

THE BUILDING OF THE PARK

Nash's plan was not accepted in its entirety. On 29 August 1811 he was summoned by the Lord Chancellor and requested to reduce the number of villas to twenty-six. He did so unwillingly, and calculated that the revenue would amount to only £45,268 15s. The site for the barracks was transferred to the eastern side of the Park and, on Lord Glenbervie's insistence, the main drive was replanned to form a continuous outer circle. Objections were raised to the canal transversing the Park and its route was altered to run just inside the boundary. Nash regretted the change—he felt the scenery lost thereby—but the commissioners were adamant; they did not intend to risk bargees landing on their select estate. On 18 October, a Treasury minute was issued, saying that although their lordships could not

> at present sanction the Plan furnished by Mr Nash . . . they concur with the Commissioners of Woods, and with Mr Nash, in thinking it highly expedient that a broad Drive or Road for exercise on horseback, in carriages, or on foot, should be immediately formed round the whole of the said property. My Lords are further disposed to assent to the idea of Mr Nash, that it may be proper to make plantations on all such parts of the Ground as are in his plan.

No further authorisation was needed and work began immediately on the roads and plantations. Notice to quit was sent to the farm tenants, at which Thomas Willan objected, asserting that his cows would adorn the landscape. Nash replied that the stench of the byres was offensive and that the cattle would destroy the new plantations.[1] Eventually, Willan removed himself, his family

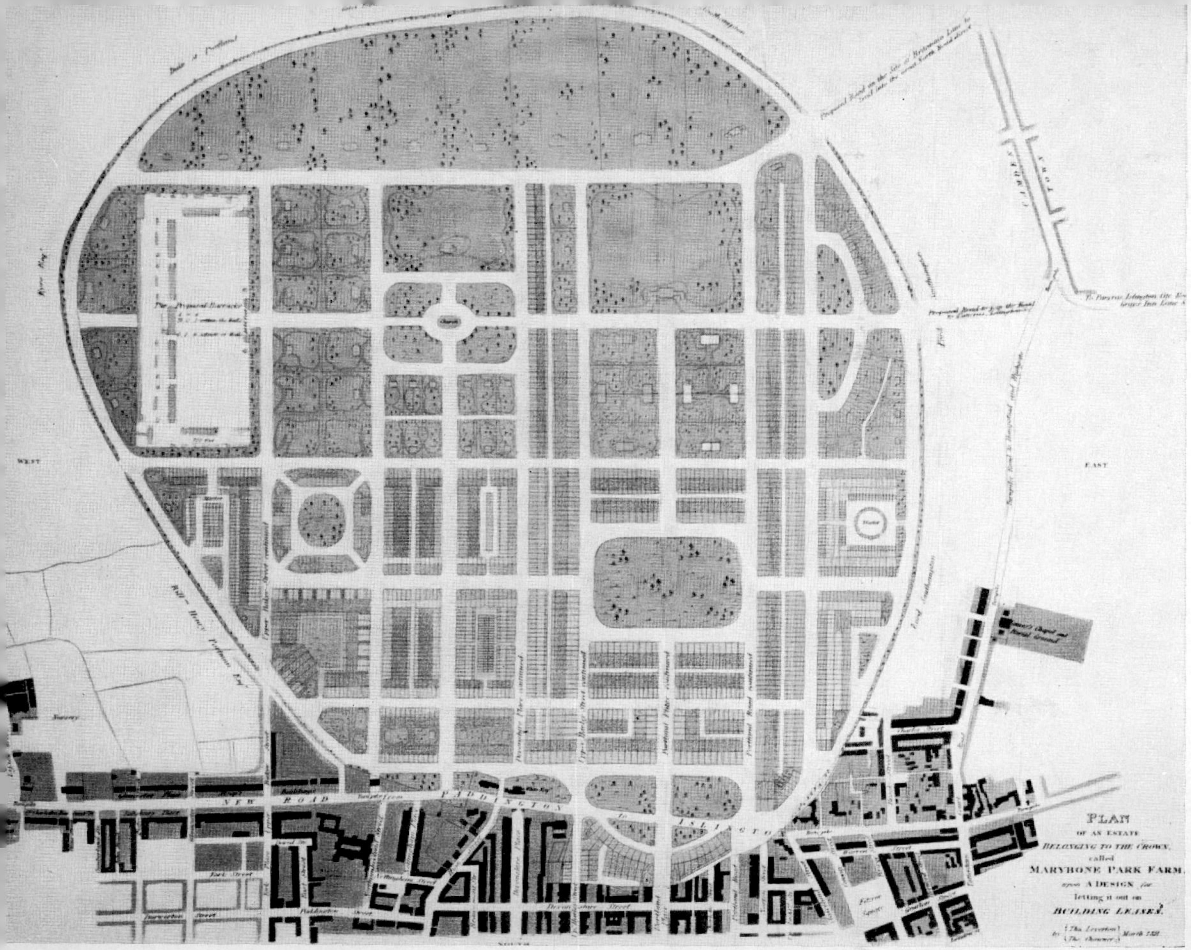

Page 89: A plan for the Park by Thomas Leverton and Thomas Chawner, 1811. This gridiron lay-out simply carries on the pattern of the Portland estate, and makes no provision for a new street linking the Park with Westminster. Note, however, the crescent following the boundary of the Dupper Field; this, under Nash, was to become Park Crescent

Page 90: (above) and (below) Sections of a Panorama of Regent's Park as first conceived by John Nash, 1811 (Public Record Office, M.R.1045, 1047). These drawings, probably made by A. C. Pugin, bear no resemblance to reality but were prepared to impress the Prince Regent and the Commissioners. The originals were drawn on brownish paper and are badly stained and faded and his cows to West Twyford in Middlesex, where he became lord of the manor and built a splendid Gothic mansion with William Atkinson as his architect. Observers viewing the projected expansion of the town said that the head was growing too big for the body and prophesied 'You metropolitans will have half a day's journey . . . ere you can get a mouthful of fresh air.'[2] But the proprietors of the 'Jew's Harp' and 'Queen's Head' immediately leased new sites in the eastern, tradesmen's sector and suffered their old premises to be pulled down. John White was shocked at the arrangement—'Public houses . . . ought never to have been tolerated in a royal or ornamental Park'[3]—but the commissioners took no notice. Later a fire broke out in the ruins of the 'Queen's Head', causing the death of a poor woman sheltering there and destroying all that remained of old Marylebone Park.

The £1,000 premium for designs was paid out in November 1811. Nash received £600, Leverton and Chawner had £300 between them, and £100 was sent to John White. No specific arrangements were made for paying Nash for his work on the Park; during the first year he must have continued on his original arrangement of £100 retainer plus a guinea a day when working, but in November 1812 an agreement was negotiated on the arbitration of Samuel Pepys Cockerell, an architect of great integrity, whereby Nash was to receive five per cent of expenditure on public works, such as roads, rails, lodges, and open spaces, one and a half per cent on the sale of old materials and on valuations, and half a year's value on the ground-rent of all sites let. From 1811 to May 1812, his bill was £71 12s 9d, to the end of 1813 it was £2,682 17s 0d, and to Christmas 1814 £2,847 7s 11d, which indicates the speed of work on the Park. In addition, Nash received an *ex gratia* payment of £1,000.[4] The commissioners had driven a hard bargain with him, for the amount of work and time needed was immense, but when Nash was personally interested in a scheme he neither counted the cost to himself nor thought of the financial risk, though he realised that he was ill paid and was still saying so in 1828.[5] Leverton and Chawner asked to be employed on the new estate and the commissioners agreed.

The commissioners presented their first report on 4 June 1812 and were able to say that the drive and the plantations were nearly complete,[6] that enquiries were coming in about villa sites, that some leases near to the markets had been taken up already, and that Mr Charles Mayor, who had previously built houses on the Foundling estate, had leased the whole of the circus at the top of Portland Place. It seemed as though Nash's confident prognostications would come true. But when the second report was presented in March 1816 the commissioners had to confess to an expenditure of £53,650 4s 2d, though Nash's original estimate had been £12,115.

Everything had gone wrong during those four years. There was trouble over the canal; the grand circus was yet unbuilt, its lessee a bankrupt; no site could be agreed upon for the parish church; the Duke of Portland refused to remove his railings from the north end of Portland Place; the villa and terrace sites failed to let; the new street proceeded so slowly that it became a general laughing stock; and everything cost far, far more than anyone had ever expected or even imagined it could. One general cause, the wars with France, underlay the majority of these particular troubles. James Malcolm, in his *London Redivivum,* noted in 1803 that 'this present war has been a great check to the enterprising spirit of builders,'[7] and though, in fact, government and public expenditure on building was high during the first four decades of the century, the years between 1815 and 1819 marked a regression in the building industry, especially as far as private undertakings were concerned, and it was by private enterprise, as we shall soon see, that Regent's Park and Regent Street were built. The price of materials had risen, money was scarce, and the Crown, unlike other great landlords, did not lend money on easy terms to those who took up building leases. It was nine years before matters improved and nine years is a long time. Throughout the entire period, Nash refused to be discouraged and the Prince Regent never lost confidence in him. Regent's Park and the new street were only built after an heroic struggle. We will speak of the problems one by one, remembering always that Nash was harassed and vexed by them several at a time.

The Regent's Canal was one of Nash's speculative ventures.[8] The suggestion of a cutting to link the Grand Junction Canal at Paddington with the Thames at Limehouse had been projected as early as 1802 by an entrepreneur called Thomas Homer, and John Rennie, the engineer, had calculated that some 800,000 tons of goods would be carried annually by such a communication. Homer first suggested driving the canal straight through London, but the costs of buying up land and conciliating various interests were obviously too great and too likely to arouse opposition, so the scheme was dropped until 1811 when the proposed development of the Park became common knowledge. Homer then approached Nash to whom the possibilities and difficulties of the scheme appealed. He suggested taking the canal round London in a loop eight and a half miles long, and he incorporated a stretch of it in the Park. A company was formed, the Prince Regent lent his name to the enterprise, a capital of £254,000 was raised to acquire the necessary seventy acres of land, and the commissioners agreed to grant six acres, two roods, and three and a half perches of land in the Park in perpetuity for £2,347 17s 6d. Lord Glenbervie readily bought £3,200 worth of shares in the new venture. He and Nash were on the friendliest terms, writing to each other cordially and visiting when Lord Glenbervie was in the Isle of Wight where Nash lived.[9] The Regent's Canal Bill was drafted in February 1812 and went before Parliament three months later. Then the trouble began.

The wharfingers at Paddington saw their livelihood threatened; local landowners did not like the thought of a canal cutting across their estates; it was said that the stagnant water of the canal would impair the health of the population; and Mr Creevey attacked the Bill with acerbity during debate.

> Mr Creevey complained that, notwithstanding the sums drawn from the Treasury, no improvements had been made in Marylebone Park, except a long gravel walk being laid out, and some plantations of trees which no one was permitted to approach. He thought the projected Regent's Canal was a mere job, intended to benefit Lord Glenbervie and Mr Nash, at the expense of the Crown; and concluded by moving for papers.
>
> Mr Wharton reprobated these unjust aspersions on the characters of Lord Glenbervie & Mr Nash, and said that, when the plan was completed, there would be an increased annual revenue to the Crown of 30,000£,[10]

Poor Lord Glenbervie complained in his diary of the 'violent and unjustifiable attack made by that *accusateur officieux*, Mr Creevey,'[11] but he held Nash responsible for the trouble and thereafter considered him as an archfiend, which did not make the architect's work any easier. The Bill finally became an Act, though it cost the company £12,724 to obtain instead of £4,241 as they had budgeted, but their troubles were not ended there. Landowners threatened lawsuits and one of them, Mr Agar of St Pancras, forcibly defended his property against James Morgan and the navigators, as the canal diggers were called, when they wished to start work, and it was Morgan who was arrested and marched before the justices for disturbing the peace. The unfortunate man was made engineer to the company but he, knowing nothing about canal construction, bought and installed an expensive patent lock that would not work and had to be sold off for £400.

The Grand Union Water Company declared that they could not supply the necessary water, so land supposed to contain fertile springs was purchased on Finchley Common, but the springs proved inadequate. The Eyre estate would only sell land in St John's Wood on condition that houses of a superior class should be built along the canal banks, and they enforced the condition rigorously.[12] Finally in 1815, Homer, the original promoter of the scheme, embezzled most of the company's remaining capital, and though he was tried and transported that did not bring back the money. Nash poured in his own fortune, taking out shares in his own, his wife's, and doubtless several other people's names; he afterwards said that at one point he held 1,100 £100 shares.[13] The cut round the Park was completed by 1816, but in 1818 Nash had to take up, as a private person, all the wharf leases for the Regent's Park basin, since the company were unwilling to honour their obligations and the sites would not let.[14] At last, on 1 August 1820, the canal was completed and ceremonially opened by Lord Macclesfield, the chairman, Nash and the managing committee, who floated along it in the City state barge which had been lent for the occasion. Next day, *The Times* gave Nash all the credit for the achievement and did not even mention Homer's name. Nash deserved it.

The circus, which had begun so auspiciously, was another series of disasters. The whole site was taken up in 1812 by Charles Mayor, a business associate of Nash's, and the commissioners were delighted to dispose of so large a part of the undertaking so easily. The matured ground-rent was to be £1,200, the houses were to be worth £2,500 each, and Portland stone was ordered in large quantities to face the buildings.[15] This last point is interesting as it would seem to indicate that Nash originally intended to use stone for the finishing but that he substituted stucco when money ran short. Had he been able to keep to his original plan, the wits might not have sung:

> Augustus at Rome was for building renown'd,
> And of Marble he left what of Brick he had found;
> But is not our Nash, too, a very great master?—
> He finds us all brick and he leaves us all plaster.[16]

Mayor called himself an architect but his employees told a different story, for they said that he lived by 'buying Deals, Bricks, and other building materials for Sale and selling the same and charging the profit thereon' and 'by making Packing Cases, Bottle Racks, Wine Binns, Cupboards, Dressers, and other articles for Domestic and Other Purposes.'[17] Mayor's manner of earning his living, however, ceased to be of importance when he proved to be a man, not of substance, but of straw. The houses he had built on the Foundling estate proved unsound, the management of the circus got out of hand, and Mayor went bankrupt to the sum of £22,000. A committee was appointed to deal with his estate, and they found that he owed money everywhere—£59 6s 8d to John Stock of Poplar, schoolmaster, for the instruction of his two sons, £23 13s 6d to John Brown of Dorset Street, baker, £34 4s 11d to Messrs Thompson & Co of Charlotte Street, who were 'Dress, Pelisse and Frock Makers, Specialists in Ready Made and Child Bed Linen', as well as much larger sums concerned with his business—£2,079 0s 3d to John Fowler, iron-founder, and £376 13s to Robert Young, glasscutter. Creditors' meetings dragged on for ten years, the wretched Mayor alternately refusing to answer questions and then insisting he had been defrauded of his rights.[18] He wrote furious letters to the commissioners and the Duke of Wellington but they were left unanswered. Meanwhile, the six houses he had built in the south-east quadrant stood as unroofed carcasses, open to the wind and rain. 'The grass has grown on the top of the walls, reaching in some places higher than the kitchen windows', a passer-by noticed.[19]

All this time, the vestry had been vainly trying to have a site staked out for the parish church. There were four possible sites—the centre of the circus, the northern or the southern crescent, or within the Park proper, on the north side of the new road. Nash favoured the centre of the circus, with the new road diverted round the perimeter; the vestry disagreed with him and among themselves. In March 1812 they settled on the southern semi-circle, with an ornamental garden to the north, and the New Road re-aligned at right angles to Portland Place. An Act to alter the road was easily obtained but Nash did not care for the idea and so did nothing about it despite numerous reminders. Meanwhile, the Duke of Portland had made up his mind that the new church was to be on his land; if some other site were chosen, he would refuse to remove his railings from the end of Portland Place, thereby effectively blocking the new street—the main line of communication between the Park and Westminster. The commissioners realised how hard it would be to obtain an Act compelling the duke to remove the railings and wrote to the vestry asking to be relieved of their promise of a site within the circus and offering any other within the Park. The vestry hesitated and debated—and then decided to turn a chapel which they had begun to build on a corner of the old parish church site into the new church, which they had now sought after for forty-three years.[20] Their architect, Thomas Hardwick, was instructed to alter his plans, and Nash, as we shall see, changed his to take advantage of this turn of events.

In 1818, an eccentric millionaire, John Farquhar, agreed to guarantee the money for the development of the circus, and three builders took up the leases.[21] They were William Richardson of 72 Portland Street, Samuel Baxter of 306 Regent Street North, and Henry Peto of Peto & Grissel, 31 Little Britain, who acquired Mayors' six houses. In 1814 a fire had broken out in the one nearest the centre of the quadrant, and though £700 insurance money was paid to Mayor it seems doubtful whether it was spent on repairing the damage. More probably, it went into the needy man's pocket. Peto took over the houses as they stood—Nash having certified that they were satisfactory—and began to complete them, but after a terrible night of storms on 4-5 March 1818 the house where the fire had been collapsed. Peto complained to the commissioners and they in turn sent surveyors, Messrs Craig and Stevens, to view the debris and submit a report.

> The mortar has a most unfavourable appearance, and altho' the external walls are more in thickness than the Specification implies, yet it must be acknowledged the Buildings are very bad. It appears to us that in such lofty edifices, and under other circumstances which present themselves to our Minds, that if ever such Buildings and in such a distinguished part of the town required the constant attendance of an Architect or his Clerk of Works to superintend the Materials and Labour, this pile of Buildings ought to have had such a one or more persons;

> and we, with great deference, recommend the adoption of such a procedure . . . In his letter of 6th April 1818, [Mr Nash] states therein "that his Clerk attended the setting out of the foundations of the Buildings, and when they were covered in, his Clerk surveyed the Buildings, and found they were built according to the terms of the Agreement." This is what we particularly wish to draw the Commissioners attention to, it does not appear to us that these two duties performed were all, nay! not a tenth part of what was necessary to be performed.[22]

The accusations seem ironical when one remembers that Nash's original report on the design of the Park contained strictures against jerry-building and a catalogue of the results—'cracked walls, swagged floors, bulged fronts, crooked roofs, leaky gutters, inadequate drains, and other ills of an originally bad constitution.' Nash, whose faith in himself must have been sublime, delayed answering the charges until November and then replied with a long, dignified letter. He pointed out that it was the fire-damaged house that had collapsed and that Peto was a bricklayer by training and should have known better than to rebuild with damaged bricks. He, Nash, had made

> not only complete plans and elevations of the general design; but, the detailed parts for the execution of the work, and this is the principle [*sic*] duty required of architects in private practice and for which they receive a Commission of five per Cent on the expenditure . . . That Commission on one of Mr Mayor's houses would amount to 200 or 250 £, the cost being from 5 to 6 thousand pounds, the fee I received does not exceed £20. Besides the before mentioned duties I set out the foundations of the buildings, inspected them several times in their progress, and finally surveyed them previous to the granting of the Lease. I examined and filled the Drafts of the agreements and drew the plans on the Leases . . . [The houses] were built according to the Terms of the Contract—the Bricks were rough, unsightly but sound; the Timber and Stone of the very best sort; the walls even thicker than prescribed—the Mortar appeared good but no one but a man continually standing over the Labourer who mixed the Mortar and hodded the Bricks could tell whether there was the due proportion of Lime and

Sand, or whether every Brick that was used was sound, but I know that Mr Mayor had agreed with the Bricklayers that none but sound Bricks should be delivered and that there should be 1½ Loads of Lime used in every rod of Work and that he had two persons on the premises to see that these were observed and the work well performed . . . Three of the houses which I certified were bought by Mr Peto, and another has been very recently bought by him (since his complaint) and which he is finishing in a very expensive manner . . . Another of the houses certified by me (the corner house on the East side) is in the hands of Mr Mayor's assignees, is nearly finished and for which (I believe) been offered £8,000 or 9,000£ . . .

The defence was adequate. It is worth quoting in full since it shows how much work Nash put into the earliest buildings and gives some indication of the market value of the houses. The damaged house was rebuilt and the whole crescent completed and let soon afterwards.[23] The idea of a grand circus was reluctantly abandoned and Park Square was substituted for the northern half. But though Nash had cleared himself of negligence, the falling bricks had not made his relations with the commissioners any easier.

By this time he was busy with Regent Street—and several other schemes—and could not give his full attention to the Park. Estimates continued to be inaccurate and plans arrived months behind schedule. Instead of friendly letters from Lord Glenbervie, he received eleven-page epistles of complaint from the Secretary, Alexander Milne.[24]

The Board would fain indulge the hope that the sanguine prospect which you still seem to entertain of the effect of those measures upon the value of the Crown Property in Marybone Park by the letting of Building Ground therein will be realised, tho' at the same time they continue to view with very considerable anxiety the heavy and still increasing disbursements, so much exceeding the amount of your original Estimate, and of which a very small portion indeed is yet in a way of being refunded.

The worst trouble was the lack of takers for the villa and terrace sites, for not one of the original enquiries received in 1812 had materialised. Mayor's failure discouraged other investors and the slowness with which Regent Street developed was a further deterrent. Glenbervie noted gloomily in his diary: 'The project of the New Street seems to be in a deplorable way, and Nash I hear is held in universal abhorence except by his royal master and dupe.'[25] John Shaw, the surveyor to the Eton College estate, gave evidence to the Parliamentary Committee on Crown Leases some twelve years afterwards and remembered:[26]

> As [the New Street] advanced, public opinion fluctuated with respect to it; it was a common subject for laughter among the profession for a long time . . . [As for Portland Place and Park Crescent] that was dreadfully unprofitable at first; it was intended to have made [the Crescent] a Circus . . . one portion of it remained in skeleton for a great length of time and indeed some of the houses fell down; it was not until a very extraordinary man, Mr Farquhar, embarked as a speculation in the investment of a sum of money, that it was started at all; it remained a dead loss to the projectors a long time.
> He was asked:— Did that failure alarm builders as to taking ground in other parts of the New Street?—The New Street was of so great an extent that it did alarm all reasonable men, I should think. I think among the most respectable quiet-minded people of the profession it was considered a great chance whether it would be realized for a long time.

Nash, however, was neither reasonable nor respectable nor quiet-minded. He himself took up lease after lease along Regent Street and, supported by the Prince Regent, wrote sensible, soothing letters to the commissioners:[27]

> You will please, Gentlemen, to recollect that the Circus at the end of Portland Place was let as soon as the Plan was settled; that the measure of the Regent's Canal was carried as soon as it was proposed; that applications were made for Sites for Villas as soon as the Scheme of Marylebone Park was known; so far the public expectation was in unison with mine; and it cannot be expected I should have foreseen the interruptions which the Circus and Canal have met with, nor the Causes which have induced those Gentlemen who had put

> down their names for Villas to decline following up their first intentions. The failure of Mr Mayor in the middle of his progress was certainly owing solely to the sudden stoppage of those resources of credit which Builders look up to for the success of their speculations . . . Before the Roads were completed and the Park inclosed, the disposition to building became paralysed . . . The main object of the Crown, I conceive to be, the Improvement of their own Estate, to augment and not diminish it, and not to sell any part of it; a magnificent and convenient Street for the Public will be the result, not the cause. The Crown property in Mary-le-bone Park, in extent of ground, is greater than all their London Property beside; and to make it more productive in proportion as it is more extensive, only requires the Street in question; time will do the rest, and Mary-le-bone Park one day become a very prominent feature in the list of Crown Revenue.

Nash's confidence was justified, for in 1816 he at last found the backer he needed in a wealthy builder, James Burton. Burton who was one of the first men to employ on a permanent basis all the trades and crafts needed to build a house, had been responsible for most of the development on the Bedford and Foundling estates.[28] It was good solid work and he was often his own architect. Having taken up a number of sites in Regent Street, he realised he would lose his money if the Park failed to materialise, so during 1817 and 1818 he built himself a villa there, to a design by his son Decimus. Another villa site was taken at the same time by C. A. Tulk, MP for Sudbury, and a house, St John's Lodge, was built to the designs of John Raffield.

The commissioners' third report, issued in 1819, was still melancholy, since apart from the villas and the crescent they had only disposed of twelve leases for the second-rate houses in Albany Street and five wharves on the canal. Almost immediately afterwards, however, the building industry boomed,[29] every site was let before the fourth report of 1823, and the Park was virtually completed in seven years. Park Crescent and Regent Street were finished and Cornwall Terrace begun in 1820; in the next three years, York Terrace, Sussex Place, Clarence Terrace, Park

Square, and Hanover Terrace were built, and finally between 1826 and 1828, one minor terrace, Gloucester Gate, and two major ones, Cumberland and Chester, were erected. Eight villa sites had been let, and in their fifth report of May 1826 the commissioners, assured of an income of £15,000—one-third of what Nash had promised them in 1811—decided that no more villas should be built. They also abandoned Munster and Carrick Terraces, which were to have stood on the north side of the Park, and the double circus in the middle. The buildings, they felt, would 'destroy the Scenery, and shut out the many beautiful views towards the villages of Highgate and Hampstead;' they had also, in all probability, had enough trouble. The inner circle remained simply as a drive; the guingette disappeared from the plans, for by this time George IV was building Buckingham Palace. The Park as it materialised was little more than the skeleton of Nash's original plan, but even so it was the most beautiful estate in London.

Before we begin a detailed description we must consider how the Park was built, who paid for it, and what effect its building had on the rest of London. The overall plan was Nash's alone and, though he did not make all the working drawings, every façade was designed or approved by him. The layout of the roads and plantations and the siting of the buildings were his, and the commissioners', responsibility. The interiors and supervision of the construction was left to the builder or his architect—with unexpected results at Gloucester Gate and Chester Terrace. But by the time the Park was properly advanced, Nash was occupied with the metropolitan improvements that were the logical outcome of its creation, and with Buckingham Palace.

The building of Regent's Park may be said to mark the emergence of the speculative builder. Previously the division between employer, architect, and builder had been indistinct. The day of the gifted amateur, the gentleman-architect, was almost ended but the professionally trained man was only beginning to appear. Simultaneously, the master mason who could build on his own or, having received his instructions, could carry them out properly without supervision, was vanishing and his place was being taken by the speculative builder, more financier or business man than mason or carpenter. Although it was still possible for a group of craftsmen—masons, carpenters, tilers, plasterers—to work together on a row of houses, each owning a share of the result in proportion to his labour as had been done since the seventeenth century, and although this was done in Regent Street, there is no evidence to suggest that it happened in the Park, excepting possibly in the service area behind Albany Street.

Regent's Park was erected by private builders relying on private resources. It was not the creation of the Office of Works; public money was spent only on the roads, lodges, open spaces and railings. The practice was for a builder or financier—the two might be synonymous—to take up a site on a building agreement with the commissioners for a peppercorn rent, and to erect on it a terrace corresponding to Nash's façade but internally to his own design. When the building was up, a regular lease was granted for the remainder of ninety-nine years on a ground-rent assessed at so much per foot of frontage. The valuations varied according to locality—10s per foot for the markets, 15s for Albany Street, 18s for York Terrace.[30] The builder hoped to have sold the houses to private buyers before or immediately following completion. There were 1,233 building sites in the Park, originally let out in 365 leases to 220 leaseholders, seventeen of them being women. Forty per cent of the leases were held by eleven individuals. These large holdings were chiefly in the Park proper; the eastern service sector was more of a small man's investment. An attractive compendium of the leases was drawn up in 1832,[31] giving the names of the leaseholders, details of the leases, and water-colour ground plans of the sites. From it we can tell who first held the head-lease from the Crown, and therefore who was most concerned in the building.

The man who put most money and work into the Park, with the exception of Nash himself, was James Burton. He built and took up the leases for Cornwall, Chester and York Terraces, built Clarence and Cumberland, and most of the villas including his own, The Holme. Four other investor-builders were William Mountford Nurse, Richard Mott, William Smith and John Mackell Aitkens. Nurse was responsible for the western side of Park Square, Ulster Terrace, Brunswick Place (now Upper Harley Street), and part of the western half of York Terrace in partnership with Burton. Mott built Gloucester Gate, Chester Gate, and Cambridge Terrace, putting up at least part of the money for each; Smith built and financed Sussex Place, Kent Terrace, and 15-33 Park Terrace, and Aitkens undertook Hanover Terrace, one of the finer and more expensive constructions. Smith, Nurse, and Aitkens were required to give guarantees that they would complete their undertakings; Smith's was for £5,000, Aitkens' for £10,000, and Nurse's unspecified. Of these five men, only Nurse retained any of the houses he had built; in his will he bequeathed properties in each of the terraces with which he had been concerned. He left 58 and 59 York Terrace to his nurse and housekeeper, a widow, Mrs Rebecca Young. He must have considered these houses to be letting propositions and good investments, whereas Burton, Smith, Mott, and Aitkens built to sell as quickly as possible.

There were two investors, as distinct from the investor-builders. They were John and Samuel Neville Ward, probably brothers and both local men. John Ward had invested money in the canal and was an associate of Burton's. He held the leases for the whole of Clarence Terrace, for 2-14 Park Terrace, the row of smaller houses and shops behind it, and for fifteen houses in York Terrace; all the building was done by Burton. There was a strong link between the two families, for Burton's son, Decimus, was retained by Ward from 1828 onwards to develop the Calverley estate at Tunbridge Wells for him, and Decimus designed country mansions for both the Wards.[32] Samuel Neville Ward took up twenty-three leases in Albany Street and all of Gloucester Gate; in this case, the building was by Mott.

Then there were a great number of smaller builders and investors. We have already mentioned the three, Richardson, Baxter and Peto, who completed Mayor's venture in Park Crescent. There was Thomas Carpenter, a carpenter and plumber, who took up sixteen leases in Osnaburg Street (Nos 20-36), and four in Frederick Street (Nos 5-8). John Hill, an instrument-maker of 422 Oxford Street, held at least forty-five leases in Albany Street, Clarence Street and Edward Street, and his widow Elizabeth continued to hold them after his death. Michael Crake, statuary, surveyor and builder of 64 Great Portland Street, had eight houses in Albany Street, and John Peachey, the ironsmith who made the gates and lamps for Cambridge Gate, owned leases of three very superior pieces of property, one house in York Terrace and two in Cumberland. Edward and Thomas Mace, coach-builders of York Market, bought up nine leases besides the six they needed for their own premises. The Misses Joanna and Mary Myrtilla Sturch, living with their brother William at 21 York Terrace, bought twenty-one leases, and Mrs Elizabeth Jesser Reid, whom we shall meet again later, bought seven. James Boobbyer, an ironmonger in Stanhope Street, had six leases in York Terrace, and one wonders how he got on with his more aristocratic tenants. Joseph and Thomas Brindley, who ran a lime-wharf at Regent's Park Basin, leased three houses there, and Samuel Thorrington, another lime-merchant, had two in Ernest Street. The Reverend John Gibson owned five houses in York Market and Osnaburg Street and Thomas Masson, a confectioner in Great Portland Street, had three in Albany Street and Ernest Street. Sir Scrope Barnard Morland, MP, Sir George Duckett, FRS, FSA, and Thomas Barber Beaumont clubbed together to buy up five leases in Ernest Street.

Nash himself bought up all the leases that were hardest to dispose of to outside takers, being those on the east of the Park. He held all Augustus Street, most of Augustus Square, the whole of Park Village, and all the wharves along the canal, as well as the ground lease for the Ophthalmic Hospital in Albany Street. Thus eleven men—Burton, the two Wards, Nurse, Mott, Smith, Aitkens, Richardson, Baxter, Peto, and Nash—carried the brunt of the building and financing, and behind them was a host of small investors and private buyers who realised that the Park, with its fresh air and open garden surroundings, was unlike everything else in London and were willing to back their belief with their money.

The creation of the Park and of Regent Street made possible a reorganisation of London's West End. Logical development of communications, such as the extensions of New Oxford Street and of Charles Street into the Haymarket, resulted from the cutting through of Regent Street, and with the redevelopment went a clearance of slum property.[33] St James's Park was replanned, Buckingham Palace built—or at least begun, Waterloo Place and Trafalgar Square laid out, and the façade of St Martin's-in-the-Fields was revealed so that it could be seen to advantage for the first time since its building a century earlier. The long wars ended, the old city seemed young again, freshly clad in spruce, elegant apparel.

Nash had further plans for linking Bloomsbury with the West End, but the king's death and his own subsequent dismissal from the post of royal architect forced him to abandon them. Even so, he achieved more than Wren had been able to do 150 years earlier. His success depended on the royal support he received—the Park and Street are well dedicated[34]—and on Fordyce's preservation of the Park from previous development. Vested interests had defeated Wren, but the Park was mercifully free of them, and the government of the day had the power and the necessary financial machinery to buy up property along the line of Regent Street.[35] The familiar face of London owes as much to Nash as to any man.

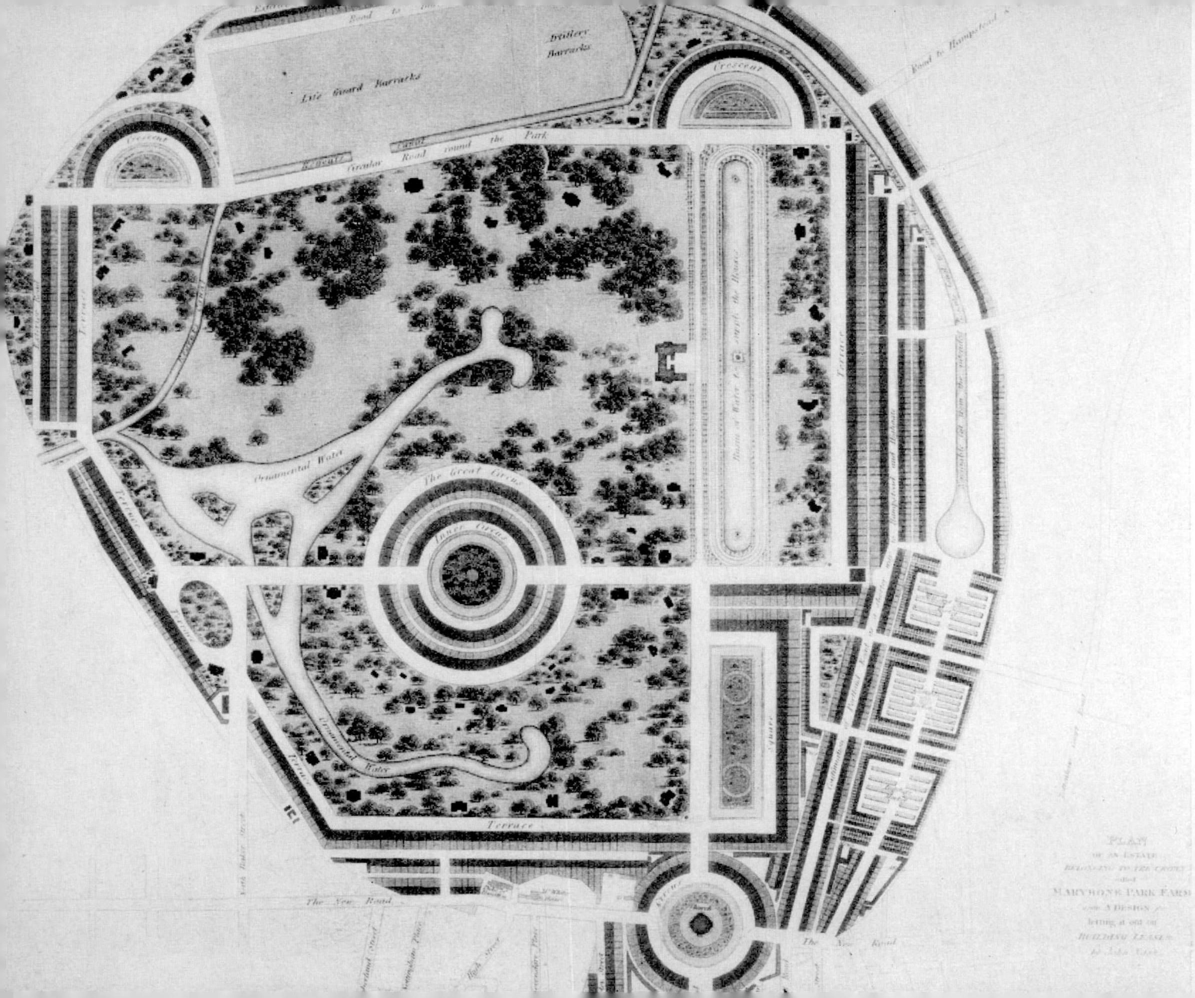

Page 107 : Nash's original plan for the Park, 1811. Note the double ring of terraces in the Inner Circle, the barracks and the crescents on the northern boundary, the circus where Park Crescent and Park Square now stand, the basin of water with a small royal palace beside it, the canal crossing the Park and the large number of villas

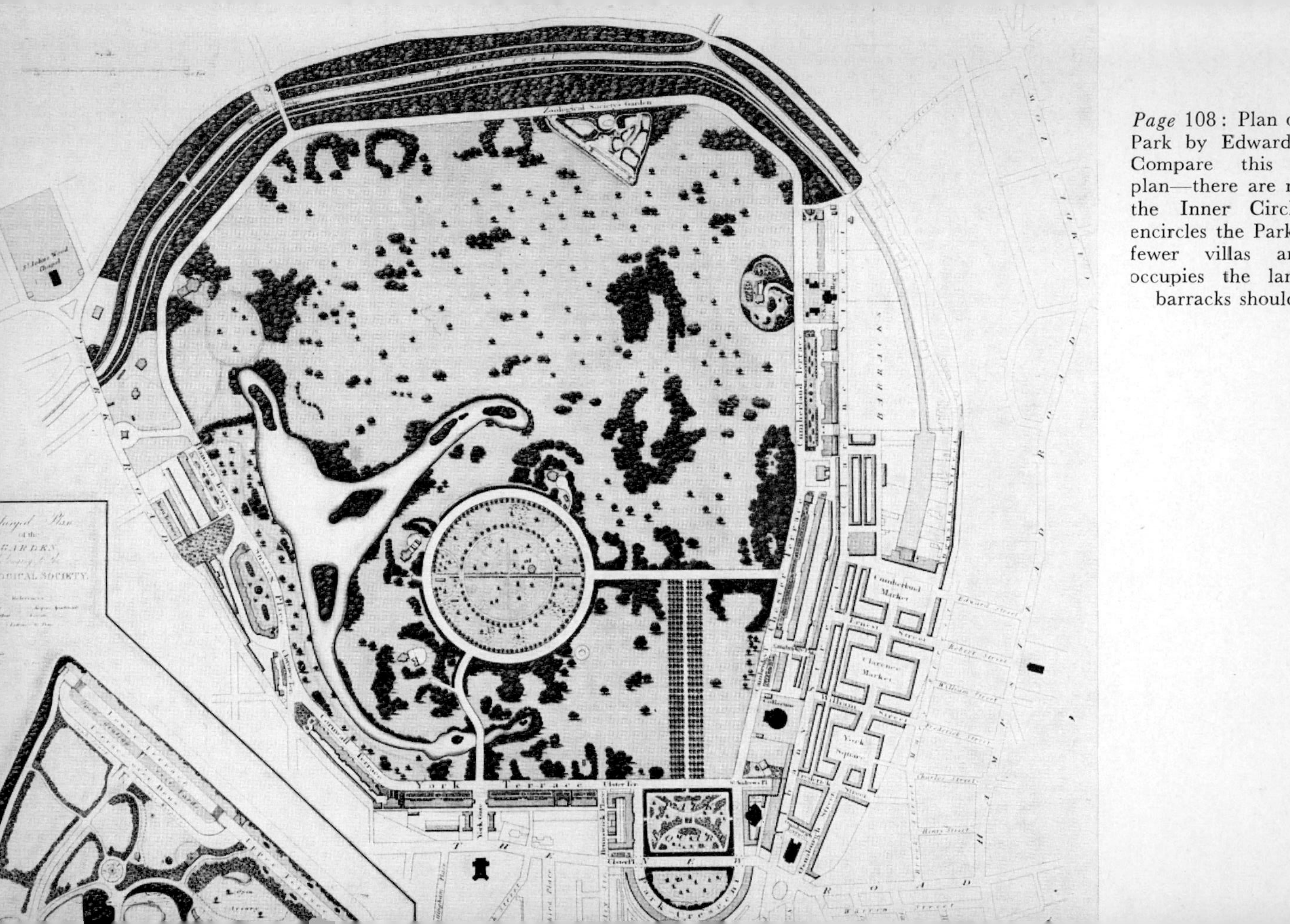

Page 108: Plan of the Regent's Park by Edward Mogg, 1828. Compare this with Nash's plan—there are no buildings in the Inner Circle, the canal encircles the Park, there are far fewer villas and the Zoo occupies the land where the barracks should have been

CHAPTER 5

THE REGENT'S PARK

Throughout 1827, Messrs Jones, the publishers, issued in parts a series entitled *Metropolitan Improvements*. Each part consisted of several engravings, based on wash drawings by the topographical artist, Thomas Hosmer Shepherd, and a text by James Elmes, a practising architect who was also an architectural antiquarian. 'No city in Europe has undergone such rapid changes and improvements as this metropolis,'[1] Elmes declared, and he compared the building achievements of the regency and rule of George IV with those of Athens under Pericles, Rome under Augustus, and France under Louis XIV. Such changes needed publicity so that Londoners should realise the excitements around them and visitors to the capital might appreciate them. Elmes devoted his first two chapters to Regent's Park and Regent Street, 'which have metamorphosised Mary-le-bone Park farm and its cowsheds into a rural city of almost eastern magnificence; and changed Swallow Street and its filthy labyrinthine environs into the most picturesque and splendid street in the metropolis',[2] and we cannot do better than follow Elmes on his tour of the new Park, adding such other information as it has been possible to collect.

The Park is best entered from Portland Place, from the northern end of which the wings of Park Crescent extend. There are twenty-nine houses in the crescent, fourteen in the western half and fifteen in the eastern. Each house had four storeys and a basement. Along the ground floor was a running colonnade with Ionic capitals, unifying the whole composition. The first floor rooms, which were the principal reception rooms, had access to the balcony above the colonnade, and the two upper storeys were separated from each other by a plain string course. Nash paid more attention to the crescent than to any other group of building in the Park; the result, restrained and dignified, is the most satisfying of all.

Park Square, which replaced the northern half of Nash's intended circus, was in fact two parallel terraces, each of five houses of moderate size. The façades were designed by Nash and the western side was built by William Mountford Nurse between 1823 and 1825. The houses, facing east and west, look into a private garden for the residents which is connected by an underground tunnel to a similar garden in the centre of Park Crescent.[3] The fine iron railings and lamps which surround these enchanting oases were the work of John Peachey, one of the craftsmen who invested money in the Park.

We are now on the Outer Circle and, turning left, we come to Ulster Terrace, built by Nurse in 1824. This is a group of individual houses rather than a terrace, with ample bay-windows and Ionic decorations similar to those which distinguished the square and crescent. Continuing clockwise round the Park, we pass Brunswick Place (now Upper Harley Street), two groups of four houses each, also with Ionic pilasters and also built by Nurse. In the original plan, there had been no opening into the Park opposite Harley Street but the outcry from the Duke of Hamilton, the younger John White, and other residents on the Portland estate was so great that Nash agreed to make another entrance, provided that all high brick walls were pulled down, that the houses of the duke and Mr White and at the ends of Harley Street and Devonshire Place were stuccoed to accord with the Park terraces, and that the residents should undertake to pay to the Crown the equivalent of the ground-rent that would have been received had the land been built over. The residents were circularised to this effect but there was little response, and in the end an entrance was made at Harley Street only. Devonshire Place lost its view, the duke and Mr White moved away and, after prolonged negotiations with the Portland estate, their houses were demolished in 1820.

On the far side of Brunswick Place is the elaborate architectural composition of York Terrace. The façade was by Nash and the work was undertaken by Burton and Nurse, Burton being responsible for the eastern half and the two men jointly for the western. York Terrace consists of two symmetrical groups of twenty houses each separated by York Gate. Each appears to be a palace, and the smaller groups of buildings, which are a part of the whole, seem to be attendant villas. There was first a group of six houses with Corinthian decorations,[4] then a pair designed as a single building and known as the Doric Villa, and then the terrace proper. The main entrances, with large sheltering porches intended for 'the reception of dressed company from carriages in bad weather,'[5] were in the mews behind; the Park façade was an unbroken whole. The wings and the centres project slightly and are rusticated on the ground floor. They are linked by a colonnade of free-standing Ionic pillars and these pillars are repeated at first- and second-floor level above the rustication. A small pediment crowns the centre of either building. In the mews behind the eastern half were York Terrace Baths, of which Elmes disapproved, calling it 'an affectation in little of East India House, divested of all its beauties of detail and invested with all its few faults.' On the other side was an archway leading to stabling.

York Gate, which divides the terrace, is one of the most magnificent vistas in the Park—or indeed in London. Nash, realising the opportunity the unfortunate vestrymen had given him, altered his plans to accommodate Hardwick's fine, if hard-won, parish church.

> The road opposite the Church will become the great central Entrance to the Park & on that Account every available circumstance ought to be seized to make it grand and imposing. [Mr Nurse and Mr Burton] have agreed to adopt one and the same Elevation, and to execute the design which I have the

> honor [*sic*] to submit to the Board; and by which it will be seen that the Church will stand in the middle between the two ranges of buildings which I propose to unite by continuing the Colonnades of the buildings across the Road as an enclosure for the Iron railing and gates, so the whole will be one uniform front, 914 feet in length; the Church and its Steeple forming a magnificent centre.[6]

The colonnade across the road was never built, but the view from the Inner Circle down York Gate to the church with York Terrace extending on either side is superb.

Directly opposite York Gate, a road leads into the Inner Circle. It goes over a bridge across the lake which Nash considered an essential part of his design, though it caused him much trouble. Originally, it was to have been supplied with water from the canal at little or no cost to the Crown, but when the canal's supply proved to be scarcely sufficient for its own needs, negotiations were opened with various water companies. The first two approached refused to tender and in the end the natural resources of the Tyburn were utilised. It was turned into a lake by judicious excavation[7] and the earth from it piled into a huge mound in the centre of the Inner Circle which added to the scenery and over which generations of children have since played and scrambled.[8] The Tyburn, which had to be carried by a small aqueduct over the canal excavations, disappeared from sight as a river for it was built into the new King's Scholar's Pond sewer which drained the Park. After flowing in at the northernmost end of the lake and out again beside Sussex Place, it was built into a brick culvert and vanished.[9] Six small islands, well fenced-off, were left in the lake to add to the picturesque effect. In the summer of 1831, the residents complained of the smell and an agreement was made with the West Middlesex Water Company to supply 23,000 tons of water annually for £200.[10]

Around the perimeter of the Inner Circle were three villas, St John's Lodge, The Holme, and South Villa. The two former were the first important buildings to be erected within the Park.

John Raffield's design for St John's Lodge was exhibited at the Royal Academy in 1818. It was a dignified, imposing building, adorned only with a pediment. The main interior feature was a fascinating well hall; the sitting rooms were all small but very pleasant, each with a view across the Park; the kitchens, as was usual, were concealed in the basement. James Burton's house, The Holme, was designed by his son, Decimus, a young architect whom Nash had trained. Decimus was only eighteen when he planned the house, probably with his father's help, and with very pretty results. It stood on the shores of the lake, with large bow-windows overlooking the water. Inside it was plain but very pleasant, suitable for as large a family as the Burtons—ten children and the staff needed to look after them all—but its position lent, and still lends it, an enchantment. Not everyone liked it however; the commissioners complained to Nash who agreed that the design was ugly—and who was then taken to task by Milne for having permitted such a building to be erected at all.

> In your observation that, "it is to be lamented, for the beauty of the Park, that Mr Burton was *allowed* to build the sort of House he has built", the Board (having recently inspected the Park and the Villa in question) command me to state to you that they entirely concur; but they cannot record this concurrence, without unequivocally stating to you, at the same time, that in their judgement the whole blame of having suffered such a building to be erected, as well as the considerable expence to which it is their further mortification to find, by your Letter, the Crown has been put in planting out [with additional trees] the deformities of this building, rest entirely with yourself; The Board consider it to be your special Duty to take care that any Building to be erected in Marylebone Park should be so constructed as not only not to deform but to constitute a real ornament and a substantial and profitable improvement . . . of the Crown's Estate."

It is hard to see why Milne disliked The Holme so much; to twentieth-century eyes, the villa is graceful and elegant. Nash's concurrence with his views suggests that the architect did not care for his chief backer; we shall find Nash and Burton at loggerheads on other occasions, though the two men were too wise to quarrel irrevocably with each other. The third house, South Villa, was not built till 1827, by an unknown architect for William Henry Cooper Esq. It was a fine house with a podium raised on an arched loggia and a bow-window at the eastern end overlooking the lake.

Returning now to the Outer Circle, after York Terrace we come to Cornwall Terrace. It was the first terrace to be built, erected during 1821, nine years after the Park had been begun. It was designed by Decimus Burton with Nash's approval, and was built by the young man's father. It has been suggested that Nash would never have entrusted the first terrace to anyone but himself, but since he had been entirely responsible for Park Crescent, begun so much earlier, the argument is scarcely valid.[12] Moreover, by 1821 he was fully occupied with Regent Street and with rebuilding Buckingham House as a palace for George IV who had succeeded to the throne a year earlier, so he was probably only too willing to leave matters to the son of the man on whose financial support he was to a good extent dependent. Nash might not have liked the father, but he was too shrewd and too fair-minded not to further the son's career, so the twenty-one-year-old Decimus was given a magnificent opportunity. The design was exhibited at the Royal Academy in 1822; it consisted of nineteen houses, their front doors opening on to the Park, the centre and wings projecting slightly and ornamented with pediments and colonnades stretching from the first- to the second-floor windows. The westernmost house has a large bay-window to the ground and first floors, decorated with four charming caryatids.[13]

The ground rent on the terrace was £200 and the houses were intended for the wealthier members of society, but since they were without gardens Burton proposed that the strip of Park opposite should be encircled with a sunk fence and reserved for the use of the residents of Cornwall Terrace. The commissioners referred the suggestion to Nash who suppressed it firmly.

I am decidedly of opinion that such a disposition of the Park ought not to be entertained even for a moment, the objections are numerous. The first and leading objection is the departure from the original purpose of forming a Park for which reason the few Villas to be allowed within its area are to have their small shrubberies surrounded by thick plantations of forest trees to *conceal* them as being *out of harmony* with *Park scenery*, and that the passenger in riding round the Park might recognize nothing but a park. The next is—that if such *ornamental plantations, walks and seats* should be allowed in the Instance proposed it is impossible even to hope that it could be extended to the whole of the park and its incongruity in that case must be felt and would be censured by every person who should possess common sense—much less taste—but even if such an incongruity could be allowed the project would be found impracticable—who is there to contract to *preserve it when made for 99 years*? & what *kind of security* could be given for *such* a purpose? If Mr Burton could assure to the Board (and I am sure I wish he could) that he should live 99 years and that he should be as able to perform such a Covenant during that term as he now is, his personal undertaking might be sufficient and I know of no other he could offer. Mr Burton it may be presumed builds the houses for sale and when he has sold them will care (naturally enough) as little for the plantations in question as he does for the planted squares he has made in Bloomsbury. The speculation I can easily conceive may answer Mr Burton's views which I take to be *Rents* from the inhabitants of the houses for permission to walk in them . . . The question is whether a *Public Garden* shall be cut out of the Park which might and probably would end in a Tea Garden—a *subscription* tea garden *perhaps*—but still as arrant a public garden as White Conduit House was and as Smiths and other tea gardens now are and when Mr Burton shall have filled his list with *genteel* subscribers he may let it or sell it and slip his shoulders out of the responsibility.[14]

No more was heard of the garden with its ornamental pavilions 'serving the purpose of seats and gardeners' tool houses.'

Beyond Cornwall Terrace was an entrance from Baker Street called Clarence Gate after the next terrace westwards. A small and charming lodge was designed by Nash and iron gates were made by John Peachey. The whole undertaking cost £1,317 2s, the largest items being the bricklayers' work—£278 12s—and the gates themselves which cost £279 10s.[15] Clarence Terrace was designed by Decimus Burton. His original plan[16]—a large central block linked to side-wings by an open Ionic colonnade and decorated with caryatids and sarcophagi above the cornice—was more elaborate than the modest terrace built in 1823, which was the smallest in the Park consisting of twelve houses only. The building was a cramped version of the first design, with two houses inserted behind the colonnades which consequently made them dark, but Elmes approved and wrote of its 'pleasing composition', for the apparent separation of the parts made it lively and the details were well finished. Decimus' designs met with general approval; Sir Charles Arbuthnot, addressing the parliamentary enquiry into the management of the Office of Works in 1828, said that his attention had been held by Decimus' buildings above all others in the Park for their elegant correctness and that he had therefore recommended the young architect for other public works in Hyde Park.[17]

The next terrace was Sussex Place, the one eccentric group of buildings in the Park. Nash designed it for the builder William Smith, who gave him £200 for the detailed drawings.[18] It consists of twenty-six houses with curved wings, three-sided bow-windows, ten pointed domes, and fifty-six Corinthian columns. Sir John Summerson points out that the design resembles Nash's unused plans for rebuilding Carlton House and the thrifty architect may well have made use of what he had in hand.[19] His contemporaries did not approve of the result; Elmes wrote 'It presents a singular contrast to the chaster beauties of the other terraces,' and Messrs Britton and Pugin, in their *Public Buildings of London,* declared that 'The whole has too much the air of being an experiment in brick and mortar.'[20] The houses sold well, however, and to modern eyes have an endearing and piquant charm; they seem a piece of stage scenery, intended to be seen from a distance, but they enjoy the most picturesque view in the whole Park for they look out on to the prettiest part of the lake. The curve of the terrace, though Britton and Pugin declared it was 'not only a positive defect . . . but absolutely productive of no beauty whatsoever in the elevation . . . as ungraceful to the eye as it is incommodious for interior arrangement,' permitted a private garden which made the immediate outlook as agreeable as the distant prospect was romantic. It also enabled the architect to bestow pretty oval spiral staircases, rising the whole height of the buildings, on some of the houses.

Behind Sussex Place, Smith and Burton built Park Terrace, a row of small houses and shops with agreeable plain elevations. Northwards on Park Road Smith erected Kent Terrace, a severe building with restrained Ionic columns. Britton and Pugin disapproved, saying that it backed so closely on to Hanover Terrace in the Park as to be injurious to the 'insulated and salubrious character' of the latter, but Nash felt that Kent Terrace would have a good effect on the neighbourhood as a whole for he wrote to the commissioners on 10 March 1827 :

> If Mr Smith will erect this line of Building and plan the extremities and lay out the ground in front in an ornamental manner, they will give respectability to the neighbourhood of the Alpha Cottages.[21]

These cottages were a small street in St John's Wood which had acquired—without real justification—a slightly doubtful reputation. As Mr Smith lived near to them, on South Bank by the canal, he may have been trying to improve his own surroundings.[22] The only peculiarity of Kent Terrace was the roof, for in November Nash was writing :

> The houses are flat roofs covered in with a recently invented covering called zinc, the which being metal and of the nature of copper, I do not see that I can object to its use, although I have no experience of its properties.

Directly in front of Kent Terrace, facing on to the Park, was Hanover Terrace, which Nash designed in a more scholarly mood than usual. Its twenty houses were arranged as one group with three porticoes linked by a continuous loggia. The porticoes have Doric columns to the first and second floors and pediments adorned with sculpture which Elmes thought 'the architect would do well to remove' for they were in 'a wretched style of art.' He approved of the setting however :

> The situation of this very pretty terrace is near the north western extremity of the western branch of the lake which embellishes and refreshes the Park. The islet which faces its northernmost wing sweetly diversifies the scene, and gives a charming sylvan character to the prospect from the houses.[23]

Hanover Terrace was built by John Mackell Aitkens of 9 Chapel Street, Grosvenor Place. It was one of the finer and more expensive buildings—the ground rent was £440—and Aitkens had to produce a guarantor, a Mr Alexander Birnie, to stand surety for £10,000. After their experience with Mayor the commissioners were not taking any more chances. The accommodation inside was the usual compact London terrace house—the kitchen in the basement, two reception rooms on the ground floor, a double drawing room on the first, and three bedrooms on the second and third floors, but in Hanover Terrace, the drawing room was really superb.[24] Each house had a small private garden and the building agreement specified that the brick front should be faced with cement or Francis and White's mastic, a type of stucco which Nash favoured. Behind the terrace was Abbey Lodge, a neat Gothic villa built by Aitkens about 1826 for George Birnie, who was surely a relative of his guarantor. It was so unlike anything else in the Park that one is tempted to think that Birnie and Aitkens designed it between themselves and that Nash accepted their design because the building was screened by trees from the Park and seemed more a part of the rural Alpha Cottages.

Beyond Abbey Lodge was an entrance at Hanover Gate for which Nash designed a quaint little lodge with niches for statuary, and to the north was a belt of trees through which the canal wandered, and five villas, Albany Cottage, Hanover Lodge, Grove

House, Hertford Villa, and Holford House. Albany Cottage, or as it was sometimes called, North Villa, was a pretty cottage ornée built for the diarist, Thomas Raikes. The ground floor was raised and entered from a curved flight of steps which led to a small verandah, edged with urns and an iron balustrade. There was only one upper storey, the kitchens being in a half-basement. The centre of the house was set forward a little and ornamented with four neat little columns. Hanover Lodge, the home of Sir Robert Arbuthnot, had 'greater pretensions to architectural character than its rural neighbour' and was designed by Nash himself. It was a plain, dignified two-storey building with four Doric pillars to its portico and a hall with marble columns and a tessellated pavement. There was a large dining room and three parlours. 'A stone stair-case of good proportions leads to the upper storey, which comprises nine handsome bed-chambers, a bathing room with every accommodation for that healthful luxury, dressing rooms, and other requisites for a respectable family.'[25]

Hertford Villa and Grove House were both designed by Decimus Burton and probably built by his father. The Marquess of Hertford had the largest villa in the Park which, though otherwise of restrained design, had a spectacular portico with eight large free-standing Corinthian pillars. On the far side of the canal was Grove House, the home of George Bellas Greenough, an eminent natural scientist. This villa was one of Decimus' most successful achievements. It was erected in 1822 and the building agreement specified that it should not be of less value than £3,500. The site, which covered nearly three acres, was leased at 10s the square foot, unlike other villas which were charged £100 for the first acre and thereafter at £20 the acre. Nash was particularly anxious that the building on this site should be imposing, for the ground rises slightly and any villa was bound to have a commanding position, visible from the Park. The canal was at the bottom of the garden, which Greenhough was at pains to lay out to the best advantage, and though no access was given to the banks the water added to the picturesque setting. Grove House faces on to Prince Albert Road and a small amount of land had to be purchased from the Eyre estate for the site. The entrance was from a small portico leading into a circular hall, beyond which was a rotunda with marble floor and eight marble columns with Corinthian capitals, their order copied from the Temple of the Winds in Athens. To the left was a dining room and beyond that a billiard room, both fine and well-proportioned; to the right were two libraries for which Decimus designed all the library furniture, which is still there. Immediately behind the rotunda was a gracious drawing room looking across the garden, the canal and the Park; outside its windows was a semi-circular portico with six pillars and three steps leading into the grounds.[26]

Although it was not constructed when Elmes made his perambulation, another villa, the most spectacular of them all, was built by Decimus on the northern boundary of the Park. This was Holford House, built in 1832 for a wine-merchant, James Holford, to the value of £6,000—the most expensive villa by £1,000 at least. All the villas were somewhat Italianate, but Holford House was a fantastic palace, with a huge, pedimented portico, semi-circular bays at either extremity of the front with cupolas and a balustrade round the roof adorned with large urns. It was nearly as large as Hertford Villa and certainly more breathtaking. The grounds were extensive and well wooded. The owner lived there in solitary state, looked after by twelve families of servants, till his death in 1855.

The north-eastern corner of the Park has been occupied by the Zoological Society ever since 1828, and then came the eastern entrance, a roadway and two footpaths spanned by a screen with Doric columns and a lodge on either side. The first group of buildings on the east side was Gloucester Gate, a terrace of eleven houses with some detached dwellings at the northern end.[27] They were built by Richard Mott with John Joseph Scoles as his architect. Scoles did not care for Nash's façade so, hoping to improve it, he doubled the scale of the moulding on the Corinthian capitals. This was in 1827, when Nash was in difficulties over building Buckingham Palace, and he never noticed the change but just murmured 'The parts looked larger than he had expected.'[28]

Beyond Gloucester Gate was St Katharine's Hospital. This institution had existed since the thirteenth century under the patronage of the queen consort as a hospital and home for poor men and women of clerical connections.[29] In 1825, its site near the Tower was sold to the St Katharine's Dock Company and in spite of appeals from the inmates and protests from those who wished to preserve the hospital for antiquarian reasons, the last sermon was preached in the chapel on 29 October 1825 and demolition began the next day. A site was provided in the Park and the Dock Company undertook to pay £36,000 towards the cost of a new chapel and house for the master, the brothers, sisters, and bedeswomen. These had become royal appointments, grace and favour houses with a clerical bias; the 2,000 real poor whom the old hospital had sheltered had been dispersed and were relying on the poor rates of Stepney. The new buildings were designed by Ambrose Poynter, a young architect whom Nash had trained and whom he thoroughly disliked. The older man declared himself 'astounded at the phenomenon' of Poynter's being commissioned.[30] The buildings bore no resemblance to anything else in the Park, being Gothic in style and bare of stucco. The fittings of the old chapel—the choir-stalls, pulpit and the Duke of Exeter's tomb—were re-installed, and the houses for the master, the brethren and the sisters were plain and grey. Poynter exceeded his estimate and £15,000 worth of repairs had to be done by the middle of 1833.

Southwards from St Katharine's was Cumberland Terrace, which was designed by Nash and built by William Mountford Nurse with James Thomson as architect on the site. Begun in 1826, it is the most splendid of all the terraces, for it was designed as a royal prospect since it would have stood opposite the prince's own palace had that been built as originally planned. It consists of three separate blocks linked by decorative arches with a small group of houses at either end. The ground levels change on the site so Nash planned a mews with the stables in the basement and small pair of houses behind the linking arches. James Thomson was a careful architect and added several ideas of his own to the details so that the finished result is unusually successful. The pediment of the central block was adorned with figures by George Bubb representing Britannia with the 'various arts, sciences, trades, etc., that mark her empire.' The sculpture is not very good when examined at close range, but seen from a distance, as it is meant to be, it creates a fine effect. Altogether, this building is Nash's greatest individual achievement as an architect and the grandest thing in the Park.

Chester Terrace, which follows Cumberland, gave more trouble than any other. It was built by James Burton and was his last undertaking in the Park so that he was particularly anxious to make it a success. On March 30 1825, Nash wrote to the commissioners saying that Burton was willing to take up the site and to build a terrace:

> The Extent of the Elevation is 900 feet, nearly equal to the Tuileries and of one regular design. The Centre presenting to the road . . . a portico of eight Corinthian Columns and one also at each end of the like number and in each of the spaces between the centre and the extremities a Colonade [*sic*] of six Columns making in the whole line 36 Corinthian Columns. This front will recede 90 feet from the side of the Road with wings advancing to the road where there are also Colonades of eight Columns making on the whole 52 Cols: on each of which it is proposed to place a Statue . . . The Columns, Capitals and Statues will cost Mr Burton at least £4,000; at the same time that they do not contribute to the comfort or real value of the building, but as they will essentially contribute to the value of the Park I recommend as a remuneration to Mr Burton, or rather as an inducement to him to carry such a magnificent Facade into effect, that no charge be made for the planted ground at each end and that an abatement be made

> in the rent of 1125£ (say of 75£ per Annum) . . . Mr Burton is so pressing that I should report on his proposition—not considering the immense length of time such an Elevation take in the Drawing after it has been digested, thus I am induced to present it in an unfinished state, well knowing that his success in the undertaking (at least £140,000) will depend on his immediately beginning it.[31]

Nash accompanied the letter with a very rough sketch of the proposed ground plan. The commissioners agreed and the work began at once.

In the following February, Nash wrote to the commissioners complaining that the two detached pairs of houses which had been substituted for wings blocked the light and view of the houses behind in the main terrace; 'Nothing can be more ugly than seeing the front of buildings in the rear of others—the impression being that some ill-natur'd fellow, having the right, has built Houses before his neighbours windows.' He requested that they should be pulled down for he had never intended that they should look 'so disgusting'. Burton naturally claimed compensation and Nash then wrote again saying that, apart from the offending houses, Burton had departed from his design in numerous details and that the sculpture, which was being provided by George Bubb, was ludicrous.

> I entreat the favour of the Commissioners to prevent Mr Burton from exhibiting any more of those ridiculous figures on the top of the cornice—the ridicule which every new figure excites is so painful to the ears of a professional Man, that I hope you will persuade the Commissioners not only to prevent any more of them being put up, but order those already placed to be removed . . . One of the figures is the late Mr Watt, also Mr Smeaton, worthy men no doubt, but never before I believe claimed as British Worthies. Another is of a Man reading a Book; a worthy employment, no doubt, but if every Man who reads a Book is to be admitted into the class of British Worthies they would reach round the whole park.

According to Nash, Burton had omitted some of the balustrades and had doubled the scale of others, had omitted window-sills and plinths, the cornices and mouldings were not straight and were 'very badly executed,' and 'the railing on the wall in front is mean and squat'. Burton replied with a long and dignified letter and enclosed a copy of another by James Lansdown, the builder to whom he had subcontracted the work. Lansdown wrote:

> In answer to these charges, I scarcely know how to reply, because I cannot bring myself to believe Mr Nash has ever examined the Materials & Workmanship, or he would not I am sure make an accusation as untrue as it is uncharitable & unjust, nor can I for a moment think any Man influenced alone by Public Duty would bring forward charges which cannot with any degree of propriety be substantiated . . . The front railing of which Mr Nash complains was made upon his approval of the design, the drawing of which I waited on him with in December last & obtained his sanction as to its execution.

Similarly, the list of statues had been submitted by Bubb to Nash himself before the work was begun and had been approved. Lansdown went through the complaints, refuting them one by one. The matter was referred to the architect, William Wilkins, who agreed that the statues were bad and should be taken down at once, but declined to support Nash's other objections. He gave valuations for the eight houses under dispute—£1,567 6s 6d for the pair at the north end of the terrace, £2,011 for those at the south end, £3,954 13s for Nos 4 and 5, and £2,300 5s for Nos 39 and 40. In all, he calculated £11,711 18s 6d would be due to Mr Burton and £8,132 18s 6d to Lansdown, if the offending houses were to be demolished. The Treasury, reasonably enough, declared that Nash should have watched the work more closely and made his objections earlier, and they would not sanction such a sum for compensation. The houses remained, the statues disappeared, and Nash designed arches to link the pairs of houses with the main terrace.

One wonders what became of the sculpture and whether some of the figures may not, after all, have found their way into the

Page 125: (above) Park Crescent having collapsed during building, 1820. Wash drawing by an anonymous artist (British Museum, Crace collection, Views portfolio XXX, no 135); (below) The Crescent, Portland Place. Aquatint by Rudolf Ackermann, 1822. The trees, which today grow high and obscure the Crescent, were only saplings when this engraving was made and the elegant line of Nash's masterpiece can be seen clearly. The parish church can be seen in the distance

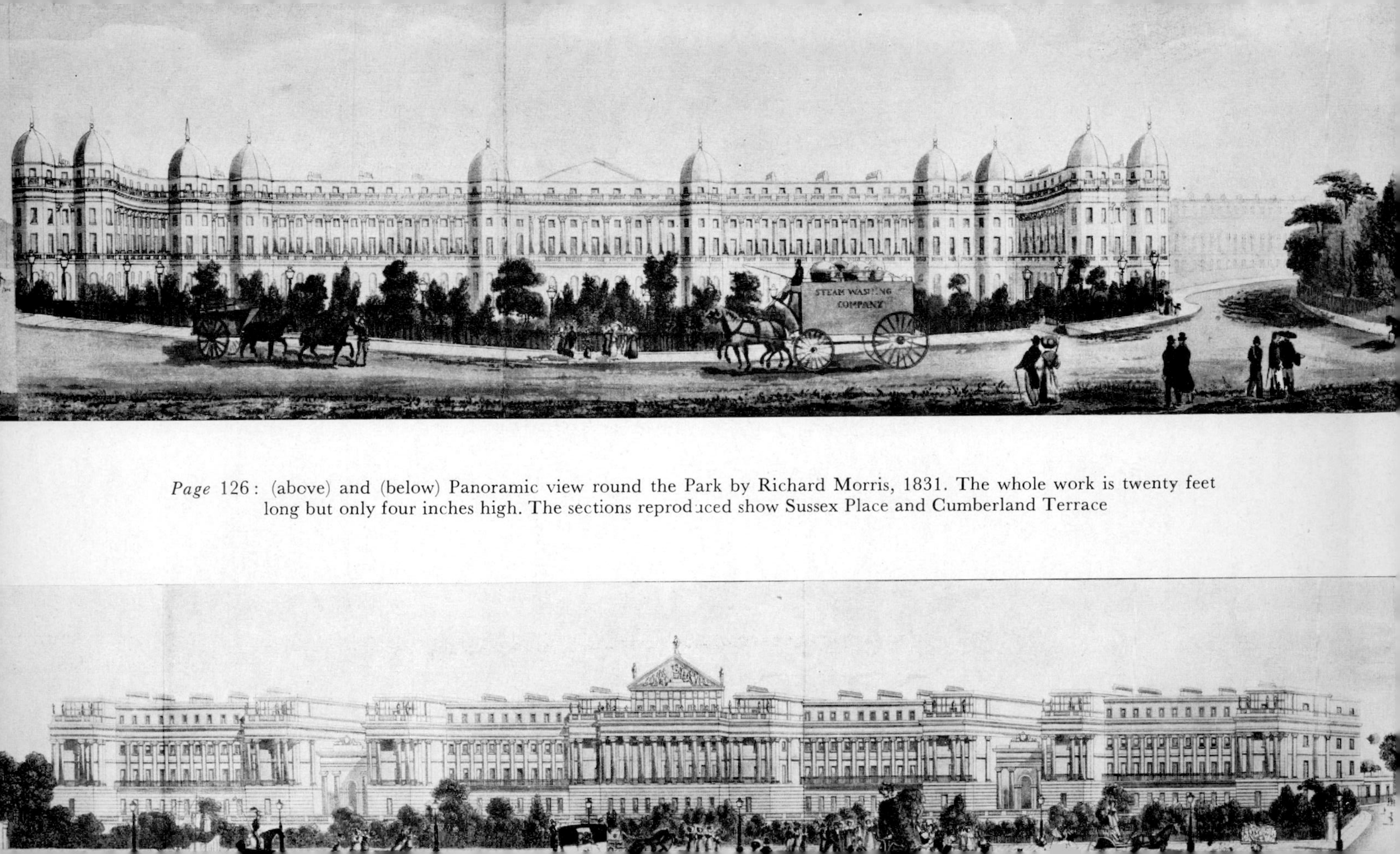

Page 126: (above) and (below) Panoramic view round the Park by Richard Morris, 1831. The whole work is twenty feet long but only four inches high. The sections reproduced show Sussex Place and Cumberland Terrace

Park. Cumberland Terrace was built a year later than Chester, and all the statues which embellish it came from Bubb's workshop. It would have been hard to resist the temptation to slip in a few of the despised worthies. Nash was of course an old man, much harassed with other work, when the argument broke out, but it would suggest that personalities were involved when he could question Burton's window-sills and balustrades and yet not notice the alterations Scoles made to the mouldings at Gloucester Gate. There had probably always been an antipathy between the two men; Burton was very much a man of his word who believed in saying exactly what he meant, whilst Nash was rather the opposite. Nash was too dependent on Burton's financial support to risk an open argument but he made difficulties whenever he could. He had disparaged Burton's own villa, The Holme; there were letters to Milne which prevented Burton building two villas, with considerably more profit to himself, on the site of Grove House; there had been a villa begun opposite the opening of Harley Street which Burton began and was forced to demolish;[32] the ornamental garden in front of Cornwall Terrace was prevented; there was trouble over Chester Terrace; no one thing significant in itself, but signifying much in aggregate. Curiously enough, Elmes approved of the offending houses:

> Let me call your attention to the pavilion-like houses that project at each end, and are connected with the main body of the terrace by the Corinthian arches, as productive of a fine and novel effect.[33]

But he did not care for the detail of the terrace:

> It is of the Corinthian order of architecture, of a feeble and effeminate character in its details, surmounted by a balustrade of lanky proportions and tasteless forms. The capitals do not spread sufficiently for the graceful beauty of the gay Corinthian, and the volutes are too small and are pinched up, as if the acanthus, whence the Callimachus of Chester Terrace gathered them to decorate his order, had been withered by a frost.

The houses in Chester Gate were built by Mott, who was also responsible for Cambridge Terrace, a very plain group of houses. Southwards was a most unusual building, the Colosseum.[34] It was built between 1824 and 1827 to house a panorama of London, painted by a young artist, E. T. Parris, from sketches made by an ingenious surveyor, Thomas Horner of Robert Street in the Adelphi. Horner had made the drawings—some 2,000 of

Park Village East, by Thomas Hosmer Shepherd, 1827

them—in 1822 from a cabin on the dome of St Paul's when the ball and cross were being restored. He spent some £5,000 on the work and then 'determined to erect a permanent Building for my panorama of London on a scale of unprecedented magnitude.' Decimus Burton was selected as architect and designed a sixteen-sided building 130 feet in diameter, with a superb portico and majestic cupola. He originally planned an even larger building but Nash felt it would be out of scale with its surroundings. 'Mr Horner and his Architect,' he wrote to Milne, 'have consented to reduce the portico to the size of the Parthenon and to continue Pilasters round the Circular Building, and make a visible roof, so as to give the whole an appearance as of a building instead of a blank wall.'[35] Decimus regretted the change but was forced to agree. It was hoped to show the panorama to the public in the autumn of 1827 but Parris was still painting away at it—he covered 40,000 square feet of canvas in all—a year later, and that winter Horner and his chief backer, a Mr Rowland Stevenson, absconded, leaving debts of more than £60,000 behind them.

The Colosseum was eventually opened on 10 January 1829, though Parris was still suspended in a cradle putting finishing touches to the panorama, which was displayed around two galleries, whilst a third gave access to the roof of the building whence the prospect of the real city could be seen. A small lift was installed to hoist spectators who did not wish to exert themselves by climbing the galleries, and the original ball and cross of St Paul's were there too, adding verisimilitude, for they had been dismantled and replaced when the cathedral was repaired. Around the Colosseum were elaborate gardens and a Swiss cottage designed by P. F. Robinson, the author of *Village Architecture*. An enterprising dress establishment, Messrs B. Read of Bloomsbury Square, issued a series of fashion plates set in Regent's Park—the most fashionable part of the town—and several of them give views of the Colosseum against which elegant well-corseted persons displayed their finery. The name 'Colosseum' was a reference to the size of the building, which of course bore no resemblance to the Colosseum in Rome but was rather a Grecian version of the Pantheon, as pundits such as Elmes were swift to point out.

Southwards was the Adult Orphan Asylum, where the grown-up daughters of penniless officers and clergy were sheltered. Nash designed the building—a very plain one—without a fee, and the commissioners subscribed £50 a year to the asylum, which amounted to letting it without a ground-rent. Beyond the asylum was a cul-de-sac, St Andrew's Place, with two fine houses at its blind end, built between 1826 and 1828 by George Thompson and Henry Crake. The lamp standards were identical with those at Clarence Terrace. The small terrace at right-angles to these houses matched Ulster Terrace on the far side of Park Square and was built by Jacob Smith in 1823, and our circuit ends with the east side of Park Square leading back to Park Crescent.

Outwardly this side was identical with the west side and could be passed over were it not that it contained the Diorama.[36] Of the five plots, the three central ones were allotted to this building which was erected during the summer of 1823 by Jacob Smith. The Diorama was the cinema of the last century. A painting, which was partly a transparency, was displayed, and by lighting and sound effects, magic lanterns and mirror projections, was made to seem alive. The Diorama had two picture rooms and a circular auditorium which revolved so that the pictures could be displayed in turn. The interior was planned by Augustus Pugin, the machinery was designed by James Morgan and built by an engineer called Topham. It was so well poised that the whole auditorium could be turned by a single man. The Diorama opened on 29 September 1823 with paintings from Messrs Daguerre and Bouton's Diorama in the Rue Sanson in Paris depicting the interior of Canterbury Cathedral and the valley of the Sarnen; it had an immense success and Bouton remained behind in England to run the new establishment. The artist, John Constable, went to the opening and wrote to his friend, Archdeacon Fisher:

> It is in part a transparency, the spectator is in a dark chamber, and it is very pleasing and has great illusion. It is without the pale of the art, because its object is deception. The art pleases by reminding not by deceiving. The place was filled by foreigners, and I seemed to be in a cage of magpies.

Our tour of the Park is now complete, but we must remember that there was another part of the Crown estate, the eastern sector which had been planned as a market and service area for the terraces and villas. Behind Chester and Cumberland Terraces ran Albany Street, made along the line of the farm track that had served the tenant of Coneyburrow Farm. On the east side stood the 'Queen's Head and Artichoke', whose licensee, Samuel Poole, had taken up the first lease on the new estate. Beside the tavern was a row of small third-rate houses—No 34, next door to the 'Queen's Head' is the oldest dwelling on the estate—and opposite it some better property. Nos 140-8 have handsome stucco façades, for they were built by Nash's own plasterer, William Nosworthy, who took over Mrs Elizabeth Hill's leases when she, being widowed, found herself in financial difficulties.

Further along, on the same side as the 'Queen's Head', was the Ophthalmic Hospital consisting of two wards which Nash let to the government at £600 a year for seven years. The institution had been founded for Sir William Adams, the oculist, at York Hospital in Chelsea, where he gratuitously treated soldiers who had been inflicted with ophthalmia during the Egyptian campaign against France, and was moved to Regent's Park in order to provide better and more convenient accommodation. A little further along the street was Lieutenant Charles Theophilus Hall's riding school, its long manège with an elegant façade. Beyond it were the barracks built during 1820 to 1821, though Colonel Neville had applied for a site in 1810. The officers must have made use of Mr Hall's stables and expert instruction.

Beyond all these buildings were the canal and the markets. Of the three markets planned, only one had been built. The whole site of the southernmost, a meat market called York Market, was leased in 1812 by Robert Green at a ground rent of £720 a year. After building four houses he went bankrupt and the sites had to be parcelled out among other builders and speculators, who took it at 7s 6d per foot of frontage. It was built as Munster Square, 'with stucco façades of modest, delicate beauty, miraculously in scale and proportion.' Beyond were Clarence Gardens, intended for a vegetable market but also built as a residential area, though the centre was railed off to prevent idlers from congregating there and was cultivated as a nursery garden by Mr Thomas Brown of Hampstead Road for a rent of £20 a year. The third, Cumberland Market, replaced the Haymarket which was transferred there in November 1830 at the earnest request of the inhabitants of Piccadilly and St James's. The commissioners, though unwilling at first, agreed to the move and the market continued to function into the twentieth century. The first superintendent was William Kendall, possibly a descendant of the family who farmed for so long in Marylebone Park. Underneath the market was an enormous commercial icehouse, the property of William Leftwich, ice-merchant. It was eighty-two feet deep and had a capacity of 1,500 tons. The firm always maintained a ship in transit between London and Norway to replenish the supply which was delivered by the canal. The ice-well was eventually filled in with clay from the Cockfosters underground railway extension. The canal also served to deliver some of the hay and straw—the rest came in by cart—and to carry away manure.[37]

North-west of the market, in Edward Street, the 'Jew's Harp' tavern had re-opened. The new building was squat and stolid compared with the old one, but on 6 June 1819 Mrs Ames, the proprietress, advertised her thanks to the public 'for their increased patronage during the last season and to assure them that the same unremitting exertions will be continued on her part towards the present season.' She was ready to cater for 'clubs, societies, annual dinners and select parties . . . Teas and refreshments also provided for schools at their summer vacations.'

The 'Jew's Harp' enjoyed a view of the canal basin. The whole site was leased by Nash himself in 1818. At that time, the canal company was in such financial straits that it had had to cease work, the promised markets were unbuilt, and Nash, as Crown surveyor, had put a high valuation on the land. The directors reproached him with the situation and he declared that he was ready to take upon himself 'anything that was not right.'[38] The rent was £24 14s for the first seventeen years, £36 11s for the next seven, £134 for the ensuing fourteen, and £1,321 for the remainder of the term, which amounted to £1 per foot of frontage on the basin. Nash enlarged the basin, reluctantly paid between £700 and £800 for its lining, and let the wharf sites to tenants who spent £9,400 on buildings, roads, and other necessary work. Some eleven million bricks were made from the earth dug from the basin, and went to build Nash's own new house in Regent Street, the Albany Street barracks, Mornington Crescent on Lord Southampton's land, and fifty-seven little houses in Augustus Street.[39] When the fortunes of the company turned with the completion of the canal, Nash made a profit from the wharves—and found himself in a questionable position as a Crown surveyor who, having valued the site, had leased and developed it and then passed as properly constructed the dwellings he had himself built thereon. A select committee was appointed to probe the matter and declared themselves satisfied that Nash had acted honourably—but they thought it better that such a situation should not be allowed to occur again.

Nash's acceptance of responsibility for the canal basin was his most courageous contribution to the success of the Park, for when he undertook it there seemed no hope of profit. In 1824 he took on another almost equally large liability, though by this time the estate was well established, so that there was less chance of failure. He leased all the remaining land along the canal banks,[40] and built thereon Park Village East and Park Village West, a colony of enchantingly sophisticated cottages, reminiscent of the model village he had laid out years before at Blaise Hamlet in Gloucestershire. The prettiest of all was Tower House in Park Village West. No two houses were alike and the villages with their winding roads are the epitome of the picturesque. They were to inspire, with less happy results, countless suburban housing estates.[41]

Contemporary opinion about the Park varied, as was inevitable. Maria Edgeworth visited it in 1830 and was 'properly surprised by the new town that has been built in Regent's Park—and indignant at plaister statues and horrid useless *domes* and pediments crowded with mock sculpture figures which damp and smoke must destroy in a season or two,' but the lady was charmed by the Zoological Gardens. More serious criticism was levelled by John Britton and Augustus Pugin in their *Public Buildings of London*. They wrote:

> In his plans for Regent Street, Mr Nash adopted this idea of uniting several dwellings into a single façade, so as to preserve that degree of continuity essential to architectural importance: and, however open to criticism many of these designs may be, he has produced a varied succession of architectural scenery, the aggregate effect of which is picturesque and imposing,—certainly superior to that of any other portion of the metropolis; and, notwithstanding all its defects, far preferable to the naked brick walls that universally form the sides of our old streets. The "Terraces" in the Regent's Park must be considered as a continuation of this design, and, like the street, an improvement upon our usual style of private houses; yet we must also be permitted to say, that although so far commendable, they are by no means the most chaste or elegant specimens of architectural composition. Owing perhaps to the desire of abandoning the petty scale and character of ordinary houses, these buildings are designed in an air of pretension that they cannot support. On a cursory view, they present an idea of palaces, but more minute inspection shows these seemingly spacious edifices to be only clusters of common-sized dwelling-houses. The windows and doors are by far too numerous, and too closely crowded together,—a circumstance sufficiently proving the extreme economy it has been found requisite to employ with regard to space, and making it obvious that the apartments are by no means lofty, nor otherwise on a magnificent scale. There is likewise a sketchiness—if we may so term it—an inconsistency between the affected grandeur of the design, and the poverty, in many instances, of the detail, that excites no small degree of disappointment in the beholder.[42]

These are fair objections; the houses are mean inside compared with the magnificence of their façades. The detail is often poor and often showy—Nash's desire for sculpture on Chester Terrace which would not 'contribute to the comfort or real value of the building . . . but to the grandeur of the Park' is typical of the whole. Nash was aiming at a grand gesture, at creating something new, exciting and beautiful. He was not worrying about convenience or detail but was trying for a total effect.

George IV, for whom the Park had been created, understood this and sympathised, and therefore supported Nash. Almost all the names in the Park recall the titles of the royal family—Hanover for their hereditary kingdom, Clarence for the duke who was Lord High Admiral, Cornwall for the king himself who had been duke of that county; even in the poorer canal area, the streets were called after the king's brothers, Ernest, William, Augustus, and Frederick. Nothing came of a suggestion that the Park should be called after the Duke of Wellington;[43] the Regent had no intention of relinquishing his claim. He was wise; the Park and the Pavilion at Brighton are his best memorials, as even his contemporaries realised. Crabb Robinson, the diarist, delivered the verdict on the Park which would most have pleased the king and his architect:

> This enclosure, with the New Street leading to it from Carlton House, will give a sort of glory to the Regent's government, which will be more felt by remote posterity than the victories of Trafalgar and Waterloo, glorious as these are.[44]

CHAPTER 6

THE NINETEENTH CENTURY

Although Regent's Park as built was only a torso of the grand design he had proposed, Nash never lost interest in his creation. Designing cottages for Park Village was, he felt, a suitable occupation for his old age but he had to forego the pleasure for in 1825, when he was seventy-three, he was ordered by his sovereign to build a new palace on the site of Buckingham House. Nash advised against the idea from the first and when he was compelled to accept the commission he struggled bravely with lack of funds, the ever-changing whims of his royal master, and the conflicting orders of that master and the Treasury. Wings were built looking so odd that they had to be demolished; an elaborate dome was erected—and was found only to light a box-room; £200,000 was voted for the work but at least three times as much was spent. Matters ended in 1828 in a parliamentary enquiry at which Lieutnant-Colonel Stephenson of the Office of Works admitted he had no control over expenditure.

> Have you any means in your hands of checking the architect if you think he is exceeding the estimate considerably?
> —I am not generally aware of his exceeding his estimate till I find it out by the bills.[1]

Nash was required to answer to the board but he succeeded in clearing himself both then and in the following year when he was interrogated about the profits made by his speculating in Crown leases in Regent Street.[2] The ageing George IV tried to protect him and begged the Duke of Wellington to gazette his 'poor little Nash' a baronet,[3] but the duke firmly persuaded the king to postpone the honour and the monarch's death intervened before he could ask again. Several architects have been knighted but Nash is the only one for whom a higher honour has been proposed. Meanwhile, popular feeling was all against him. Cartoons appeared showing him impaled on the spire of All Souls' Church, as a toad under a harrow, as an ugly little man presenting John Bull with an endless bill, but on the king's death the old man was allowed to retire peacefully to his estate in the Isle of Wight where he died in 1835. His obituaries were unkind; John Britton wrote: 'We cannot contemplate the character of the architect without feelings of sorrow and terms of reprobation.'[4] Nash would not have cared. He had never worried about other people's opinions, and he had a more enduring monument than the gibes of a topographical journalist.

* * *

Fordyce, Nash, and the commissioners had all, from the first, intended that the Park should be a residential area for those in the highest ranks of society. Every detail—the palace for the prince's leisure moments, the studied serenity of the parklands providing an idyllic setting for the villas, the terraces resolutely turning their backs on the outside world, the canal providing a bulwark against the meaner properties to the east, the markets segregated from the terraces but there to provide for and to wait upon the needs of the residents—all indicate that the architect hoped the Park would at least rival, if not replace, Westminster and St James's as the quarter for the aristocracy. Visitors to London eulogised it as such; the Vicomte d'Arlincourt wrote:

> The Regent's Park, above all, is a scene of enchantment, where we might fancy ourselves surrounded by the quiet charms of a smiling landscape, or in the delightful gardens of a magnificent country-house, if we did not see on every side a countless number of mansions adorned with colonnades, porticoes, pediments and statues, which transport us back to London; but London is not here, as it is on the banks of the Thames, the gloomy, commercial city. Its appearance has

> entirely changed; purified from its smoke and dirt, and decked with costly splendour, it has become the perfumed abode of the aristocracy. No artisans' dwellings are to be seen here; nothing less than the habitations of princes.[5]

But once the prince had become George IV, and the idea of the park providing a retreat from the responsibilities of government for himself and his entourage had been relinquished, the impossibility of maintaining it as an exclusively aristocratic area became apparent. The inhabitants, though necessarily well-to-do, were as mixed a gathering as one would expect to find in any capital city and, as one would also expect in a commercial centre such as London, there was a preponderance of men associated with trade. The successful banker, the wealthy merchant, the fortunate stockbroker, sought to make their home in Regent's Park, where they were joined by the more prosperous members of the professional classes—the Church, the Army and Navy, doctors, lawyers and publishers—all of them prizing the rural atmosphere which was still within half an hour of the City and Westminster.

> What a prospect lies before us, splendour, health, rurality and comforts such as nothing but a metropolis can afford are spread before us. Trim gardens, lawns and shrubs; towering spires, ample domes, banks clothed with flowers, all the elegancies of the town, and the beauties of the country are co-mingled with happy art and blissful union. They surely must all be the abodes of nobles and princes! No, the majority are the retreats of the happy, free-born sons of commerce, of the wealthy commonality of Britain, who thus enrich and bedeck the heart of their great empire.[6]

So Elmes summed up the residents, and an examination based on rate books, directories and census returns shows that things did not change very much after his day, though the inhabitants included several persons who could hardly be described as 'sons of commerce'.

To compile a complete list of the occupants of the villas and terraces would certainly be possible but its perusal might well prove tedious and it seems better that a dozen of the more interesting names should stand for the hundreds who have made their homes there.[7] James Burton, the builder and Nash's partner, we already know well; when living in The Holme, he would have had as neighbour Francis Charles Seymour Conway, the third Marquess of Hertford, who owned Hertford Villa. He had been Envoy Extraordinary to Russia, was a friend of the king, owned a magnificent art collection and entertained on so lavish a scale that he was known as the 'Caliph of Regent's Park'. Thackeray modelled the Marquess of Steyne in *Vanity Fair* on him, and Disraeli introduced him into *Coningsby* as the Marquess of Monmouth. It was he who salvaged the clock with the figures of Gog and Magog striking the hour from the church of St Dunstan's in Fleet Street. He paid £210 for it, had it repaired and set up in his garden, and changed the name of the villa to St Dunstan's.

On the northern outskirts of the Park, George Bellas Greenhough, President of the Geological Society and a founder of the Royal Geographical Society, was lavishing attention on the grounds of Grove House where he lived for thirty-three years. His care was maintained by later owners and when, in the present century, the villa became the home of the artist, Sigismund Goetze and his wife Constance, they opened the celebrated gardens to the children of the Charity School nearby in Lisson Grove. They also made several gifts of sculpture to adorn Regent's Park and Marylebone; these included the great iron gates leading into the Inner Circle which were presented in 1935, and the Triton Fountain by William Macmillan in 1936.

Hanover Lodge was the home from 1846 to 1860 of the banker, Matthew Uzielli, who provided much of the financial backing for railway development in this country, in France and in Italy. After his death, the sale of his pictures at Christie's lasted eight days. His widow lived on at the lodge till 1897.

South Villa was the home from 1834 to 1861 of a wine-merchant, George Bishop. He was born in Leicester in 1785, entered a London firm at the age of eighteen and eventually acquired a fortune which he applied to his lifelong interest, astronomy. In 1836, with the approval and support of the Crown commissioners, he built an observatory in the Inner Circle and, despite being over fifty, studied mathematics sufficiently to enable him to participate in the observations and calculations carried out there. After his death in 1861, owing to the increasing pollution of the London atmosphere, the observatory was moved by his son to Twickenham where it still stands. From 1840 to 1876, Mr Bishop's neighbour at Sussex Villa was Sir Francis Grant, portrait painter and President of the Royal Academy; his grand-daughter married the next occupant, Lord Annesley, who lived there until 1906. He had entered the Army in 1851 and had been wounded at the Battle of Alma during the Crimean War and again during the Kaffir War.

Perhaps the liveliest family that ever inhabited one of the terrace houses was that of Mrs Collins at 17 Hanover Terrace where she lived with her sons, Wilkie the author and William and Charles the artists. Charles' painting, 'May in Regent's Park', is in the Tate Gallery. In 1852 the Collins' gave a dance which seventy artists and writers attended; Charles Dickens, living nearby in Devonshire Terrace, presided over the buffet and Wilkie's publisher, Alexander Strahan, who lived at 9 Hanover Terrace, may have come too. Not far away, at 24 Sussex Place, lived John Lockhart, Sir Walter Scott's son-in-law and biographer, from 1828 to 1855; his eldest son, John Hugh, was buried in the parish church.

The Army was well represented in the Park; its members showed a partiality for York Terrace. Lieutenant-Colonel Sir William Colebrook, Governor first of Antigua and then of the Leeward Isles, lived at No 10; of him it was said that he 'seemed to derive pleasure from freely imparting his just and admirable views of colonial policy, founded on the immutable basis of Christian principle'. At No 21 in the same terrace lived Elizabeth

Jesser Reid, née Sturch, with an unmarried sister. This redoubtable lady was responsible for the foundation in Bedford Square of a college for the higher education of women. Her bosom friend, Elizabeth Anne Bostock, lived at 5 Ulster Terrace, a short walk away.

Perhaps the best conspectus of the type of person inhabiting the Park is obtained by a glance at the map illustrating Charles Booth's *Labour and Life of the People of London*, first published in 1889. This map indicates in colour the wealth or poverty of the residents in any given area of London. The terraces are solidly yellow for they were inhabited by wealthy people. The sole exception is Kent Terrace which is red; its inmates were therefore 'fairly comfortable'. Albany Street shows as middle-class—Edward Lear stayed at No 61, the Rossettis lived at No 45, Francis Trevelyan Buckland, the naturalist, at No 37, Henry Mayhew at No 55, and Sir Edward Jenner spent fourteen years at Nos 8 and 12—while the hinterland around the markets varies through middle-class to mixed to poor—'18s to 21s a week for a moderate family'. There was a great contrast between the residents in the villas and those on the outskirts of the Crown estate.

* * *

In spite of the raptures of Elmes and d'Arlincourt which we have already quoted, one Londoner was less enthusiastic about the Park. Leigh Hunt wrote:

> Mr Nash is a better layer-out of grounds than architect, and the public have reason to thank him for what he has done for Regent's Park. Our gratitude on that point induces us to say as little as we can of the houses there, with their toppling statues, and other ornamental efforts to escape from the barrack style. One or two rows of the buildings are really not without handsome proportions, those with the statues among them; and so thankful are we for any diversity in this land of insipid building, where it does not absolutely mortify the taste, that we accept even the pumpkins of Sussex Place as a refreshment. We don't know what they mean nor why they are there; but there

> is something Eastern in their look, and they remind us, among other things, by a fantastic but not unpleasing link in our memory, of the time when we have sat up in a tree in this very neighbourhood, reading the Arabian Nights! . . . We have reason to be thankful that the Regent's Park has saved us from worse places in the same quarter; for it is at all events a park, and has trees and grass, and is a breathing-space between town and country. It has prevented Harley and Wimpole-streets from going further; has checked, in that quarter at least, the monstrous brick cancer that was extending its arms in every direction.[8]

The judgment was fair; approval of Nash's architecture is a matter of personal taste, but no one can deny that the Park provides north London with a fine breathing-space. Hunt might well have spoken more caustically for he could remember Willan's Farm, 'where we have eaten creams and other country messes', and no man is inclined to love the development that eats up the fields where he has played in boyhood.

Nash's work affected the growth of north-west London profoundly.

> It spared Regent's Park from the kind of mediocre development which ruined Camden Town; it secured the exclusiveness of the West End in Marylebone and Westminster; it set the tone for future developments in Hampstead.[9]

White, Nash, Leverton and Chawner had all commented, in 1811, on the poor property springing up to the west and east of the Park, on the Portman estate and on Lord Southampton's land. But the Eyre and Eton estates to the north and north-west, which were developed from the 1820s and 1830s onwards, were covered with attractive semi-detached villas and trim stuccoed terraces designed exclusively for the professional and affluent classes, and they in their turn influenced the type of property that spread up the slopes of Hampstead Hill.

The Park itself did not stand unaltered after Nash's retirement. His wife's adopted son, James Pennethorne, succeeded to much of his step-father's practice and completed the building of

Page 143: (above) The Zoological Gardens in the Regent's Park, by J. Marchant, engraved by H. Adlard, c 1850. The clock on the right is still in use; (below) View in the Colosseum. Summer fashions for 1836. Another of B. Read's fashion plates. The assembly room attached to the Colosseum was decorated by one of the Crace family. At a later period than this plate, the window shutters were lined with looking-glass so that when they were closed at night, the room became 'one effulgent blaze of light'

Page 144: (above) The Colosseum, by Edmond Thomas Parris, engraved by T. Higham, 1830. To the left can be seen the Adult Orphan Asylum, later Someries House; (below) The geometrical ascent to the galleries in the Colosseum. Aquatint by Rudolf Ackermann, 1829. The engraving shows the interior of the almost completed building. Two men, slung in cradles, presumably Parris and an assistant, are finishing the panorama. Spectators could reach the viewing platforms by a staircase or in a lift worked at first by a hand-winch and possibly the first public lift in this country. The original ball and cross of St Paul's can be seen above the platforms. A final staircase led out to the roof from which the visitor could gaze at the real London

Park Village. A terrace of miniature houses, Nos 1-7 Park Village West, are his work and are particularly charming. In 1832, the Toxophilite Society was allotted its own terrain, five acres close to York Terrace at a rent of £125 per annum for thirty-one years.[10] A small rustic lodge was built at which the residents complained bitterly; they particularly resented the red-tiled roof. The commissioners' architects inspected the building, found it unexceptional and told the residents they had a perfect right to grant the land as a villa site if they chose, which put an end to the complaints. However, so many of the younger residents soon joined the society and disported themselves with bows and arrows and social gatherings such as ladies' days and balls and a bazaar to raise money for Brompton Hospital in 1856 that the Toxophilites became an established part of life in the Park. In the winter months the grounds were flooded and allowed to freeze over and the London Skating Club joined the archers for graceful exercise.

The spiritual needs of the residents were not neglected either. Those living in the southern half of the Park naturally joined the congregation of the parish church, while the villa owners and inhabitants of Hanover Terrace were nearer to St John's Wood parish church. In 1818 the Church Commissioners were established and given a million pounds to provide new and much-needed churches for the increasing population of London. Four were built in St Marylebone: St Mary's, Bryanston Square, Christ Church, Cosway Street, All Souls', Langham Place, and Holy Trinity, Marylebone Road. The first three sites were easily chosen and Nash himself designed All Souls', incorporating it in his scheme for Regent Street, but the location of Holy Trinity was only settled after much difficulty when a plot of Crown land at the end of Albany Street fronting on the Marylebone Road was bought for £3,660 and a dignified church was built from designs by Sir John Soane. It stood where the buildings of Coneyburrow Farm had once been and the boundary between Marylebone and St Pancras had to be adjusted so that the church might stand entirely in Marylebone. An outside pulpit—probably the only one in London—was added in 1893 in memory of the Reverend William Cadman who had been vicar there; unfortunately it did not improve the façade.

The inhabitants of Albany Street and the surrounding district were served by Christ Church, Albany Street. It was the first church to be built under Bishop Blomfield's Church Extension Scheme and was designed by James Pennethorne in 1837. It is a plain brick building with an enormous lofty door, small towers at each end of the four corners and a slender steeple over the main entrance. The interior was remodelled in 1867 by William Butterfield and a stained-glass window, illustrating the Sermon on the Mount, was made from designs by Dante Gabriel Rossetti in memory of Miss M. M. Polidori, a relation of his mother's. A daughter church, St Mary Magdalene in Munster Square, was built in 1852 with funds provided by the Reverend Edward Stuart, a wealthy curate at Christ Church who later became the first vicar of the new foundation. The architect was Richard Cromwell Carpenter, who had in mind the old church of Austin Friars and he created a curiously restful interior with quartrefoil piers. Finally there was St Saviour's Hospital in Osnaburgh Street, an Anglican nursing sisterhood established by Dr Pusey in 1845—the first to be housed in this country since the Reformation.[11] Outwardly the building was ruggedly Gothic and inwardly full of corridors, but in the chapel was woodwork that had come from Buxheim near Augsburg in Germany. The altar-screen was dated 1691 and the choir-stalls and other fitments were of the same date. When the hospital was demolished in 1963, the sisters removed to Hythe, taking the woodwork with them.

Throughout the nineteenth century the Park was gradually opened up to the public. At first, no part of it excepting the roads was open but in 1835 the eastern portion and a strip adjoining the canal, amounting to eighty-eight acres in all, were opened for general enjoyment and recreation. There was such approval that another ninety-two acres were open in 1841 leaving only the grasslands around the villas, a narrow strip in front of the southern terraces, and the grounds of the Toxophilite and of the Royal Botanic Societies as restricted areas.

> The Park is always full, but on Sundays and holidays it really swarms with pleasure-seekers, who find in its trees, grass and flowers a very fair substitute for the fields of the country. During the summer months, a band plays on Sunday afternoons on the greensward by the side of the long avenue, and is the means of attracting thousands of the working classes thither.[12]

The long avenue, now known as the Broad Walk, had been planned and planted by Nash, who had died before the trees were larger than saplings. Along the southern half, a flower garden was laid out by Nesfield at the express request of the Prince Consort. A superb herbaceous border was created and huge granite urns were installed. They are still in use today and are bedded out with seasonal flowers; literally hundreds of plants are required to fill each one.

The open space available for recreation was extended still further when, in 1841, the Crown acquired Primrose Hill by exchanging land at Windsor with Eton College to whom the hill had formerly belonged. It was made into a public park. By chance in that same year, James Pennethorne created Victoria Park, a poor man's Regent's Park in Limehouse at the eastern end of the Regent's Canal.

The admission of the public encouraged gifts of sculpture, such as the splendid drinking-fountain presented by that benefactress of of London, Baroness Burdett-Coutts, in 1871. It is of bronze, granite and marble, adorned with reliefs and surmounted by a cluster of lamps; it stands at the northern end of the Broad Walk near the entrance to the Zoo, where it has attracted the destructive attention of hooligans so that it is a wreck of its former self. Similarly, Richard Westmacott's Swan Fountain, which used to stand in the middle of the Broad Walk, was irreparably damaged in 1961 and has now been replaced by Alexander Munro's 'Boy with a Dolphin' from Hyde Park. Another fountain, designed by

R. Kevile and presented by the Indian potentate, Sir Cowasji Jehangir Readymoney, in 1865, is still in position near the lake and there is another near Gloucester Gate designed by Joseph Durham which consists of a bronze statue of a girl drawing water from a natural spring, the pedestal being made of boulders from the Cornish moors.

Almost imperceptibly, the characteristics of the Park began to change. Instead of being an aristocratic precinct, it became a resort and open space for all Londoners. The residents, when it suited their convenience, altered their individual terrace houses. Colonel Fanshawe built himself a dressing-room behind 14 Cumberland Terrace; Sir Francis Grant, the portrait painter, added a studio to Sussex Villa. Though the changes were often slight in themselves—a window-box here, a window-blind there—they were enough to impair the line of the terraces. More serious were the additions of an extra attic storey whose dormers peered over the balustrades or parapets Nash had designed, and the general substitution of sheets of plate glass for the small panes in the sash windows. The property in the eastern sector was troublesome from the first. In 1831, Messrs Stephenson and Glover at 65 Chester Mews raised their building by four feet and converted a stable into a dwelling house. This was reported to Nash who wrote that it was 'most injurious to the whole neighbourhood . . . The Commissioners should repress this by every means in their power.'[13] Eight years later, Pennethorne was asked to make a report on the area.

> The opposite side of Little Albany Street is now unfortunately occupied by servants of the worst description, living in the Buildings originally built as stables and gradually converted into Houses and this has been done to so great an extent and has long existed that I fear it would be almost impossible entirely to get rid of the nuisance.[14]

Worse still was threatened in 1845 when it was proposed to convert the Regent's Canal into a railway and the promoters offered £1,000,000 for the shares—three times their market value. The residents protested passionately and the commissioners rejected the proposal.[15]

The uses to which the non-residential buildings were put began to change too. Holford House ceased to be a private villa and became Regent's Park Baptist College. The college had formerly been established in Stepney and existed to train candidates for the ministry. The Adult Orphan Asylum moved away to Ealing and the building became a private residence, Someries House. The Ophthalmic Hospital ceased to be used as such, and Sir Goldsworthy Gurney, a colleague of the oculist Sir William Adams, took over the lease and built himself a steam-carriage in the yard, for his interests were not confined to medicine. He exercised the machine around the Park until it was in sufficiently perfect condition to drive to Bath in July 1829. Then for a while the hospital was used as a factory for Perkins & Bacon's 'steam guns', a prototype of the modern machine-gun, and in 1835, just before he died, Nash leased the building to Sir Felix Booth, the distiller who had been knighted for his services in promoting Arctic exploration. After that, the building was used for a variety of warehouse purposes.

Similar fates overtook the Diorama and Colosseum. The entrance fee for the Diorama was 2s and it did very well for several years, £200 being taken on Easter Monday in 1824. Topographical scenes, such as the Castle of Stolzenfels on the Rhine or the Cloister of St Wandrille in Normandy, were the most popular; most of them were painted by Bouton and Daguerre and were shown in Paris before being brought to London. But the takings declined steadily and in 1848 the Diorama closed and was sold off for only £3,000. The lease was taken over by Sir Samuel Morton Peto, the builder and railway magnate, in 1852 and was converted into a Baptist chapel which it remained until 1921. The first minister was the Reverend William Landels who was noted for his preaching.

> He could deliver a whole series of orations without notes and without the slightest variation from his manuscript. He

> composed his public utterances with great attention to oratical effect. The sentences were decorative and delivered in a torrent of unfaltering and passionate speech. Audiences were held breathless until the peroration was finished.[16]

The congregation increased rapidly and attracted many wealthy Baptists who contributed generously to the mission work undertaken by the chapel. One of them was Lady Lush who concentrated her attentions on the desperately poor women who strove to drag up their families in Nash's once trim little streets near the canal. She first took a room in Frederick Street where 'cottage meetings' could be held and where the mothers could be instructed in first principles of hygiene and child-care as well as the Bible. Then one day her husband offered her a specially valuable piece of jewellery but she said she would rather have a hall where her mothers could meet, so he bought her a site in Charles Street (now Drummond Street) just off the Crown estate, and a mission hall was built. She often called it her diamond necklace and it is still flourishing today. The Regent's Park chapel was also noted for the breadth of its theology, for all Christians were admitted to Communion whether or not they were Baptists.

The Colosseum held out longer as a place of entertainment, though it, too, succumbed eventually. It was purchased in 1831 by John Braham, the famous tenor singer whose voice had earned him a fortune. He paid £40,000 for the building and added two marine caverns, an African glen full of stuffed animals, and a hall opening onto Albany Street which was panelled with looking-glass and decorated with painted birds, the work of one of the Crace family of artists. Concerts were given there and in the evening the shutters were also of looking-glass so that the chandeliers were reflected and the whole long room was one dazzle of light. Reproductions of antique statues were displayed and the queen visited the Colosseum in 1835, but soon afterwards affairs began to go downhill. In 1838, the new hall had been 'converted into a place of evening entertainment for man and beast at the moderate rate of a shilling admission-refreshment ticket, alias ticket for gin and water included',[17] and in 1843 Braham was forced to sell the Colosseum for 23,000 guineas and to return to the stage from which he had retired in order to pay his debts. He was supported in old age by his daughter who had married into the peerage and as Frances, Countess Waldegrave, was one of society's most celebrated and beloved hostesses.

The new owner was David Montague who 'altogether retrieved and elevated the artistic character of the establishment'.[18] The panorama was repainted by Parris, who also created a new one of London by night. The Museum of Sculpture became the Glyptotheka; a Gothic aviary, a Swiss chalet and classical ruins were built in the grounds, and it re-opened with a private view for the Queen Victoria and the Prince Consort on 3 May 1845. In 1848 a panorama of Paris was displayed and a cyclorama with ten scenes of the Lisbon earthquake of 1755 was added, but the Colosseum still could not pay its way and after a last season, when the panorama of London was put on again for the Great Exhibition, it closed and was put up for auction in 1855. The auctioneer declared that £200,000 had been spent on it but no bid came near the reserve price of £20,000 so it was withdrawn and stood mouldering in the Park, its stucco flaking and the brickwork showing bare underneath. It opened for two seasons of entertainments in 1857 and 1863 but then closed finally and was demolished in 1875. Decimus Burton was still alive and saw his work vanish. Cambridge Gate, a terrace of unattractive Victorian houses by Messrs Archer & Green, was built on the site which, though it did not accord with Nash's work around it, was at least a residential terrace and preserved the original building line. The Hall on Albany Street was replaced by a small row of houses, Colosseum Terrace. This rebuilding was the only major change in the appearance of the Park which otherwise entered the twentieth century very much as Nash had left it.

* * *

Two appalling tragedies occurred in the Park during the nineteenth century. On 15 January 1867 the ice of the lake gave way under the weight of skaters, 'its surface shattering like a tessallated pavement',[19] and some 150 people were left struggling in the water. The water was deep and the presence of islands in the lake and the underwater current of the Tyburn prevented a solid canopy of ice from forming. There were no ropes available and too few lake attendants to be of use. The gardeners from South Villa did all they could to drag people from the bitter water but forty men and boys were drowned or died from exposure. Fourteen of the victims were under sixteen, the youngest being nine-year-old Edward Jukes. The commissioners at once lowered the level of the lake and most stringent precautions against skating are kept to this day. Street ballads appeared about the tragedy and nearly sixty years afterwards eye-witnesses could still remember the horror of the sinister occasion:

> The first indication was a tremendous "Oh!" coupled with the sound as though someone had walked on a bed of dry leaves.[20]

The other serious accident occurred in the early morning of 2 October 1874 when five barges, laden with gunpowder, were being towed along Regent's Canal. The third barge was the *Tilbury*, and as she reached Macclesfield bridge, the northernmost of those spanning the canal, she suddenly exploded, damaging the bridge and the banks and blowing out all the windows of North Villa. Her crew of three were all killed, and it was assumed that one of them must have been smoking and that as he knocked out his pipe the sparks must have fired the cargo.[21] A relief fund was opened to assist the widows and children of the dead men. The scars of the explosion can be seen on a nearby plane tree.

* * *

Two learned societies, the Zoological Society of London and the Royal Botanic Society, had made their headquarters in the

Park from the beginning. The Zoo is still in its place; the Royal Botanic Society was only recently disbanded and has had a permanent effect on the appearance of the Inner Circle, since the gardens laid out there have been maintained by the Crown estate commissioners.

The desirability of a society devoted to the zoology both of the British Isles and of the whole world had been under discussion for some time among Fellows of the Royal Society and other learned men before a firm suggestion was made by the explorer, Sir Stamford Raffles, who became, with Sir Humphrey Davy, the first president. At its foundation in July 1824, the society consisted of 151 members several of whom, such as the Marquess of Hertford, were residents in the Park. Meetings were held, transactions published, a library formed and premises for a museum were acquired in Bruton Street, but it was obvious from the first that an open-air menagerie where animals could be displayed and studied scientifically was what was needed. The committee approached the commissioners and asked for twenty acres of land in the new Park.

> Our first plan would be to have a garden laid out in aviaries, paddocks for deer, antelopes, etc., stabularies for such animals as may require them, lodges, and perhaps suitable apartments for the Society to meet in; and, if possible, pieces of water for fish and aquatic birds. Our buildings would for the most part be low, and in no case offensive, and the plans would be readily submitted to you. As we find support from the public, we should eventually wish to have a museum attached to it whenever our finances admit, and this would of course be on such a scale and plan as would render it ornamental and suitable to the situation.[22]

On 16 March 1826, Sir Stamford Raffles and Lord Auckland inspected land on the northern boundary of the Park and wrote to the commissioners the next day to say the site was 'liable to many objections' and that they would prefer ground in the Inner Circle. This however was already let to a nursery gardener called Jenkins who had moved there from Lisson Grove, and since the commissioners were unwilling to interfere with an established lease, the Zoological Society had to be content with five acres to the north-east at a rent of eighteen guineas for the first three years rising thereafter to £400 a year. Later in 1826, more land was granted making up the twenty acres originally requested at a rent of £683 19s 2d for thirty-one years. *The Literary Gazette* commented tartly 'We do not know how the inhabitants of the Regent's Park will like the lions, leopards, and lynxes so near their neighbourhood.'[23] Possibly the same idea was in the commissioners' minds when they insisted on a site well removed from the terraces and villas.

Decimus Burton was appointed architect to the society and he immediately drew up a very pretty plan for the layout of the triangular piece of ground allotted to the Gardens. Only a part of his plans was put into practice and on 27 April 1828 the Gardens were opened to the Fellows who were able to inspect the animals and birds in their terraces, dens, ponds, and aviaries. The public were admitted, excepting on Sundays, on production of a letter from a Fellow and payment of a shilling; the Fellows were, of course, free to enter as they pleased, paying a subscription of two, and later three guineas a year.

No catalogue exists of the animals in the Gardens at the opening but from the newspapers we know that there were monkeys, all sorts of birds, gazelles, bears, foxes, emus, llamas, zebras, turtles, beavers, goats and jackals; they were all donations. The grounds were bisected by the Outer Circle and Burton linked them with a tunnel which is still in use today—as is his clock tower which was part of the camel house. The society expanded rapidly, numbering 1,100 Fellows within four years, and so did the collections, an elephant being added during 1828. In 1836 giraffes were acquired and Burton designed a special house for these charming creatures; three years later they bred in captivity. In 1837, the first chimpanzee, Tommy, arrived but lived for only six months, though he shared his keeper's own house and was in no way confined. The popularity of the Gardens can be gauged from the numbers of prints and lithographs which were issued showing the various species displayed and the types of human regarding them. A long account of the Gardens was published in Charles Knight's *London* in 1843, describing them as 'the most delightful lounge in the metropolis' and listing the animals exhibited, such as the Cuban bloodhound, the elephant and the rhinoceros who were friends, the terrible man-eating hyaena, and Lady Jane, a chimpanzee who sat up to table and drank her tea from a cup.

In 1845 a new open-air terrace was built for the carnivora which had hitherto been displayed in cages in centrally heated buildings and the creatures' health immediately improved to a remarkable extent. A change in the secretariat of the society ordained that the public should henceforth be admitted at a shilling a head without need of a letter of introduction from a Fellow; this opened the gardens to a wider public. The abbreviation 'Zoo' came into use about 1867, possibly from the song 'Walking in the Zoo' sung by the Great Vance, a music-hall comedian.

The Stilton, sir, the cheese, the OK thing to do
On Sunday afternoons is to toddle to the Zoo.
Week days may do for Cads, but not for me and you;
So dressed right down the road, we show them who is who—
The walking in the Zoo,
The walking in the Zoo,
The OK thing on Sunday is the walking in the Zoo!

The reference is to the Gardens being restricted on Sundays for the use of Fellows.

The Gardens had been expanded steadily and land on the far side of the canal was rented to house the ever-increasing and more varied collections. There was a record number of visitors in 1851 when all England came to London to see the Great Exhibition and the Gardens were thronged again for the International Exhibition of 1862 and again in 1876 when the Prince of Wales, later Edward VII, brought a collection of animals from India; the admissions for that year exceeded 900,000. There was a similar increase in 1882 when a moody African elephant was sold to Barnum's Circus for £2,000 and the press distorted the sale into a story of monstrous cruelty to animals, alleging that Jumbo was separated from his mate, Alice, who pined for him. In fact the two animals had never mated and Alice remained in the best of health and spirits although all the errand boys in London were singing:

> Jumbo said to Alice: 'I love you!'
> Alice said to Jumbo: 'I don't believe you do!
> If you really loved me
> As you say you do
> You wouldn't go to Yankee land and leave me in the Zoo!'

The money from the sale of Jumbo made it possible to build a new, long-desired reptile house. Previously, in 1868, a new elephant house had been designed by Anthony Salvin and a second improved open-air arrangement for the lions, tigers and other carnivora, which finally convinced the Fellows that it was best to keep animals in a captivity that as nearly as possible resembled their natural surroundings.

A million visitors came in 1912 to see the animals which the Prince of Wales, later George V, brought back from India, and in 1913 the new terraces presented by J. Newton Mappin, and named after him, were completed. The Zoo suffered very little during the First World War and continued to expand thereafter, one great attraction being the Giant Panda which arrived in 1938. During the Second World War the Zoo remained open, though some animals were evacuated to Whipsnade Zoo. All poisonous snakes and insects were destroyed and the Aquarium was drained—very fortunately for the building received a direct hit which would have released a quarter of a million gallons of water had the tanks been full. Though feeding presented a problem, careful arrangements were made; had the Zoo disbanded itself, it would have cost an incalculable amount of money to replace the stock and some famous breeds, such as certain giraffes, would have died out altogether.

After the Second World War, the Zoo once again became the Londoners' favourite outing but the society realised that an extensive redevelopment scheme was needed. Like all pioneers, the society was working with superseded equipment; more modern methods of display, permitting the animals to be seen behind fewer bars, were desirable and a greater economy in running costs had become essential—there were, for example, thirty separate central-heating boilers all of which had to be stoked individually. In 1959 a plan was devised by Sir Hugh Casson and Mr F. A. Stengelhofen, the society's own architect, for a complete remodelling of the Gardens. Since the Crown estate was unwilling to allot more land to the Zoo, higher buildings are being erected and service units centralised; Burton's camel house and clock tower, giraffe house and ravens' aviary and bear terrace are to be retained for historical and sentimental reasons, and so are the Mappin terraces; a new attraction is an aviary designed by Lord Snowdon. The entire scheme will cost between two and three million pounds, of which £250,000 was donated in 1960 by Mr Jack Cotton, the financier. The society itself will be provided with a new meeting-room in the Institute of Comparative Medicine, hitherto homeless, which the Nuffield Foundation is building on the Outer Circle. When the work is completed, the Fellows and Londoners in general will have a Zoo as modern as any in the world of which to be proud. It is worth mentioning that the Fellows' subscription has not been raised for 150 years but is still three guineas, though they have lost their last privilege, the exclusion of the public from the Gardens on Sunday mornings.

The Botanic Society was founded in 1838 and received a royal charter the following year. The creation of such a society and its location in the Park had been suggested as early as 1812 by William Salisbury, a nurseryman well known in his day at the Botanical Gardens in Cadogan Place. There was need for such a garden—that belonging to the Apothecaries' Company at

Chelsea was—and is—restricted to medicinal plants and the Royal Gardens at Kew were not open to the public. Nothing came of Salisbury's suggestion but it was made again in 1827 by Dr John Robert Thornton who declared he would be 'the happiest man in the world' if such a society were to be set up. Nash approved of the scheme and offered to subscribe £1,000 towards it but matters lapsed again until 1838 when the Royal Botanic Society of London was founded, mainly through the efforts of James de Carle Sowerby, who became the first secretary and was succeeded in the post by his son and grandson.

Eighteen acres which had been leased to Jenkins, the nursery gardener who had supplied trees for the Park, were rented; once again Decimus Burton was commissioned to act as architect and in conjunction with Richard Marnock he laid out the Gardens. Marnock had been curator to the Botanic Gardens in Sheffield but came to London on being offered the post there; he was appointed on the advice of the great landscape gardener, John Claudius Loudon. In spite of the heavy yellow clay which was difficult to work, the grounds were laid out with winding paths, a terrace on the northern boundary and several specialised gardens—a Linnean arrangement, medical, agricultural and manufacturing collections, an experimental garden, an American garden, a rose garden, a geographical arrangement of plants, and large borders for display of all other varieties. The mound of earth excavated from the lake was made a feature of the Gardens. A conservatory of iron and glass—the first of its kind—was built by Messrs Turner of Dublin, and huge tents—so large that they had to be watched all night because of the wind-resistance of such an area of canvas—were erected for the flower shows held in May, June and July, which became a feature of the London season. Queen Victoria was the first patroness and took great interest in the Gardens, visiting them regularly with her children. Ladies were encouraged to become members, as had been the case with the Zoological Society, and soon club premises were built and lectures, both popular and specialised, were given, as well as instruction in flower-arrangement. Several unusual plants were grown in the conservatory and borders, including the banana plant from which Queen Victoria first sampled the fruit, and a giant Amazon water lily on the leaves of which the secretary was able to sit on a chair, such was the buoyancy of the plant.

The society at first suffered from lack of funds and in 1839, having spent £12,000 on the laying-out, asked for the remission of a year's rent. This was refused and so were similar requests in 1840 and 1841 but eventually matters righted themselves and the Gardens flourished through the nineteenth century. The azalea shows by Messrs Waterer were particularly beloved. Unfortunately, the society's funds were not large enough to bear the increase in rent when the original lease ended and it was forced to disband itself in 1932, after nearly a hundred years of useful existence.[24] The care of the Gardens was taken over by the Royal Parks Department and the trust has been well preserved, though there was some protest when the conservatory was demolished and trees were cut down under the new arrangements. Her Majesty Queen Mary was much concerned about the fate of the land and, in compliment to the interest shown, the area was named Queen Mary's Garden. As we have already noted, elaborate iron gates were presented for it in 1935 by Sigismund Goetze.

It is sad that the two sister societies—if they may be so described—could not both contrive to continue in the Park. There was, of course, no official connection between the Zoological Society and the Royal Botanic Society but it was somehow very right and fitting to have two learned bodies in the Park, one devoted to animal and the other to plant life.

CHAPTER 7

THE TWENTIETH CENTURY

Although Regent's Park entered the twentieth century very much as Nash had left it, the buildings on the estate underwent great changes in use if not in appearance as the century progressed. In 1908 the lease of South Villa was acquired by Bedford College, the oldest establishment for the higher education of women.[1] The college, as we have seen, had been founded in 1849 by Elizabeth Jesser Reid whose parents, the Sturches, had been among the original leaseholders and who had herself spent most of her life at 21 York Terrace. In spite of disapproval and indifference, her establishment in Bedford Square had grown and flourished and needed newer and larger premises. When the lease of South Villa, which for many years had been the home of two old ladies, Mrs Abbot and her sister Miss Adamson, came on the market, the college bought the remaining sixteen years with permission to replace the villa with a fully equipped academic building which was designed by Mr Basil Champneys and completed in 1913. The residents did not take kindly to the new tenants and protests were staged in the Park. Part of the grounds of South Villa were reserved by the Crown and were made into a public walk along the edge of the lake but this was described as a 'paltry sop' by both residents and the general public who felt that an encroachment was being made on their claim to open air and space for recreation. In spite of the opposition, the college moved in and the buildings were opened by Queen Mary on the splendidly fine afternoon of 1 July 1913. Mrs Reid would have been delighted to have seen her college installed in such good premises near to her own home.

Page 161: (above) The Holme, by Thomas Hosmer Shepherd, 1827. All the engravings of this date by Shepherd were done for James Elmes' *Metropolitan Improvements*; (below) A morning drive in the Gardens of the Zoological Society, by James Pollard, c 1830. The charming vehicle is a cabriolet, a design made fashionable in England by the Count d'Orsay. It was desirable that a very large horse should be offset by a very small tiger or groom

Page 162: (above) Macclesfield bridge by Thomas Hosmer Shepherd, 1830; (right) damage caused by the explosion of the powder barge, the *Tilbury*, at Macclesfield bridge on 2 October 1874. The metal piers of the bridge can be seen sticking out of the rubble

THE ILLUSTRATED
LONDON NEWS

REGISTERED AT THE GENERAL POST-OFFICE FOR TRANSMISSION ABROAD

No. 1833—VOL. LXV. SATURDAY, OCTOBER 10, 1874. WITH EXTRA SUPPLEMENT

That was the last cheerful thing to happen in the Park for some time, for by the end of the next summer the First World War had broken out. The Park suffered no direct damage but inevitably repairs to the houses and terraces were neglected. Otto Kahn, the owner of St Dunstan's Villa, surrendered the lease in 1917 so that the house could be used as a training centre for blind and disabled soldiers and sailors. This centre had been established by Sir Arthur Pearson and to it the villa gave its name—St Dunstan's Institute for the Blind.[2] St John's Lodge was taken over as a hospital for disabled officers; the expense of alterations and equipment was borne by Sir John Ellerman, the shipping magnate. When in 1921 it was no longer needed as a hospital, St Dunstan's moved to the other villa and made its headquarters there until 1937. The Royal Hospital of St Katharine's, which had been disbanded in 1914 since it no longer served a useful purpose, was used throughout the war as a hospital for British and American officers, the necessary alterations being financed by William Salomon of New York; after the war it became the West London Hospital for Nervous Diseases.

The end of the war gave a new life to the Park. Social conditions made the comparatively small terrace houses desirable to those who would formerly have kept a larger establishment in Mayfair. The increasing commercialisation of the West End made the Park seem even more attractive, for the clause in the Crown leases that each dwelling should be used for residential purposes only and by no more than one family, was strictly enforced. Notable figures in London society made their home there; Lady Ribblesdale, whose husband's stables were famous, arranged tennis tournaments at Sussex Villa to raise money for charity; Rear-Admiral David Lord Beatty lived at Hanover Lodge till 1925; Herbert and Cynthia Asquith were at 8 Sussex Place and Mrs Wallis Simpson at 7 Hanover Terrace. For the arts, there were Alfred Noyes, H. G. Wells and Edmund Gosse in Hanover Terrace, E. V. Knox and George Sims in Clarence Terrace, and Hugh Walpole in York Terrace.

During the 1920s, the original ninety-nine-year leases began to fall in and the Crown policy was to renew them for a further twenty-one years at a higher rental. As a result, the Baptist College moved out of Holford House in 1927 and built a new college at Oxford while the villa was let out in apartments. Such circumstances do not keep a property in the best of repair. St Dunstan's stood empty through the 1920s and then from 1935 to 1936 was the home of Lord Rothermere, the newspaper owner, who restored the clock after which the villa had been named to the church of St Dunstan's in Fleet Street, where it is today. After his tenancy the villa was demolished and Winfield House was built on the site for Barbara Hutton, the daughter of the founder of Woolworth's.[3] It was a plain brick residence but, despite the lack of stucco, the architecture was sufficiently restrained not to look out of place in the Park, especially as it did not stand near a terrace and was well screened by trees. Park Village had already been spoiled, for half of it was swept away in 1906 when the Euston railway cutting was enlarged.

By the end of the 1920s, the economic situation of Europe and America began to be felt as much in the Park as everywhere else. Immediately after the war leases sold readily, but by 1931 'For Sale' boards appeared on the terraces and remained there. Houses stood unoccupied, which did no good to their structure or decorations.[4] The Toxophilite Society declined in membership and had to disband itself in 1922 when the lease came up for renewal. The grounds were taken over by the commissioners and, after the buildings had been pulled down, were opened to the public. An unattractive alteration was the children's paddling and canoeing pool which was opened on the western boundary in 1930. The residents protested loudly against this excavation which however undoubtedly gave—and gives—delight to many small children.

An open-air season of *Twelfth Night* was put on by Sidney Carroll in 1932 in a roped-off enclosure in the Inner Circle; Phyllis Neilson-Terry played Olivia and Sir Nigel Playfair was

Malvolio. Since then similar theatrical productions have become a regular feature of London life during the summer months, their success or failure depending on the weather. On a fine summer's night, there can be no more perfect setting for *A Midsummer Night's Dream*. By the time the Open Air Theatre was founded, a springtime spectacle had become an established event. This was the Van Horse Parade on Easter Monday. The parades had started in 1904 and, with wartime breaks, they have continued to the present day, the most successful of all being in 1922 when 705 horses and their owners took part.

The Second World War took a far heavier toll of the Park than the first had done. Although the Zoo remained open, almost everything else was affected. Barrage balloons were moored in the Inner Circle, the villas and terraces stood forlorn and deserted for the most part and many were damaged; Holford House, the Master's House at St Katharine's and part of the western sector of Park Crescent were destroyed by bombs. More insidious harm was caused by inevitable neglect and by the building restrictions which made all but absolutely essential repairs illegal. By 1945, there was scarcely 'a single Terrace . . . which does not give the impression of hopeless dereliction; there are, in fact, few more lugubrious experiences in London than that to be obtained from a general survey of the Nash Terraces in Regent's Park.'[5]

That was the verdict of the committee under the chairmanship of Lord Gorell which was set up by the government to consider what should be done for the best with the decaying terraces. The commissioners had already given their fullest attention to the problem. Two-thirds of the houses were empty; few remained undamaged from blast or bombing; many were no longer weatherproof. The possibilities were: to rehabilitate and to re-let the terraces as before the war, to demolish the whole of Nash's scheme and to redevelop the estate, or to adapt the existing buildings to the needs of London life in the mid-twentieth century. But the fate of the Park was too important to be decided by the commissioners alone. When it was first laid out by Nash, it was a matter of building on hitherto undeveloped ground, but the Park, once built, had become a part of the national heritage, and an attempt to tear it down might easily have become a major political issue. As an interim measure, the commissioners leased 212 of the 374 terrace houses to the Ministry of Works for seven years on a repairing lease, and they also asked Mr Louis de Soissons, an architect both imaginative and scholarly, to devise a plan whereby Nos 6 to 23 York Terrace could be converted into eight houses and sixteen flats. They then consulted the Royal Fine Art Commission on what should be done with the Park as a whole.

The commission recommended that:

> The general lay-out of the main Terraces should be retained, and the front and end elevations preserved or restored with a view to reconstructing the houses behind the façades in the most advantageous and economical way, having regard to post-war requirements.

They also advised that Someries House (the Adult Orphan Asylum), Cambridge Gate and Cambridge Terrace could all be demolished and redeveloped. The asylum, though designed by Nash, had been very much altered; Cambridge Gate, which had replaced the Colosseum, did not fit in with the other terraces and Cambridge Terrace was the least interesting of the original buildings. At this point, the newly elected Labour government set up the committee headed by Lord Gorell. It consisted of the chairman and six members—Mrs I. M. Bolton, Sir Edward Forber, J. H. Forshaw, Sir Eric Maclagan, Sir Drummond Shiels, and John A. F. Watson; they met seventeen times during 1945 and 1946, heard evidence from forty-seven witnesses, examined seventy written memoranda, and consulted 'the views of all parties professing an interest in the subject [and] also the opinion of all local and public bodies affected, and of learned and professional institutions and expert persons.'[6]

Not very surprisingly, they received views and evidence that conflicted. The London County Council said that all the terraces should be preserved, so great was their architectural importance, and that 'nothing less than the restoration of the buildings to their former state can be contemplated' but St Marylebone Borough Council thought that everything should be demolished and 'blocks of multi-storey flats of a mixed character' should be erected, whilst St Marylebone Labour Party said that Nash's architecture was not worth preserving and that the whole area should be redeveloped for the working classes. The committee appointed their own expert, Dr Oscar Faber, to examine the structural condition of the terraces, which he found to be very bad; apart from bombing, blast, subsidence and neglect, dry rot had attacked almost every house. 'We saw beautiful large bodies of Merulius, about 12 inches by 24 inches, reddish brown at the centre and white at the edges . . .' he reported with professional relish. Several residents, including the novelist Miss Elizabeth Bowen, declared that the houses were far more solidly constructed than any modern dwelling. There was similar disagreement about the cost of restoration and the length of life of the buildings once restored. Estimates varied from £1,350,000 for rehabilitation—or patching up—to £6,000,000 if the buildings were to be demolished, rebuilt with façades identical to those designed by Nash but with interiors suitable to modern living, and faced with Portland stone. Mr de Soissons considered that the terraces, if converted and modernised, could be guaranteed a life of no longer than fifty years, which would scarcely have justified so great an expenditure; Dr Faber thought a hundred years was equally possible.

Faced with so many contradictions, the committee made up its mind for itself. The members announced that:

> We are unanimously of the opinion that the Nash Terraces are of national interest and importance and that .... they should be preserved as far as that is practicable and without strict regard to the economics of 'prudent' estate management.[7]

Park Crescent, York Gate, Sussex Place, Hanover, Cornwall, Chester and Cumberland Terraces were to be preserved at all costs, and York Terrace if possible. They advised that the terraces should be reconditioned as they stood or converted behind the original façades on plans such as those devised by Mr de Soissons. They emphasised that the Park should remain for residential use only but agreed that Someries House, Cambridge Gate and Cambridge Terrace could be pulled down and replaced by a hostel for students at London University, and a music centre. They insisted that 'the present building line should be adhered to in perpetuity' and added that 'we would greatly deprecate any further building within the Park itself'. Finally, they advised that the opportunity should be taken to remove attic storeys and other additions to Nash's original plan. They closed the report with some strictures on the way in which the commissioners had managed the Park over the years, saying that they could not understand why such additions had been permitted and that they found it 'difficult to believe that more could not have been done, during the war years and since, to put damaged buildings of this importance into at least a weatherproof condition'. The criticisms were understandable but undeserved. It is very difficult to restrain tenants who have purchased a long lease from doing as they like in their own houses, and it is easier to say after a war what should have been done in some instance than it is to try to effect the measure during the emergency. Had the commissioners diverted men and materials for the repair of the half-empty terraces, they would have been blamed and with much justification. At least the terraces were still standing at the end of the war, and nothing rash had been done to interfere with the general conception of the Park, 'that unique example of early town planning'.[8]

After the Gorrell Committee had handed in its report, nothing happened for a further ten years in the Park itself but there were great changes in the Albany Street area. The Crown Commissioners had purchased from the Regent's Canal Company the remainder of the wharf leases, and in 1942 and 1943 had had the easternmost arm of the canal filled in since it was no longer used for transport and was nothing but an unhealthy expanse of stagnant water.[9] In 1951, the commissioners sold to St Pancras Borough Council the thirty-two acres of land on which Munster Square, Clarence Gardens and Cumberland Market stood. All that area had been heavily bombed and stood forlorn and desolate. The borough council began to redevelop it as a housing estate for 1,700 families and today it is an advanced and interesting example of community planning. As far as possible, traffic has been excluded and the land bounded by Hampstead Road and Albany Street has been treated as a precinct. Some of the earliest blocks of flats on stilts, with playgrounds at their feet, made an appearance here. Shops and public houses have been made part of the plan; the 'Queen's Head and Artichoke' is still in Albany Street though the 'Jew's Harp' vanished in the bombing. The architects for the scheme are Frederick Gibberd, Thomas Sibthorp, Messrs Davies & Arnold, and Edward Armstrong and Frederick MacManus.

In 1956 the Commissioners of Crown Lands were reorganised and became the Crown Estate Commissioners, who under the chairmanship of Sir Malcolm Trustram Eve[10] considered the future of the terraces. In November 1957 they issued a statement announcing:

> That a number of Nash Terraces will definitely be preserved for effective use for many years to come.
>
> That an attempt will be made to secure the same result for all the other Terraces designed by Nash or his contemporary, Decimus Burton, if this can be achieved without undue capital cost.
>
> That, while an assured future cannot yet be foreseen for all the Nash and Decimus Burton Terraces, present plans do not provide for the demolition of any such Terrace, or for the elevation of any such Terrace to be altered.

The statement was a brave one, considering that the cost of restoration had risen from five or six million pounds to between eight and ten million. The commissioners decided, as a first step,

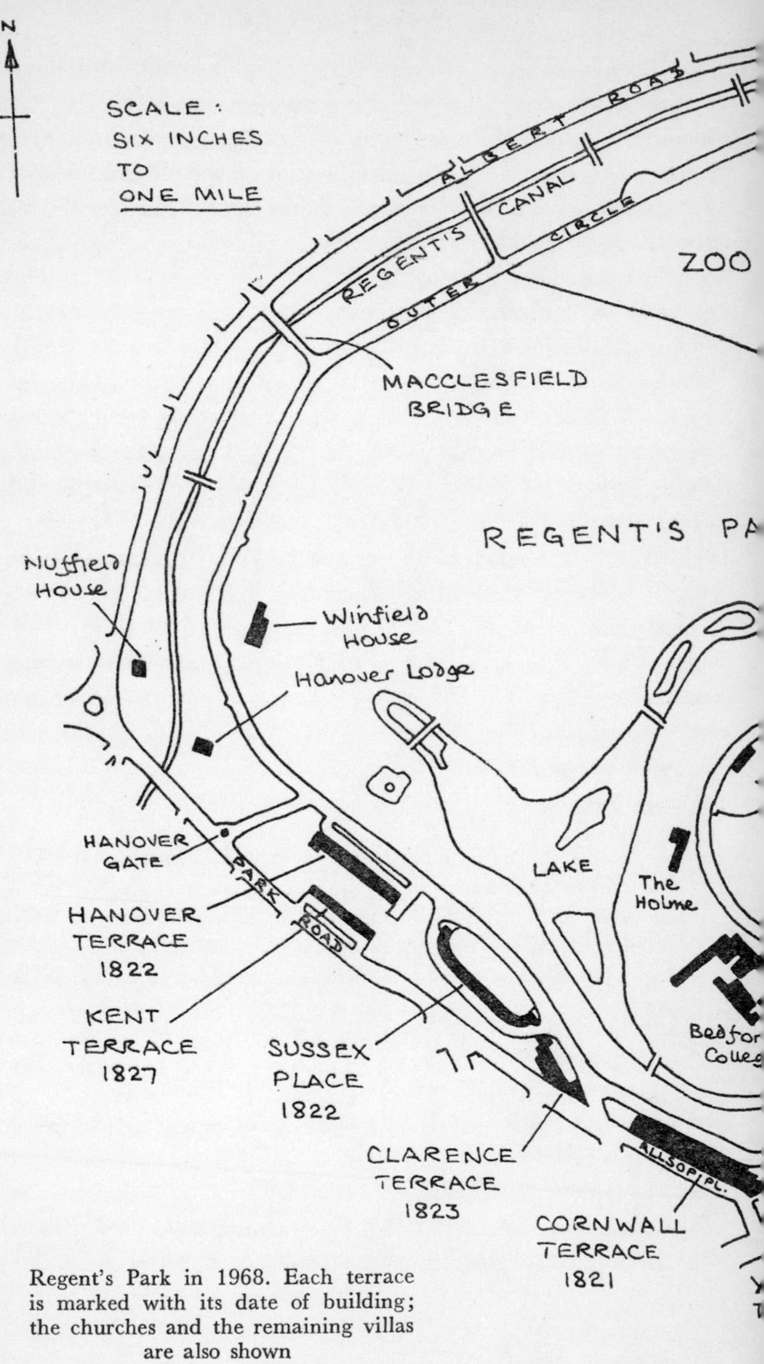

Regent's Park in 1968. Each terrace is marked with its date of building; the churches and the remaining villas are also shown

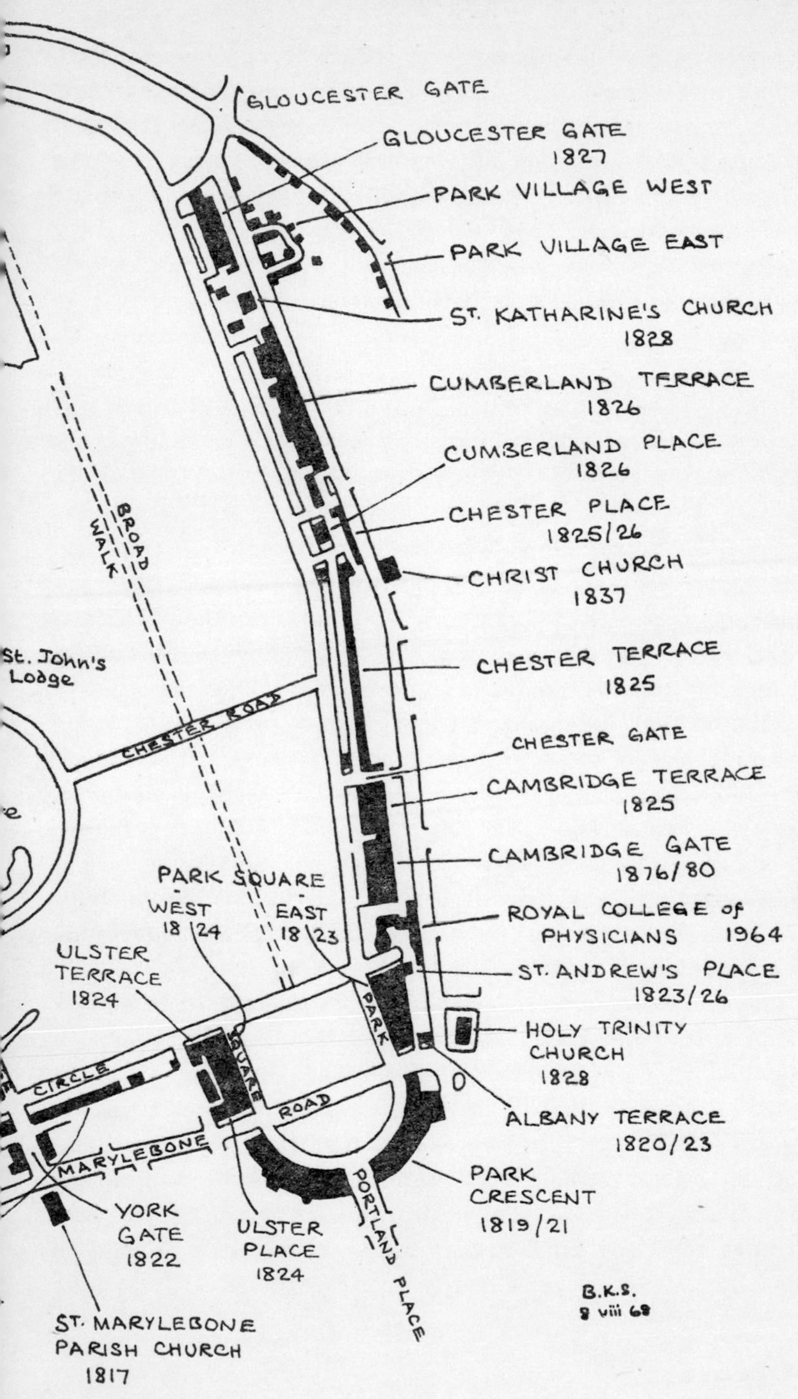
GLOUCESTER GATE
GLOUCESTER GATE 1827
PARK VILLAGE WEST
PARK VILLAGE EAST
ST. KATHARINE'S CHURCH 1828
CUMBERLAND TERRACE 1826
CUMBERLAND PLACE 1826
CHESTER PLACE 1825/26
CHRIST CHURCH 1837
BROAD WALK
St. John's Lodge
CHESTER TERRACE 1825
CHESTER ROAD
CHESTER GATE
CAMBRIDGE TERRACE 1825
CAMBRIDGE GATE 1876/80
PARK SQUARE
WEST 18 24
EAST 18 23
ROYAL COLLEGE of PHYSICIANS 1964
ULSTER TERRACE 1824
ST. ANDREW'S PLACE 1823/26
PARK
SQUARE
HOLY TRINITY CHURCH 1828
CIRCLE
ROAD
MARYLEBONE
ALBANY TERRACE 1820/23
PARK CRESCENT 1819/21
PORTLAND PLACE
YORK GATE 1822
ULSTER PLACE 1824
B.K.S. 8 viii 68
ST. MARYLEBONE PARISH CHURCH 1817

to preserve or where necessary to rebuild Park Crescent, Park Square and York Gate. 'These Terraces, comprising sixty-one houses, constitute the main southern entrance to the Park and are, in our view, its most important features.'[11] Next, residents in Hanover and Kent Terraces, which had always been in private hands and had never been taken over for office use, were given new twenty-year leases provided they undertook necessary repairs. Then, the commissioners decided to convert Cumberland Terrace into flats.[12]

> It is clear that we cannot expect anything like a normal commercial return from this expenditure. We feel however that any large landowner with the necessary means should be ready to make some unprofitable contribution to preserve lovely buildings. This will be our main contribution to the Park.

Mr de Soissons was appointed as architect. Cambridge Gate and Someries House were to be demolished, Cambridge Terrace was reprieved, and Sussex Lodge, which had been bombed, was pulled down to make way for a new building for the Royal College of Obstetricians and Gynaecologists. The provision of accommodation for learned societies and professional bodies became a feature of the redevelopment. These plans accounted for 153 of the 374 houses in the terraces and the commissioners, turning even as Nash had done to the private speculative developer, concluded by saying that they were anxious to receive suggestions from experienced property developers in the hope that it might be possible to save all the terraces by converting them into modern accommodation.

The conversion of Cumberland Terrace and the restoration of Park Crescent and York Gate then began, and by the summer of 1965 the whole appearance of the Park had changed for the better. Instead of derelict skeletal terraces, there were newly painted façades that glistened as they had done when first built. The statues and capitals were restored by ingenious remodelling and copying of the old, and behind this outward elegance there are now flats and small houses suited to the scale of modern living and equipped with lifts and central heating. Let us retrace the circuit which we made with Elmes as our guide in 1827 and observe the alterations that have been made.

Park Crescent was the first to be renewed. Owing to bomb damage and general deterioration, it was completely demolished section by section and rebuilt behind a façade identical with that designed by Nash. Drawings were made by architects, checked by expert auditors, and then corrected to serve as master drawings. Attics and other additions have been removed and the sky can now be seen through the balustrade edging the roof. Inside, the accommodation has been adapted to suit the needs of professional bodies and learned foundations, such as the Medical Research Council, the National Spastics Society, the Gulbenkian Foundation, and the Royal Institute of Public Administration. An International Students' Hostel occupies the six houses at the Marylebone Road end of the eastern wing; the architect was Sir Thomas Bennett whilst the rest of the wing was developed by Mr S. B. Harbour with Mr J. T. Cornall as his architect. Park Square was found to be in good enough repair for the leases to be extended and the houses are much used as consulting rooms for the medical profession, as might be expected so near to Harley Street.

York Terrace presented the worst problems of any. Nos 44-9 were a small separate terrace but, having been completely destroyed by bombs, it is hoped they will be rebuilt to the original design as a small block of houses or flats. Nos 42 and 43, the Doric Villa, have been rebuilt as private houses with the original façade preserved. Owing to the narrowness of the site, the main terrace will be redeveloped as flats, the eastern half by the International Students' Trust, and the western by a subsidiary of the Taylor Woodrow Group. The east side of York Gate has been restored as commercial offices, for which the developer, Mr Max Rayne, and the architect, Mr Elsom, won a Civic Trust award, and the west side will receive similar treatment from Messrs Taylor Woodrow with Sir Thomas Bennett as architect.

If we follow the road into the Inner Circle, we find that the villas there have all become part of London University. South Villa has been replaced by Bedford College, which also took over The Holme in 1948 as a students' hostel. St John's Lodge housed the Institute of Archaeology from 1937 until 1958, but the building now belongs to Bedford College, too, and has been renovated to provide a flat for the principal and rooms for post-graduate students. The garden has been opened to the public and is one of the most agreeably secluded retreats to be found in London. A variety of roses and herbaceous plants are grown here, and a fountain, 'Hylas and the Nymphs' by Henry Pegram, RA, and a statue, 'The Shepherd Girl' by C. A. Hartwell, are there to please the wayfarer.

This is perhaps the right place in which to describe the commissioners' policy with regard to open space. Their aim is always to preserve, and, where possible as in the case of St John's Lodge, to extend it. The Park now covers 487 acres; of these, 400 are open parkland freely available to everyone. The land to the north and north-east is used extensively by school children and by adults for cricket, football, hockey and athletics; there is a running track on the northern boundary near the Zoo; rowing and sailing can be enjoyed on the lake; tennis and instruction in golf are also available. This successful endeavour to make the Park a real amenity for Londoners is reinforced by the care bestowed on the trees, plants and birds. The Victorian urns and the borders—two acres of them—along the Broad Walk still flourish; Queen Mary's Garden, with its rosary and herbaceous beds, seems to grow lovelier every year, and a garden of miniature plants has been made at the foot of the mound just inside the southern gate of the Inner Circle. A great number of varieties of duck, as well as swans, moorhens and geese, live and breed on the lake. It is the delight of children from all parts of London to feed these colourful creatures. In addition to these natural delights, the Open Air Theatre, now capable of seating 4,000, still bravely ventures new productions each summer, and the offices of the

Royal Botanic Society which, after the society was disbanded, had served as a tea-house, have been replaced by the Polygon Restaurant, a building of amusing and fanciful design.

Returning to the Outer Circle, we come to Cornwall Terrace which will remain in the occupation of the Ministry of Works for some time to come. At Clarence Terrace, settlements and general structural weaknesses made restoration impossible and flats have been built behind a replica of Burton's façade by the Dolphin Development Company with Mr Guy Morgan as architect. Sussex Place is being rebuilt for the London Graduate School of Business Studies; the front walls will be preserved, and the architects for the work are Messrs B and N Westwood, Piet & Partners. Next comes the newly built College of Obstetricians and Gynaecologists designed by Mr de Soissons. This building is very much in harmony with its surroundings; it is of brick with arcading on the Park Road front and houses a library, committee and lecture rooms.

Hanover Terrace is in relatively good structural condition and is to remain as private houses, though it, too, may need reconstruction eventually. No 10, where Vaughan Williams lived, has been taken as an official residence for the provost of University College. Behind it, in Kent Terrace, each house has been strengthened separately and let as a house or maisonette. Behind the newly spruced-up lodge at Hanover Gate stood the main group of villas, of which only two have been left in any semblance of their original form. Abbey Lodge was replaced by a block of flats in the 1920's; North Villa was altered out of all recognition by Lady Ribblesdale and in 1948 was taken over as an Islamic cultural centre. It is their intention to erect a mosque—Nash would surely have been delighted. Hanover Lodge has become part of Bedford College and has been diligently restored. Beyond it, a block of one-room flats for students has been built. Grove House stands virtually unaltered on the far side of the canal and is now the headquarters of the Nuffield Foundation who have renamed it Nuffield Lodge. The grounds are well kept and as beautiful as ever. On the site of St Dunstan's is Winfield House, now the residence of the American Ambassador. The ruins of Holford House have been cleared away. The Zoo is still in its proper place.

Gloucester Gate and the detached houses beside it remain untouched at the moment. At St Katharine's, the Master's Lodge was destroyed by flying bombs in 1944; the site has been cleared and the church and adjoining premises have been made over to the Danish Church in London. The chapel is being restored and a beautifully furnished community centre has been opened; a replica of the runic Jelling stone has been erected in the gardens beyond the church.

Cumberland Terrace has been restored by the commissioners themselves. When their architect, Mr de Soissons, died in 1962, Mr K Peacock took his place. The original thirty-three houses have become forty-four flats and twelve houses, the flats let on thirty-year leases, the houses on sixty. Cumberland Place, Chester Place and Chester Gate, with the other small terraces—St Andrew's Place, Albany Terrace, Ulster Place and Ulster Terrace—will all be restored eventually. Chester Terrace has already been restored by Hallmark Securities Ltd with Mr David Hodges as their architect, almost in its original form—as forty-four individual houses. The mews behind has been demolished and a group of small houses and flats has been built round a courtyard. They are really delightful and behind them in Albany Street an exclusive little dress boutique has opened—a sure sign that the property is being let successfully.

It is hoped to restore Cambridge Terrace and Cambridge Gate, the one terrace in complete disharmony with the rest, has been reprieved till 1976 at least. Someries House has been replaced by a new building, designed by Mr Denys Lasdun, for the Royal College of Physicians; the result is extraordinarily interesting for the building, which was opened on 5 November 1964, is modern and functional. Its core is the Pannelled Room, which dates from before the Great Fire of 1666 and which the college have preserved from their former premises, but everything else, from the superb sweeping staircase to the hexagonal, partly-sunken lecture theatre at the side of the main building, is as much of the twentieth century as it can be, yet the whole accords astonishingly well with Nash's designs around it.

The commissioners should be believed when they say 'The task of giving the Terraces a new lease of life is in our blood'. The Park was built as a place for men and women to live in and not as a museum of early nineteenth-century architecture to be preserved unaltered for all time. The needs of domestic accommodation have changed in a century and a quarter, and if a house cannot be adapted to suit the needs of today, it will be allowed to decay just because it serves no useful purpose. The houses, flats and premises for learned societies which are now being built will still be desirable accommodation at the end of their leases; this ensures that they will still be well cared for and still in good condition. And it should also be remembered that if Nash were alive today, it is possible he would side with those who wished to demolish the Park entirely and to redevelop it on different lines. In retaining the Park as it is, a great scheme has been preserved but a great opportunity has been foregone.

We should be content with what we have. Forest has given way to farmland, and farmland to urban development which still retains a rural atmosphere. Nash's scheme was 'an achievement in planning, landscape and architecture unique in this country, and in fact with no parallels abroad'.[14] The 'grand design' is being saved and the buildings are being given another century of useful life. Regent's Park, which has served so many purposes—as foraging-ground for pigs, as a royal hunting park, as a mortgage for a king in need, as farmland supplying the capital, and as the finest of the 'metropolitan improvements'—continues to serve the community as London's loveliest park, which is at once both town and country.

CHAPTER 8

A WALK IN REGENT'S PARK

A book should be used as well as read. By this, I mean that, unless you go out and explore Regent's Park as well as reading about it between these two covers, you will only be half-using the volume. So, to make such an exploration easy and, I hope, more rewarding, I have described a walk around the Park. Of course, the Park is too large to be covered on foot in a single afternoon—the exploration seems to me to require at least three expeditions, two for the Park and one for the Albany Street area—but this guide can be used for quick reference just as and when it is needed. If one has a car then one can start at any point but I am writing for those who are making the exploration on foot and who are reaching the Park by public transport, in which case they will use either the bus (Nos 1, 2, 13, 18, 23, 27, 30, 59, 74, 113, 134, or 159) or will take the Underground to Baker Street (Bakerloo, District, Inner Circle or Metropolitan lines) or to Regent's Park station. Let us start at the latter.

Emerging from the Underground, we find ourselves facing the Marylebone Road with the gardens of Park Crescent behind us. If we turn to the right and then right again at the eastern horn of the crescent, we can admire the uncluttered elegance of Nash's masterpiece with the sweeping linked porticoes and the plain lines of the building above it, and we can remember how much trouble it cost to build. The original lessee, Charles Mayor, went bankrupt when he had built only six houses at the Portland Place end of the south-east quadrant. A fire broke out in the house nearest to the centre of the quadrant and when the work was taken up again by other backers in 1818, the damaged house fell down

Page 179: (above) East Gate, by Thomas Hosmer Shepherd, 1827. This entrance to the Park is now known as Gloucester Gate; (below) York Gate, Regent's Park, and Marylebone Church, by Thomas Hosmer Shepherd, 1827

Page 180: (above) View of the Royal Hospital of St Katharine, by Ambrose Poynter, 1827; (below) Hanover Terrace was one of Nash's most restrained and classical compositions—it is next to his most exuberant design, Sussex Terrace

after a night of storms on 4-5 March, and Nash was—unfairly—much censured for the collapse. The houses were at last completed and since then have been shaken by bombing, completely demolished, and rebuilt again to an exact replica of Nash's façade but with accommodation behind more suited to twentieth-century needs. In the case of Park Crescent, the needs considered have been those of learned societies and charitable institutions, as the explorer can discover from an examination of the discreet brass name-plates on the doors.

The crescent is divided by Portland Place—'the finest street in London', Nash called it—and even today, when the enchanting symmetry of Robert Adam's majestic boulevard has been shattered by haphazard rebuilding and insinuating parking-meters, the width and proportions of the street are superb. Nash made this the beginning of his New Street which was to be at once a swift means of communication between the Park and Westminster and a triumphal way linking Carlton House, the Prince Regent's palace, with the new Park called after its occupier. The street became Regent Street, hinging itself upon those twin hubs of London, Oxford and Piccadilly Circuses, but before it was completed the Prince Regent became George IV and Carlton House was pulled down, considered redundant once Buckingham Palace was built. Regent Street, however, remains, rebuilt so that Nash would not recognise it today and so crowded with traffic that a drive from the Park to Westminster must, only too often, go at a snail's pace.

The western quadrant matches its fellow. As we walk past, we can remember that underneath the garages at the rear there is buried an icehouse, once rented by a Mr Samuel Dash for three guineas a year. And then we are back at the Marylebone Road, laid out in 1757 as London's first by-pass. As we pause before crossing, we may recall that the crescent behind us follows the curved field boundary of the Dupper Field and that if we had stood on this spot in 1803 we should have looked out across the open fields to Hampstead and Highgate [Illustration, page 71].

Closer to us, we could have seen two pleasant public houses, the 'Jew's Harp' and the 'Queen's Head and Artichoke', either of which would have been delighted to have served us with 'the best Wines, Spirituous Liquers, Cyder, Perry, Fine Ales, etc', while on the other side of the road, where the garden of Park Square stands today, stood the public gallery which housed the picture collection of Count Truchsess, brought all the way from Vienna at immense expense, and there we could have fed our souls and intellects by gazing on paintings by Rembrandt, Michelangelo and Durer.

We cross into Park Square and reach the Outer Circle. To our right, we can see the noble line of the Broad Walk planted out with saplings in Nash's day, saplings which have now grown to their full majesty. It runs across the Park continuing the line of Regent Street and Portland Place and was an integral part of Nash's design. A very pleasant hour can be spent wandering along this walk admiring the huge stone urns, planted out with seasonal flowers, the Dolphin Fountain, moved here from Hyde Park, and the flower-beds, laid out at the request of Prince Albert, or sitting on the seats provided at convenient intervals, but we will turn to our left and go clockwise around the Park. The first houses we come to are Ulster Terrace and then the Doric Villas (Nos 42 and 43 York Terrace), damaged by bombing but now renovated so that they look like new. Sir Charles Wyndham, the actor-manager, and his wife, the actress Mary Moore, lived there from 1918 to 1929, and gave many theatrical garden parties at the house, which is today marked with a blue plaque. The eastern half of York Terrace comes next. Nash had first planned the terrace as one unbroken line but he altered his plan when Thomas Hardwick's fine parish church was built and split the terrace into two halves so as to create a vista centreing on the church [Illustration, page 179]. The mews behind York Terrace are worth exploring; Nash wanted to present an unbroken façade to the Park side so that it would seem as if the church were flanked by two long palaces, so he put all the front doors at the back. The eastern mews harbours the former Royal York Baths, with a façade like a little classical temple.

It is worth walking down York Gate towards the Marylebone Road again to look more closely at the parish church with its little cupola supported by eight gilded angelic caryatids, cast in artificial stone by Charles Rossi, who once had a manufactory for making statues and keystones and garden ornaments just inside the Inner Circle, which we shall be exploring in a moment. But before we turn back into the Park, we can look towards the beginning of Marylebone High Street and remember the tiny village that once stood there. The parish church was on a site to the east of the present building, its position marked today by a little paved garden. The original parish church dedicated to St John had been a mile away on the Oxford Road but in 1400 it was moved to this site and rededicated to Our Lady so that it became St Mary's church by Tyburn, thereby giving its name to the whole area—St Mary by the bourn—St Marylebone. Opposite it was the manor house, first mentioned in 1279 and probably rebuilt about 1500 by Thomas Hobson, one of Henry VII's senior auditors, who acquired the whole manor. Three generations of Hobsons lived there, and then in 1538 Henry VIII decided to make a new hunting park to the north of London. His choice fell on Marylebone and so young Thomas Hobson had no option but to sell his land to the king in exchange for property near Southampton and in the Isle of Wight where he settled and prospered. The manor house was leased to Sir Anthony Denny, a trusted servant of the king's, and some 550 acres to the north were emparked with a ring mound and a wooden fence. Here the old king and the children who succeeded him—Edward VI, Mary and Elizabeth—hunted; here Edward entertained ambassadors from France and Elizabeth an embassy from Russia. Elizabeth's successor James I, hunted here too but, always short of money, he sold the manor house and all the land to the south to Edward Forsett from whom it passed to the Austen family. It was then sold to the Duke of Newcastle, passed to the Earl of

Oxford and afterwards to the Dukes of Portland, becoming the Howard De Walden estate in the nineteenth century, which it still is today.

We know that the old entry from the village into Marylebone Park was opposite the end of the High Street but there is no entry there now—the Royal Academy of Music and York Terrace stand where there were once a wooden gate and two lodges where the gamekeepers lived. So we turn back up York Gate and, crossing the Outer Circle, go over a little bridge into the Inner Circle and turn left. We can walk round the road and then explore inside the Circle.

The first hundred yards of road follow the line of an old cart track linking the main farm with the village. Almost immediately we come to the red brick buildings of Bedford College, founded in 1849 by Elizabeth Jesser Reid who lived at 21 York Terrace. The college outgrew its premises in Bedford Square and acquired, in 1908, a lease of South Villa which was demolished and the present academic buildings put up. But South Villa stood on the site of something still older—the main farmhouse of what had been Marylebone Farm. The house might have been built first for Sir William Clarke who, during the Civil War, was first Cromwell's and then General Monck's secretary but who, along with his second master at the Restoration, became the king's man and was mortally wounded at the Battle of Harwich against the Dutch in 1666. He had a house in the Park which was left empty on his death and may very well have been taken over by the leading farmer in the neighbourhood. At the beginning of the eighteenth century it was owned by a farmer called George Daggett, who was always quarrelling with his neighbours, stopping up rights of way, shooting night-soil where it had no business to be, falling behind with his rent, and generally making a nuisance of himself. He was succeeded by William Francis whose widow, Mary, went bankrupt during the great cattle plague of 1745 so that her creditors could only be paid 2s 4½d in the pound on what she owed. The farm eventually passed to the Willans, father and son, who added the surrounding fields to it until it became the largest farm in Middlesex.

As we walk on round the circle, we can remember how matters went here during the Civil War—how Charles I mortgaged the Park to Sir George Strode and to John Wandesford in return for supplies of gunpowder together with 'Musquette Match and Pikes', and how the two worthy men lost their money and the security for it with the defeat of the Royalist cause. The Park was sold to Parliamentarian supporters for £13,215 6s 8d and they proceeded to cut down the trees, which made some £5,000 for them, and to let out the Park as farmland. When Charles II came into his own again, the Park was a park no longer. Strode and Wandesford were allowed to collect rents from the farmers there until they were repaid in full for what they had laid out in the late king's defence, and the property then reverted to the Crown and was leased out to a series of tenants-in-chief, who in their turn sub-leased it to three farmers (for the disposition of the farms, see page 60).

Two of the villas still stand on the edge of the Inner Circle; they are The Holme and St John's Lodge, and both now belong to Bedford College and are used as hostels for senior students and staff. We come first to The Holme, the second villa to be erected in the Park. It was built for Nash's supporter, James Burton, a builder who was responsible for the financing and building of much of Regent Street and many of the terraces and villas. The architect was his son, Decimus, who designed it when only eighteen years of age—surely a splendid and generous opportunity for any father to give to his son! Decimus proved worthy of the trust his father put in him—the villa is elegant, attractive and supremely 'livable-in'. The young man went on to train in Nash's office and, as we shall see, was responsible for other buildings in the Park. A little way further on, we come to St John's Lodge, the first villa to be constructed. It was designed by John Raffield for Charles Augustus Tulk, Member of Parliament for Sudbury, and its most famous occupant was the Marquess Wellesley, the

Duke of Wellington's elder brother, who lived here from 1829 to 1833. Its gardens have recently been opened to the public and one can sit behind the high hedges admiring the broad herbaceous borders and rose-beds and believe London to be a hundred miles away.

We must enter the Inner Circle through one or other of two pairs of magnificent tall iron gates presented to the Park by Sigismund Goetze, a German artist who made his home in this country, lived on the perimeter of the Park in Grove House and gave many generous gifts to the borough of St Marylebone. Inside these gates, we can wander on grass or past flower-beds and sit under trees or in the sunshine. We can climb the Mound, made from the spoil when Regent's Park Lake was dug out, up and down which children have scrambled and run for generations, or listen to the sound of the Triton Fountain, an elaborate and successful group in bronze by William Macmillan erected in memory of Sigismund Goetze. The gardens here were laid out by the Royal Botanical Society and, when that institution ceased to exist, were taken over by the Royal Parks Division of the Ministry of Public Building and Works. The rosary, one of the most beautiful in the country, is called Queen Mary's Garden, as a tribute to the interest which that much loved and respected queen took in it. If we wish, we can watch a play during fine summer weather in the Open Air Theatre or refresh ourselves at the Polygon Restaurant, of whose unexpected shape and design Nash would surely have approved. Finally, if we take up our stand on the roadway of the Inner Circle on the morning of Easter Monday, we can watch all the equipages—drays, barouches, traps, landaus and gigs—and the fine or trim animals that draw them which make up the Van Horse Parade.

Returning to the Outer Circle and proceeding clockwise, we pass Cornwall Terrace, a pleasant, rather unexciting façade. It has, however, one interesting feature—a bow window running from the ground to the first floor and adorned with caryatids. There is a nice story told about this window. The terrace was planned to extend further northwards, but Mrs Siddons, the actress, who lived in York Place (now Baker Street) behind the Park, complained to George IV that the prospect from her drawing-room window would be spoiled, so the end of the terrace was altered and adorned. Unfortunately, I have found no contemporary evidence for the tale and the position of Mrs Siddons' house in relation to the Park does not quite seem to fit in.

Clarence Gate, the entrance to Baker Street, comes next and then Clarence Terrace. This was the work of Decimus Burton and is altogether an elaborate and magnificent design. The building is in fact modern, for as with Park Crescent the terrace has been completely rebuilt, with a replica of the original façade disguising the modern flats behind. Opposite the terrace, inside the Park, is a little bridge over one arm of the lake and here the multiplicity of breeds of duck that throng the lake gather most closely, waddling and quacking greedily, for a visit to feed the ducks in the Park is an afternoon treat for many small Londoners, and it is at this point, so near to Baker Street and to transport, that they tend to scatter their largesse of stale crusts and cakes. There are islands in the lake that look very pretty, and on the opposite side of the water are beds of flowers which glow resplendently whatever the season, for their contents are constantly changed and replenished—tulips give way to dahlias, and dahlias to chrysanthemums—but the lake here has been the scene of a dreadful tragedy for on 15 January 1867, when a crowd were skating on the frozen waters, the ice gave way and forty men and boys were drowned or died from exposure. The level of the lake was at once lowered and skating is forbidden to this day, for the flow of the Tyburn and the islands in the lake prevent the ice from forming thickly. The tragedy bit deeply into people's consciousness, and the victims were lamented in street ballads:

They clung to the ice, until benumbed with cold,
  The ice in their grasp broke asunder.
One lady on the shore in grief did behold
  Her husband exhausted go under;

Two sisters were screaming and calling for aid,
   Their sorrow, poor girls, could not smother,
In anguish rang their hands and frantically said,
   For God [*sic*] sake save our poor brother.

The most mournful part remains to be told,
   As the bodies to the dead-house was taken,
At the workhouse gate two thousand young and old,
   The scene it was truly heart-breaking;
One body was owned by an old gentleman,
   'My son can't be dead' he said when crying,
'He left me but two hours, was strong and cheerful then,
   For a father so old it's very trying.'

But this was a hundred years ago, and we walk on keeping inside the railing that cuts off the roadway and following the path beside the lake until we reach the children's boating pond and playground, where we can either turn to the right over a bridge into the interior of the Park and spend the rest of the afternoon wandering on the grass, or to the left and rejoin the road opposite Hanover Gate.

By this time, we have passed Sussex Place and Hanover Terrace, both by Nash and totally dissimilar in appearance. Sussex Place is gay and extraordinary, with little cupolas and a large garden between it and the road. It enjoys the best view across the lake in the whole Park and looks as if Nash were using up designs left over from the Pavilion at Brighton. Hanover Terrace, in contrast, is grave, restrained and classical, its pediments adorned with rather isolated statues. Behind it, facing on to Park Road, is Kent Terrace where E. H. Shepherd, the illustrator of A. A. Milne's Winnie-the-Pooh books, spent his childhood which he has recorded most delightfully in *Drawn from Memory*, a book to be read and treasured. Beyond Kent Terrace is a block of flats, Abbey Lodge, which has replaced the villa whose name it bears. The villa was the home from 1851 till 1903 of Baron and Baroness de Bunsen. He was a German nobleman, and she the daughter of the Quaker banker, Samuel Gurney, who in 1840 visited Germany with his sister, Elizabeth Fry, on a tour of the prisons there, taking his daughter with him. An acquaintance was made which eventually developed into a romance and the young couple were given Abbey Lodge, which adjoined Samuel Gurney's house at 20, Hanover Terrace, as a wedding present.

On the far side of Hanover Gate, inside the Park, is Hanover Lodge, today newly renovated and a part of Bedford College; beyond it is a block of students' one-room flats which overlook the canal, and Nuffield Lodge which was once Grove House, originally the home of the scientist, George Bellas Greenough, who was responsible for laying-out the lovely gardens there. It later belonged to Sigismund and Constance Goetze, to whom the Park owes so many of its statues and adornments. The road goes uphill a little here, and we have passed the old boundary of Hill Field beyond which lay Sedge Field and Sparrowhawk Wood—expressive names! On our right are gates and a high hedge which shelter Winfield House, the private residence of the American Ambassador to London. St Dunstan's Villa stood on the site originally; it was built by Decimus Burton in 1825 for the Marquess of Hertford who, in 1830, purchased the clock with the striking figures of Gog and Magog from St Dunstan's church in Fleet Street and installed it in the garden, naming the villa after it. From 1916 to 1921, the villa housed a training centre for those blinded during the war and in its turn gave the name to that noble association. Then in 1934, Lord Rothermere occupied the villa and gave the old clock back to St Dunstan's church where it can be seen today in good working order. The villa was demolished in 1937 and the present house built.

There is a long quiet stretch of Outer Circle to walk along after Winfield House, until on our left we can see an iron bridge over the canal, leading to Avenue Road. This bridge was the scene of the second disaster to occur in the Park. On the morning of 2 October 1874, a barge called the *Tilbury*, loaded with gunpowder, was moving ponderously along. Suddenly, as she reached the bridge, there was a great explosion. Her crew of three were all killed instantly and it was thought that one of them must have been smoking and may have knocked out his pipe carelessly against the cargo. As we stand on the bridge a barge passes underneath us, not laden with explosives but with children and sightseers, for she is the *Jason*, the gaily-painted vessel that, starting from Paddington Basin, makes excursions up and down Regent's Canal: a voyage well worth making. Access to the tow-path can be gained by the steps beside Primrose Hill bridge and a whole afternoon can be spent wandering by the water.

Returning to the Park, we pass through the Zoo, the animals' quarters being on either side of the roadway. Since the Zoo needs a book and deserves a visit to itself, and since, with the fine programme of modernisation now in progress, the arrangements are constantly changing, we will not attempt to describe what may be seen there, except to say that the best view of the new elephant house—an exciting piece of architecture if ever there was one—can probably be obtained by walking round the outside of the Zoo, rather than by going inside.

Beyond the Zoo, on the Camden Town side of the Park, is Gloucester Gate. Two hundred yards inside the Park, where the south-eastern corner of the Zoo touches the Broad Walk, was Lodge Field, where there was once a gamekeeper's dwelling and where the standing may have been erected from which Queen Elizabeth and the Duke of Anjou watched the hunting when he came, unsuccessfully, to woo her in 1578. On the roadway we pass the group of houses known as Gloucester Gate, then St Katharine's Church. The building, of brick, angular and Gothic, flanked by two blocks of dwellings, is unlike anything else in the Park. It was the work of Ambrose Poynter, who had studied under Nash and had never been on good terms with his teacher, who declared himself appalled at the church in the Park. Nash's strictures are not really fair and the church is an interesting memorial to a great London charity. In 1147, Queen Matilda, wife to Stephen, founded a monastery and hospital dedicated to St Katharine beside the Tower of London. The hospital flourished until the Reformation and continued thereafter as a purely charitable institution, but its site was eventually needed for a new dock and on 30 October 1825 the last service in the old church took place; on the next day demolition began and the poor of East London had to look elsewhere for help. The hospital was refounded in the Park as a home for elderly clergy or their badly-off widows, until St Katharine's was dissolved altogether in 1914, since it was felt that the charity no longer served a useful purpose. The church and buildings today belong to the Danish Church in London and are very well cared for; behind the cloister-like arcade to the right of the church as you face it, is a replica of the runic Jelling stone—an unexpected but exciting sight.

Beyond St Katharine's is Cumberland Terrace, the most spectacular and theatrical of all Nash's designs. This terrace was to have terminated the view from the little palace that the Prince Regent had planned for himself in the Park; when the palace failed to materialise, Nash did not abate the magnificence of his building. The main block has a pediment full of sculpture, of which we shall have more to say in a moment. Beyond it is Cumberland Place, a group of pretty, well-proportioned houses, and then Chester Terrace.

This was built in 1825 by James Burton to Nash's designs, but the two men fell out badly over the work. Nash planned a building adorned with Corinthian columns and statues representing celebrated figures of history but, busy with Buckingham Palace, his designs and his attention to their execution were perfunctory. When at last he went to see what Burton was putting up, he did not like what he saw and begged the commissioners to force Burton to pull down or modify the terrace and, at all costs, to get rid of the statues—'The ridicule that every new figure excites is so painful to the ears of a professional Man', he wrote to the commissioners. Burton claimed compensation and there was a great argument. In the end, the statues were removed but the terrace remained unaltered.

Behind both Cumberland and Chester Terraces small modern

houses and flats have been built in the old mews; they have been designed very successfully for they fit in well with Nash's façades and yet are ideal for modern town living. Beyond Chester Terrace, with its elegant archways at either end, is Chester Gate which connects the Park with the outside world, and then Cambridge Terrace, a rather unexciting composition. Cambridge Gate was built in 1875 by Archer and Green to take the place of the Colosseum which had just been demolished. The Colosseum was built between 1824 and 1827 to designs by Decimus Burton. It housed a panorama of London painted by a young artist, E. T. Parris, from sketches made by an ingenious surveyor, Thomas Horner, who had ascended to the top of the dome of St Paul's early every morning for some months to sketch the City before it became shrouded with a pall of smoke that would obscure his view. The panorama was opened to the public gaze in 1829 but was never a great success. Other attractions were added and a variety of entertainments were tried, the ownership of the huge building passing from hand to hand, but at last it was closed down and demolished and its place taken by this rather unattractive terrace.

Immediately beyond it is something more exciting architecturally—the new Royal College of Physicians designed by Denys Lasdun and opened in 1964. It took the place of Someries House, the old Adult Orphan Asylum. The college is completely modern and functional, the main building in the shape of a 'T' with its long arm towards the Park, and beside it a curious half-sunken lecture hall. The astonishing thing is that the college looks absolutely right in its setting and perfectly in harmony with the older buildings around it. On the far side of it is a pleasant cul-de-sac, St Andrew's Terrace, and then we have completed our circuit and are back at Park Square again. The three centre houses on the east side once the Diorama—a nineteenth-century forerunner of the cinema—today have become the Arthur Stanley Clinic for the Treatment of Rheumatism, having been a Baptist chapel from 1852 to 1921.

We will now leave the Park and, walking along the Marylebone Road past Albany Terrace, turn northwards up Albany Street. This street and the land to the east of it were planned as the service area for the Park. Three markets, for hay, meat and vegetables, were planned but only one, the hay market, was built and was called Cumberland Market. The whole of this area was badly bombed and has been redeveloped since the war by St Pancras Borough Council, so for our walk we will concern ourselves chiefly with Albany Street and the villages that lie at the northern end of it.

At the southern end of the street stands Holy Trinity Church opposite Great Portland Street Underground station. The church was built in 1828 to the designs of Sir John Soane on the site of some farm buildings belonging to Mr Rhodes and Mr Allaley which were demolished soon after 1811 when the Park buildings were begun. The outside pulpit—one of the very few in London—was added in 1893 as a memorial to the Reverend William Cadman. For a while, during the 1930s, the crypt of the church was rented by Messrs Allen Lane, publishers of Penguin Books, a venture then in its infancy; today it is the headquarters of the Society for the Promotion of Christian Knowledge. Just beyond the church is the White House, a nine-storey block of flats built in 1936 to designs by R. Atkinson, and then on the east side of Albany Street, we come to the 'Queen's Head and Artichoke' public house. The façade of the public house is not particularly attractive and it is ordinary enough inside though very pleasant and welcoming, but any admirer of Nash will drink a toast to his memory here, for it was the landlord of the old 'Queen's Head and Artichoke' in Marylebone Park who was the first to take up a lease on a site on the new estate, in which courageous gesture he was joined by the proprietor of the 'Jew's Harp'. The new 'Jew's Harp' stood in Edward Street, but disappeared in the bombing and was built over with the St Pancras estate; the 'Queen's Head' still stands and is likely to continue to do so. The small houses next to it are the oldest buildings still standing unaltered on the

Crown estate. Opposite the 'Queen's Head' is a graceful row of white houses with nice plasterwork—the property was owned by Nosworthy, Nash's own plasterer, who presumably adorned the outside of his investment as prettily as he could. In one of them, No 55, lived Henry Mayhew, the journalist who wrote so well and so feelingly of the plight of London's poor; a blue plaque marks his residence. Further along, past some small old pleasant shops, we come to another public house, the 'Prince George Duke of Cumberland'. Built in the 1820s, the façade with its Corinthian columns remains unaltered and the interior has much style though it lacks the sentimental memories of the 'Queen's Head'. Beyond it are small modern flats and houses and opposite it stood, until 1968, the Ophthalmic Hospital built by Nash for the men whose sight had been damaged in the wars against Napoleon. After some years of useful life, the hospital closed and the buildings were put to a variety of uses, the most exciting being the provision of accommodation for Sir Goldsworthy Gurney's steam car which he exercised round the Park till it was sufficiently perfected to be driven to Bath in July 1829.

Just beyond the site of the hospital is Christ Church, Albany Street, designed by James Pennethorne in 1837. It is a plain brick building with one window, depicting the Sermon on the Mount, made from designs by Dante Gabriel Rossetti in memory of his mother's relation, Miss M. M. Polidori. A little further on we pass the extremely utilitarian Regent's Park Barracks, and then we come to Park Village West and what remains of Park Village East. These groups of charming little cottages and houses were begun by Nash and completed by Pennethorne. They include such delights as the Tower House in Park Village West. They have been described as the homes of not entirely respectable ladies, and that excellent novel, *Fanny by Gaslight* by Michael Sadleir, is partly centred on one of them, but in fact the occupants included people like Edmund Kean, the actor (at Bute Cottage) and Dr James Johnson, Nash's own doctor and physician-extraordinary to William IV (12 Park Village West). A few doors away at No 8 Park Village West lived James Wyld, Geographer to Queen Victoria and Member of Parliament for Bodmin. During the Great Exhibition in 1851, he constructed and displayed in Leicester Square a huge model of the Earth, some sixty feet in diameter, which had to be viewed from four galleries, one above the other; one wonders whether he was inspired by the panorama in the Colosseum.

With the villages, our tour of the Park is ended and we can walk down Parkway to Camden Town Underground station, and then go home. But the Park is a place to return to again and again, whether it is to admire Nash's terraces, to sit in the garden of St John's Lodge, to look upon the splendour of the geraniums in the urns off the Broad Walk, or just to wander in and enjoy the 400 acres of open parkland, which the pertinacity of John Fordyce, the genius of John Nash and the determination of the Prince Regent spared and adorned for us.

Princess Mary of Teck presenting prizes at the Royal Botanic Society

NOTES AND REFERENCES

INTRODUCTION

1 Henry Crabb Robinson, *Diary, Reminiscences and Correspondence*, ed. T. Sadler, 1872, vol 1, p 310.
2 FitzStephen's *Description of London*, in Sir Frank Stenton's *Norman London*, 1934.

CHAPTER I

1 Now merged in the larger administrative unit of the City of Westminster.
2 The name Teoburnham first appears in two charters of King Edward dated about 959; Birch, *Cartularium Saxonicum*, 1048 and 1351. The reference is not to the village but to the stream which was used as a boundary of a grant of land to the Church of St Peter at Westminster. *See* M. Celling, *The Boundaries of the Westminster Charters* in *Transactions of the London and Middlesex Archaeological Society*, New Series, vol 9, pp 101-104. For the River Tyburn, *see* N. Barton, *The Lost Rivers of London*, 1962.
3 C. Hart, *The Early Charters of Essex*; *The Norman Period*, 1957. Charter no 79.
4 A translation of the Domesday entry reads:

> Land of the Abbey of Barking. In Ossulston Hundred, a manor. The Abbess of Barking holds Tyburn of the King. It was assessed at five hides. The arable land is three carucates. In demesne are two hides. And there is one plough. The villeins have two ploughs. There are two villeins with half a hide each. And one villein with half a virgate, and two bordars with ten acres each. And three cottars. There is pasture for the cattle of the vill, wood for fifty swine, grassland worth forty pence. Altogether it is worth fifty-two shillings. When received it was the same. In the time of King Edward a hundred shillings. The manor belonged always and still belongs to Barking Abbey.

For a discussion of the entry, *see* A. Ashbridge, *St Marylebone and its Anglo-Saxon Manors*, in *Transactions of the London and Middlesex Archaeological Society*, New Series, vol. 4, pp 56-74.
5 In 1727 and 1822, when two successive parish Court Houses were built there, and in 1892 when drains were being laid. *See* Smith, p 60, and *Marylebone Times and Independent*, 25 Nov, 1895.
6 Dugdale's *Monasticon*, vol 1, p 445.

7 For information about Gilbert de Sanford and his works in Tyburn, *see* J. H. Round, *The King's Sergeants and Officers of State*, 1911, p 133, Rhymer, *Foedera*, vol 50, 121, and R. R. Sharpe, *Calendar of Letter Book A of the City of London*, pp 14-15.

8 See text of Hundred Roll for 1279 given in P. Vinogradoff, *English Society in the Eleventh Century*, 1908, p 482.

9 Register of Robert Braybrook, f 348, at Fulham Palace.

10 *Calendar of Patent Rolls, 1374-77*, pp 38-39.

11 *Calendar of Inquisitions Post Mortem*, vol 4, p 314. John, Duke of Norfolk, asserts his claim to part of Tyborne Manor, alias Marylebone. This entry, in 1462, is the earliest written appearance of the name that I have been able to trace so far.

12 *Calendar of Patent Rolls, 1441-1446*, p 251; Feet of Fines for Middlesex, p 240; *Calendar of Inquisitions Post Mortem*, vol 4, p 378.

13 British Museum, Harleian MS 756, p 102, gives his descendants but no ancestors.

14 R. Somerville, *The Duchy of Lancaster*, 1953, pp 441. For the Burne Park grant, Pat. 1, Henry VIII, p 1, m.1 and m.12.

15 *Calendar of Close Rolls, 1485-1500*, no 567; *Calendar of Close Rolls, 1468-1476*, no 970; text of the inquisition held at Hobson's death which gives details of his lands is document C 142/26 in the PRO. Unfortunately the parchment is so worn that it is unreadable in places.

16 Probate Court of Canterbury, Fetiplace, 1511, f 7.

17 C 150/478.

18 SC 12/23/65.

19 C 66/871, membranes 42-43. Grant to Henry Sidney, see infra p 25.

20 W. C. Richardson, *History of the Court of Augmentations, 1536-1554*, 1961.

21 Dugdale's *Monasticon*, vol 1, p 445.

22 See Appendix for translation.

23 The mill may have been at the north end of the village on the home farm, but there was a Mill Hill Field, marked on Henry Pratt's survey made in 1708, beside Oxford Street; the name still lingers, as Mill Hill Place, in Messrs Debenham & Freebody's car park.

24 *State Papers of Henry VIII, 1539*, p 342.

25 E 315/256/f 66.

26 *State Papers of Henry VIII*, vol 15, p 217. There is a copy in the House of Lords' Muniments, 32 Henry VIII. The location of Palmer's land is a deduction. We know that his son, Jerome, sold land to Sir Armigell Wade who held the manor of Belsize.

27 Eton College Records, vol 39, no 160; the tenant, John Slaning, received £11 14s compensation.

28 *State Papers of Henry VIII*, 242, f 198.

29 E 315/253/f 73.

30 SP 1/50.

31 Transaction in Court of Augmentations, E 318/603; deed of sale between Henry VIII and Hobson, E 305/D/1; patent roll entry for the sale and exchange, C 66/735, membrane 18.

32 SP 30/Henry VIII, no 1191, (10); E 315/214, ff 74b-75a; E 315/235, f 91.
33 In the Ashbridge Collection, City of Westminster Public Library.
34 SP 1/183/f 20.
35 E 315/249/ff 34-35; E 315/250/ff 38-39; *State Papers of Henry VIII*, vol 21, pt 1, no 963 (93).
36 Crest 2/737; Crest 6/84; E 101/474/21. For full text see Appendix.
37 Possibly where the lake is today.
38 New York, Folger Library MS L b 41; formerly among the Loseley Manuscripts.
39 C 66/871/membranes 42-43.
40 *Calendar of Patent Rolls, 1 Mary*, vol 1, p 59.
41 Ibid, p 435.
42 Star Chamber 4/bundle 2/piece 50. The parchment is much torn and half is missing.
43 PC 2/7/p 75.
44 *Calendar of Patent Rolls, 6 Elizabeth*, pt 6, no 377.
45 E 101/544/29. For full text see Appendix.
46 Salisbury Papers, Hatfield House. Tottenham Court was occupied by Daniel Clarke, Master Cook to Queen Elizabeth and James I. For possible associations with the 'Queen's Head and Artichoke' public house, see infra p 66 and *Survey of London*, vol 21, pp 120-121.
47 *Middlesex County Records*, vol 1, pp 41, 59, 182, 231, 258; also Chanc. Misc. 31 Eliz., bundle 68, file 10, no 271.
48 Sir Robert Naunton, *Fragmenta Regalia*, 1641, p 38.
49 J. Larwood, *The Story of the London Parks*, 1881, p 11.
50 J. Nichols, *Progresses of Queen Elizabeth*, 1823, vol 3, p 519.
51 C 66/1904, membranes 14-17.
52 British Museum, Lansdowne MS 166, f 118.
53 SP 14/LIV/23; SP 39/4; Sign manual vol 55, no 56.
54 Venn, *Alumni Cantabrigienses*. Forsett was of a literary and religious turn of mind. He wrote a comedy in Latin verse, *Pedantius*, and two treatises, *A Comparative Discourse of the Bodies Natural & Politique*, 1606, and *A Defence of the Right of Kings*, 1624, which he dedicated to James I; the monarch and his Justice had much in common. Forsett died in 1630, leaving everything to his son and daughter and asking that alms should be given to the poor of St Marylebone. He was buried in his own vault under the parish church and a carved panel on the wall indicated the place. This panel was restored in 1962 and placed on the wall of the present church on 5 July 1963. His will is to be found in P.C.C., 46 Scroope.
55 *Middlesex County Records*, vol 2, p 75.
56 *Weekly Account*, 4 October 1643.
57 W. H. Black, *Docquets of Letters Patent*, 1837, p 405.
58 He was not directly related to that William Strode who was one of the Five Members. Details from *Miscellanea Genealogica et Heraldica*, 2nd series, vol 4, p 184; *Calendar of the Committee for the Advance of Money*, vol 1, p 371; Kent County Archives, Warde MS, U 678. For both Strode and Wandesford, see *The Papers of Capt Henry Stevens*, ed M. Toynbee, Oxfordshire Record Society, 1961, pp 68-69, and *The*

Royalist Ordnance Papers, ed I. Roy. For Wandesford, see H. B. M'Call, *Story of the Family of Wandesford*, 1904.

59 E 112/447/418.

60 *Camden Miscellany VIII*, 1883, pp 14-15.

61 Introduction to *A Discourse of Holy Love*.

62 For a full account of the Parliamentary Surveys, see S. J. Madge, *The Domesday of Crown Lands*, 1938.

63 E 320/1/31. For full text see Appendix.

64 SP 1/62/488.

65 *Middlesex County Records*, vol 3, p 190.

66 E 320/L/31.

67 E 121/3/4.

68 SP 18/XV/15.

69 C 54/3713/11

70 SP 18/XVII/71.

71 E 112/444/164.

72 Crest 6/2/224-226. For full text see Appendix.

73 SP 29/21. Bolton's shop in Leadenhall Street was broken into and pillaged three times in the early 1650s. The family moved out of the City but in November 1657 Colonel Barkstead and his men had 'besett and brake open his house, & all the Dores, trunks and chests therein with much violence, & with drawne swords and Pistolls forced the chamber of your Petitrs. neece, Major Woods wife, who being then big with child miscarried, not without hazard of her life, and your Petitrs. husband was put into such an extreame ffright as that hee being almost quite worne out with so many yeares persecution and sorrow, & well nere totally ruined in his estate, within foure moneths after dyed.' Mrs Bolton had removed to Shepton Mallet, Sir George Strode's birthplace, and the Park may well have been mentioned to her by the family there.

74 E 112/444/164.

75 Stow, *Survey of London*, 1755, vol 2, p 64.

76 T 1/6/no 27, pp 108-110.

77 SP 29/232/309; SP 29/142; SP 29/186/112.

78 Crest 6/10/p 380. She sold it to Lord Wootton who purchased the fee simple for £1,000.

79 PRO 30/32/44, pp 82-84, 152.

80 T 4/6/p 97; T 1/6/no 27, pp 108-110.

CHAPTER 2

1 Middlesex Record Office, Hearth Tax no 2, 1664, and Hearth Tax no 51, 1674. The Marylebone rate books, lodged at the Old Town Hall, Marylebone Road, start in 1684 and are complete from 1704; the early ones are unindexed and are not paginated. The vestry minutes are also there, complete from 1729. This chapter is based on these documents. A more antiquarian account of the agriculture of the Park in the eighteenth century by the present author can be found in *London and Middlesex Archaeological Society Transactions*, vol 21, part 3, 1967.

2 British Museum, Harleian MS 18238, ff 44, 49.
3 British Museum, Harleian MS 18239, ff 18-20.
4 Pehr Kalm, *Kalm's account of his visit to England*, translated by J. Lucas, 1892. pp 49, 81-84.
5 Reports from Commissioners, Cattle plague, 1866, Command Paper, 3591, pp viiii-xi; Royal Society Transaction, 21 Nov, 12 Dec, 1745; 9 Jan, 1746. One gentleman said that he had 'sent for some milk as usual from the Vineyard at St James's Park' which curdled in the tea and tasted odd; the cow died forty-eight hours later.
6 Crest 2/736.
7 C 11/1633/34.
8 M P E 315.
9 Jones rose early every summer morning to make his survey of the estates north of the New Road; *see* Ashbridge Collection. For an account of this good and faithful servant of the parish, whose portrait by Northcote hangs in the Old Town Hall, Marylebone Road, *see* Sheppard, pp 161-164.
10 At present in the possession of Messrs Knoedler, St James's Street.
11 Information gathered from T. Baird, *General View of the Agriculture of the County of Middlesex*, 1793, especially p 21; W. Marshall, *Minutes . . . on Agriculture in the Southern Counties . . . To which is prefixed A sketch of the Vale of London*, 1799, especially p 39; John Middleton, *View of the Agriculture of Middlesex*, 1797, pp 48, 289-91.
12 Crest 2/736.
13 In the possession of the Crown Estates Office.
14 In the possession of the City of Westminster Public Library.
15 Wash drawing by Samuel Hieronymus Grimm, British Museum Additional MS 15542, f 139.
16 Crest 2/736.
17 Positions of marks given on John Jones' 1799 map, in Ashbridge Collection.
18 J. T. Smith, *Book for a Rainy Day*, 1905, p 22, and *Survey of London*, vol 21, pp 120-121.
19 A complete history of the Count's collection and its subsequent history has been prepared by Dr Gerda Kircher to whom I am deeply indebted for help and advice. It is to be published soon. Printed accounts of the collection have already appeared in *Blätter fur Gemäldekunde*, 1904, nr 2, pp 23-28, and in *Diocesanarchiv von Schwaben*, 1902, no 8, pp 113-128.
20 C. A. Goede, *The Stranger in England*, 1807, vol 3, pp 14-19.
21 B. Silliman, *Journal of Travels*, 1820, vol 1, p 307.
22 Messrs. Coutts' archives, Ledger S, 1802-3.
23 F. Lugt, *Repertoire des catalogues des vents publiques*, 1938. Nos 7049, 7072, 7100. The Truchsessian sale catalogues have some delightful descriptions of the paintings for sale. Lot 75 was 'Annib. Carracci. The Assassination of Pompey. Capital.'
24 Then the Grossherzoglich Hessisches Landesmuseum, now the Hessisches Landesmuseum.

CHAPTER 3

1 R. B. Pugh, *The Crown Estate, an historical essay*, HMSO, 1960.
2 *First Report of the Commissioners*, 1787, p 18.
3 British Museum Additional MS 33056, f 211.
4 British Museum, Additional MS 35128, f 480, a letter from Fordyce to Arthur Young, asking him about manure and promising him an interesting and agreeable time if he will visit Ayton. Fordyce's house there was burnt down in 1834 and has been rebuilt since.
5 Crest 2/738.
6 The younger John White [d 1850] was District Surveyor for St Marylebone. The book is called *Some Account of the Proposed Improvements of the Western Part of London, by the formation of Regent's Park*. The second edition, 1815, is much fuller than the first.
7 Milne and Pillar were paid £600 a year rising to £700 after twenty years' service; the commissioners had proposed a scale of £700-£800 but the Treasury cut it down. The surveyors and architects received a guinea a day when working and a shilling a mile when travelling, in addition to a retainer of £100 a year. There were four senior and ten junior clerks, the whole establishment costing £10,585 a year, £186 more than the old arrangements had done, but the commissioners were certain that 'advantages infinitely greater to counterbalance the small additional Expenditure would result from it.' The services of Catherine Kitson, office cleaner, were retained for her lifetime, though it was felt she was not really needed. Milne worked very hard. He was examined by the 1833 Select Committee on Land Revenue [p 109] and was asked:

    Your hours?—They commence before and extend after the usual office hours, frequently, almost daily.

    Are you occasionally under the necessity of devoting part of Sunday to the duties of your office?—Yes, sometimes.

8 Sir John Summerson's *John Nash*, second edition 1949, is by far the best account of the architect's life and work. I have been able to do little more than confirm his findings. The quotation is from a letter to Sir John Soane, given in full in *John Nash*, p 259. Mrs Arbuthnot rather confirms the unflattering description: 'Mr Nash is a very clever, odd, amusing man, with a face like a monkey's but civil & good humoured to the greatest degree.' Harriet Arbuthnot, *Journal*, edited by Francis Bamford and the Duke of Wellington, 1950, vol 1, p 334.
9 *The Letters of George IV*, ed A. Aspinall, vol 1, Letter 163. The letter is dated 2 October 1812, soon after the establishment of the Regency, when the Prince needed all the support he could get.
10 She had five adopted children whom she said belonged to a distant relative, but the suspicion was that they were hers and the Prince's. One of them, James Pennethorne, was an architect and succeeded to much of his adopted father's practice. Descendants have destroyed any evidence of Mary Anne's liaison. Mrs Arbuthnot said she was a 'vulgar bore'.
11 Sir John Summerson, *Georgian London*, 1962, p 160.

12 Joseph Farington, *Diary*, vol 6, p 249. '18 March 1811. Smirk called. He dined with Sir Thos Bernard in Wimpole Street on Saturday last. West, Beechey, Nash an architect and P[rince] Hoare were there . . . Nash seemed to put himself very forward as having had much to do in forming plans for improvements in the Marylebone district.'
13 Letter from T. Moore to James Corry, 24 October 1811, quoted in *John Nash*, p 107.
14 Printed in full in *First Report of the Commissioners*, 1812, pp 86-95.
15 Ibid, pp 95-115.
16 Guingette—a curious French word meaning a pleasure resort outside the jurisdiction of the municipal licensing authorities.
17 This plan is discussed in some detail in Sir John Summerson's *Georgian London*, pp 175-76. It was published by a firm of auctioneers, Spurrier & Phipps, but they were not the designers, who remain unknown. Accommodation on the projected estate was chiefly in pairs of semi-detached villas, this being the first appearance of a now familiar arrangement.
18 C.-N. Ledoux, *L'Architecture considerée sous le rapport de l'art, des moeurs et de la legislation*, 1804. Vol 2, Maison de M le Président Hocquart and Maison située Rue Poisonniere are particularly relevant. For a discussion of Ledoux's influence, see Summerson's introduction to Terence Davis, *The Architecture of John Nash*, 1960, p 14.
19 Report of the Select Committee on the Office of Works, 1828, p. 74.
20 See supra, p 49.
21 MR 1045, MR 1047.
22 Louis Simond, *Journal of a Tour and Residence in Great Britain*, 1817, vol 1, p 64.
23 Stucco was first used by Adam in Hanover Square in 1776, but its use did not become general until after the building of the Park. It was always scored to look like Bath stone—which Nash used when he could afford it. See infra, p 95.
24 Albert Fein, *Victoria Park, its origins and history*, in *East London Papers*, vol 5, no 2, pp 73-90.
25 This in turn was replaced, on a different social level, with Ebenezer Howard's recommendation of eight houses to the acre so that each family could enjoy its own little Park, or garden. Highview, Pinner, in Middlesex, or the Hurst-an-Clays Housing Estate in East Grinstead, Sussex, are a far cry from the dignity of Regent's Park but there is a relationship.

CHAPTER 4

1 Crest 2/741.
2 Ephraim Hardcastle [i.e. W. H. Pyne], *Wine and Walnuts*, 1824, vol 2, pp 200, 320-321.
3 John White, *Observations*, p 34.
4 Figures from Crest 2/744 and Crest 2/1736.
5 Report from the Select Committee on the Office of Works, 1828, p 73.

6 They did not report that Messrs Jenkins & Gwyther of Lisson Green, who were supplying syringa, berberis and broom for the Inner Circle, had overcharged by £369 3s 1d, or that the Treasury had suspended tree-planting while they tried to grow potatoes and mangel-wurzels for profit in the Park. The experiment was tried but 'the produce from the sale of Potatoes has exceeded only in a small degree the cost of their cultivation; but the digging of the ground has been found to be beneficial to the young Trees.' Tree-planting was resumed in 1812 with Messrs Kennedy & Lee of Hammersmith providing eight-foot oaks and Spanish chestnuts at £3 3s the hundred as well as mountain ash, Turkey oaks, sycamore and tulip trees. Jenkins & Gwyther were later forgiven and received other orders.

7 J. P. Malcolm, *London Redivivum*, 1803-7, vol 1, p 5. See also H. A. Shannon, *Bricks—a trade index 1785-1849*, in *Economica*, new series 1, pp 300-318; E. W. Cooney, *The Origins of the Victorian Master Builders*, in *Economic History Reviews*, second series, vol 8, pp 167-176; A. E. Cairncross and B. Weber, *Fluctuations in Building in Great Britain, 1785-1849*, in *Economic History Review*, second series, vol 9, pp 283-297; D. J. Olsen, *Town Planning in London*, 1964. Numerous barracks, the commissioners' fifty new churches, the Houses of Parliament, the new General Post Office, docks, customs houses at London and Liverpool, University College, King's College, several hospitals, the National Gallery, the British Museum and Buckingham Palace, were built between 1815 and 1840.

8 The records of the Regent's Canal Company are in the possession of the British Transport Commission. For accounts of the Canal, as it relates to the Park, see *John Nash*, pp 171-174, and for a full history see H. Spencer, *London's Canal*, 1961. Other documents in Crest 2/938.

9 See *The Glenbervie Journals*, ed W. Sichel, 1910, pp 148-9. By coincidence, Nash purchased Ningwood and Hamsted, two of the properties Thomas Hobson had received nearly 300 years before in exchange for Marylebone Park. Mrs Arbuthnot did not find Nash's houseparties to her taste.

10 *Gentleman's Magazine*, vol 82, 2, p 370.

11 *The Glenbervie Journals*, p 156.

12 Evidence of John Shaw to Committee on Crown Leases, 1829, p 46.

13 J. Farington, *Diary*, vol 8, p 299, November 1821.

14 When the Select Committee on Crown Leases discussed this in 1829, there was a nice exchange with Alexander Milne.

> The Board admitted Mr Nash in place of the [Canal] Company?—Yes.
>
> They look to Mr Nash as a responsible person?
>
> I suppose so, but they always look to the buildings as the best security.

15 Crest 2/752. Nash and Mayor were in agreement to build two houses in Langham Place.

16 *Quarterly Review*, 1828, vol 34, p 193. The ryhme must have been current before then.

17 Bankruptcy Proceedings, B3/3363, pp 4-5. Evidence of John Day, Mayor's clerk, and George Bayley, his foreman. A former apprentice,

Robert Roe, described Mayor as a carpenter; 'He told me that he would furnish me in the business of a Carpenter and a Joiner and would make a man of me if I was a good lad.'

18 Crest 6/ vol 149, pp 262-282.

19 W. Thornbury and E. Walford, *Old and New London*, 1892, vol 5, p 269.

20 Vestry Proceedings for New Churches, 19 June 1813; 1, 5 Jan, 2, 5, 29 March, 2, 5, 9 April, 14 May, 4 June 1814.

21 *Dictionary of National Biography* and Report of the Select Committee on Crown Leases, 1829, p 50.

22 Crest 2/763 for the charge and for Nash's answer.

23 Although Mr Richardson was still complaining in 1819 that 'the entrance from the New Road is nothing more than a barren waste and [the trench] a Receptacle for Filth of every Description'. Crest 2/760.

24 Crest 24/vol 4/pp 78-9. 20 February 1814.

25 *The Glenbervie Journals*, ed F. Bickley, 1928, vol 2, p 199. Entry for 16 August 1816.

26 Select Committee on Crown Leases, 1829, pp 46, 50.

27 Printed in full in Second Report of the Commissioners, 1816, pp 114, 122.

28 James Burton, 1761-1837. See H. M. Colvin, *Biographical Dictionary of English Architects, 1660-1840*, 1954, pp 113-4; D. J. Olsen, *Town Planning in London*, 1964; and John Britton, *Auto-biography*, 1850, vol 2, pp 172-3. for the claim to have been the first master builder, which is more usually accorded to Thomas Cubitt.

29 Evidence of Thomas Lothian to the Select Committee on Crown Leases, 1829, p 80: 'You have said that in 1824 there was such a speculating spirit abroad that persons would have built upon almost any terms; was that the same in 1819?—I do not recollect, but I think not so much in 1819; but that was the very height of the disposition in 1824.'

30 Crest 6/ vol 142, pp 273-6; Crest 2/774. The ground rents were moderate. Land in Piccadilly or Portland Place let at £5 5s per foot of frontage. Evidence of Edward Driver to Select Committee on Land Revenues, 1833, p 84.

31 M.P.Z. 14; made by George Cornell, a clerk in the Office of Woods, working in his spare time. He was paid £181 2s for his pains. Crest 2/788.

32 Holwood House, Keston, Kent, for John Ward, whose London home was in Devonshire Place, Marylebone, and Baston House, Baston, Middlesex, for Samuel.

33 The New Street was immediately much used as a thoroughfare and proved very noisy—witness a letter by J. Shakespeare [Crest 26/177]: It is really impossible to suffer the Annoyances we complain of without remonstrance. At this moment there are three large Shut carts blocking up the Passage entirely across Oxford Street & surrounded by a mob of Vagabonds—One fellow ringing a Bell, another blowing a Trumpet, and a third beating a large Gong or Drum that may be heard to Charing Cross.

34 It was suggested that the Park should be called after the Duke of

Wellington and J. M. Gandy went so far as to design and exhibit, in 1816 at the Royal Academy, a villa in the Park in which His Grace might live, but nothing came of the idea. See Sir John Summerson, *Heavenly Mansions*, 1949, p 131, and infra, p 135.

35 £300,000 was lent by the Bank of England [Bank Ledger for 13 June 1817] and another £300,000 by the Royal Exchange Insurance Company [Report of the Select Committee on the Office of Works, 1828, p 104.]

CHAPTER 5

1 James Elmes, *Metropolitan Improvements: or London in the nineteenth century*, 1827-28, p 6.

2 Ibid, p. 7.

3 Earlier this century, it was known as the Nursemaids' Tunnel, equally suitable for a professional conversation when the rain fell in the gardens or for an assignation with one of the soldiers from Albany Street Barracks.

4 Now bombed.

5 Elmes, *op cit*, p 44.

6 Crest 2/771.

7 Three contractors, Butt, Hamilton and McIntosh, had to be called in. McIntosh completed the work in the autumn of 1815 for £273 7s 4d. Crest 2/753.

8 Charles Knight, *London*, 1841-44, vol 5, p 317. Miss Helen Barlow says she can remember the squabbles for the possession of the summit that raged about 1890.

9 Nicholas Barton, *The Lost Rivers of London*, 1962, pp 30-6, and map at end of the book; A. D. Webster, *The Regent's Park*, 1911, p 24, and plate opposite for photograph of culvert.

10 Crest 6/ vol 158, p 117.

11 Crest 24/4.

12 Summerson's *John Nash* for discussion of this point. The documents in Crest 2/767 prove that the design was indeed Burton's.

13 The story is that the terrace was cut short and turned into a bay on George IV's orders, so that the view from Mrs Siddons' windows at 27 Upper Baker Street should not be obscured. Unfortunately, I have been unable to find any contemporary evidence for this delightful theory.

14 Crest 2/771.

15 Crest 2/766.

16 Reproduced in *The Architectural Review*, 1905, p 113, as an illustration to an interesting article by R. P. Jones, *The Life and Work of Decimus Burton*, pp 109-118, 155-164.

17 Select Committee on the Office of Works, 1828, p 123. Sir Charles stressed how closely Decimus kept to his estimates.

18 Royal Institute of British Architects, Shide Ledger, f 56.

19 *John Nash*, p 191.

20 J. Britton and A. Pugin, *The Public Buildings of London*, 1825-26, vol 2, p 363. For a modern description and photographs, see *Country Life*, 5 July 1962.
21 Crest 2/786.
22 The only unrespectable inmates of the Alma Cottages on record were Ugo Foscolo, the Italian poet, who had to be imprisoned for debt, and Charles Heathcote Tatham, the connoisseur and designer, who went bankrupt in 1834.
23 Elmes, *op cit*, pp 48-9.
24 The communicating rooms measured 20 ft 6 in by 18 ft, and 12 ft 6 in by 18 ft.
25 Elmes, *op cit*, p 50; Crest 2/768.
26 Arthur Bolton's description in *Country Life*, 22 March 1913.
27 There were originally three houses, one detached and two built as one, but the pair were periodically thrown into one, which is confusing.
28 *Dictionary of National Biography*; no source is given. C. J. Mathews, an architect who had trained with Nash but who became an actor, wrote: 'If a column or a window was found on being drawn from his measured sketch to be a foot or two too much to the left or right, he would say: "Never mind, it won't be observed in the execution"'. *Life of C. J. Mathews*, vol 1, pp 252-3. The surveyors measuring up Park Crescent for rebuilding in 1961-2 said that no two levels were the same, no corner a right angle, and that there was a kink in the curve of the eastern half.
29 See Catherine Jamison, *The History of the Royal Hospital of St Katharine*, 1952.
30 *John Nash*, p 291, quoting information supplied by Mr C. F. Bell, Poynter's grandson.
31 All quotations on Chester Terrace come from Crest 2/768, Crest 2/1737 or Crest 2/1749.
32 Crest 24/5. Burton claimed £700 compensation but did not get it. This was in 1817.
33 Elmes, *op cit*, p 67.
34 Burton's drawings are now in the Richardson Collection in the Victoria and Albert Museum. See also: *A Brief Account of the Colosseum*, 1829; J. Timbs, *Curiosities of London*, 1855, pp 221-224; Britton and Pugin, *op cit*, vol 1, pp 368-375; and Hugh Honour, *The Regent's Park Colosseum*, in *Country Life*, 2 January 1953.
35 Crest 2/771.
36 For a full account of dioramas in general, see Olive Cook, *Movement in Two Dimensions*, 1962; for the Park Square Diorama, see Britton and Pugin,*op cit*, vol 1, pp 362-367, and J. Timbs, *op cit*, pp 252-3.
37 See the Revd J. Clutterbuck in *Journal of the Royal Agricultural Society*, new series, vol 5, p 13. He said Cumberland Market was better arranged than Smithfield or Whitechapel haymarkets.
38 Select Committee on Crown Leases, 1829, pp 70-113.
39 The bricks were made at first by Mr James Ellis, who had demolished Willan's farm and had made the roads in the Park, and then, on his disagreeing with Nash on the weather-worthiness of the bricks, by a Mr Boyle. Ellis valued the bricks at 42s to 45s the thousand; Frederick

Lewis, a dismissed contractor, said they were not worth 15s. The Committee were worried lest Augustus Street should have fallen down.

40 Crest 2/778. This contains Nash's original proposition to take on the land. It is annotated 'Nash is the only person to want it in ten years.'

41 *John Nash*, chap 5; T. Davis, *op cit*, pp 69-88; *Survey of London*, vol 19, pp 153-158.

42 Issued between 1825 and 1828. Pugin, as we have already seen, was a French refugee who worked for Nash as a draughtsman. Britton was a voluminous writer on architectural and topographical subjects. The exception is from vol 2, pp 362-3.

43 Unidentified newspaper cuttings, c 1815, in Westminster Public Library; see supra, p 206, note 34.

44 Henry Crabb Robinson, *Diary*, ed T. Sadler, 1872, vol 1, p 310.

CHAPTER 6

1 Report from the Select Committee on the Office of Works, 1828.

2 Report from the Select Committee on Crown Leases, 1829.

3 George IV, *Correspondence*, ed A. Aspinall, vol 3, letter 1514 for reference to 'poor little Nash'; Letter 1563 for the Duke's refusal to confirm the honour. See also *Wellington and his Friends*, ed Seventh Duke of Wellington, 1965, letter 104, and Mrs Arbuthnot's *Journal*, vol 2, p 289.

4 J. Britton, *Auto-biography*, 1850, vol 1, p 441.

5 Charles d'Arlincourt, *The Three Kingdoms*, 1844, vol 1, pp 24-5.

6 Elmes, *op cit*, p 21.

7 Enid C. Samuel, *The Villas in Regent's Park and their Residents*, 1959. This excellent little book lists all the known residents; I have only mentioned a few.

8 Leigh Hunt, *The Townsman*, nos 2, 3 & 4. Reprinted in *Political and Occasional Essays*, ed L. and C. Houtchens, 1963, pp 289-290.

9 *Greater London*, ed J. T. Coppock and H. C. Prince, 1964, p 103.

10 Crest 2/787 and *A History of the Royal Toxophilite Society* . . . by a Toxophilite, 1867.

11 T. J. Williams and A. W. Campbell, *The Park Village Sisterhood*, 1965.

12 W. Thornbury and E. Walford, *Old and New London*, vol 5, p. 266.

13 Crest 2/1741.

14 Crest 6/ vol 163, p 333.

15 Crest 2/796; Crest 6/ vol 180, pp 254-67.

16 A. C. Underhill, *A History of the English Baptists*, 1947, p 240.

17 Briton and Pugin, *op cit*, vol 1, p 373; Hugh Honour, *The Regent's Park Colosseum, Country Life*, 2 January 1953.

18 J. Timbs, *op cit*, p 224.

19 Middlesex Coroner's Records in the possession of the Greater London Council at County Hall. Quotation and details from the depositions of Lawrence Barrett Phillips and W. A. Pointer, an ex-sailor who helped

to drag people from the Lake. Illustrated accounts appeared in the *Illustrated London News* during January 1867.

20 Letter in *The Times*, 26 March 1926.

21 The bridge was called after Lord Macclesfield, the first chairman of the Regent's Canal Company. Accounts of the explosion in the *Illustrated London News*, October 1874. The coroner's records for the relevant dates are missing.

22 The two standard histories of the Zoo are P. Chalmers Mitchell's *Centenary History*, 1929, and H. Scherren's *The Zoological Society of London*, 1905.

23 26 May 1826, p 282.

24 Information about the Royal Botanic Society from their Guide to the Gardens, 1900. When the Society was disbanded, its records were deposited in St Marylebone Public Library, now Westminster Public Library.

CHAPTER 7

1 M. J. Tuke, *A History of Bedford College for Women, 1849-1937*, 1939.

2 Sir Ian Fraser, *My Story of St Dunstan's*, 1961.

3 The lady at the time was the Countess Haugwitz-Reventlow. It was after her marriage with the film star, Cary Grant, was dissolved that she gave up the house.

4 Statement by Mr Osborne, Crown estate surveyor—Nash's direct successor. The sale notices referred to the leases not to the actual properties.

5 Gorell Report, Cmd 7094, p 10.

6 Ibid, p 5.

7 Ibid, p 21.

8 Ibid, p 12.

9 Since the war, it has been possible to make cruises along the remaining stretch of canal on the beautiful barge, the *Jason*.

10 Besides the chairman, it consisted of Ronald Harris, Michael Berry, Lord Bradford, D. H. Cameron of Lochiel, W. C. Farnsworth, Sir Edward Gillett, and Lord Williams.

11 The Future of the Regent's Park Terraces, Statement . . . 1957, p 3.

12 Ibid, p 3.

13 The Future of the Regent's Park Terraces, Third Statement, 1962, p 9.

14 Third Statement, p 5.

APPENDICES

APPENDIX I

Public Records Office, Special Collections, Rentals and Surveys, Portfolios, (S.C.1./23/65) [Translation].

THE MANOR OF TYBURN IN THE PARISH OF MARIBONE

Survey made there by Geoffrey Chamber, surveyor and receiver general of the lands acquired by the lord king in the month of June in the thirtieth year of the reign of Henry VIII by the Grace of God King of England and France, Defender of the Faith, Lord of Ireland, and on earth supreme head of the Anglican Church.

The Manor of Tyburn, lands and buildings acquired from Thomas Hopson [*sic*]
The scite of the manour with the pasture therto adjoyng. From the issue of the site of the said manor with two orchards, whereof one contains 3 roods, 12 perches, and the other one rood and a half, and two gardens containing half an acre between them by estimation, which are valued annually at 36s. 8d.

From the issue of four pieces of meadow adjoining the said site containing between them 13 acres, whereof two of them are called Welmedowes, 10 acres, and the other two are called Dovehouse-medowe, 2 acres, and Swanmedowe, half an acre, which are valued at the rate of 5/- the acre, in all 65/- a year. Richard Jaquett holds by indenture from William Hollis, the guardian of Thomas Hopson, son and heir of Richard Hopson, dated 28 March 1523, all that farm or tenement in which the said Richard Jaquett now lives, with all the buildings, gardens, fields, pastures, lands both arable and common appertaining to the said farm or tenement, in as full a manner and form as ever the aforesaid Richard Jaquett held, occupied or enjoyed theretofore, by virtue of a grant or concession made to the said Richard Jaquett by Richard Hopson, reserving and excepting to William Hollys the woods and underwoods and the windmill with the gravell pyttes and Clay pyttes, To have and to hold the said farm or tenement with all and singular the premises excepting the aforementioned, from 29 September last past before the date of the said indenture, until the said Thomas Hopson shall come to the full age of 21 years, or for as long as William Hollys shall have, occupy and enjoy the said premises by reason of his custody of the body of the said Thomas Hopson, or by reason of any other feofment or last will of the aforesaid Richard Hopson the father of the said Thomas. And he shall pay quarterly at the four usual terms, excluding 60/-, deducted and allowed to the same Richard Jaquett from the rent of 12 acres of meadow part of the premises and now enclosed in the Park of our Lord the King, as will be shown £10. 16s. 8d.

Thomas Holte holds by indenture, as is stated, one windmill, 20/- £11. 16s. 8d.

Rents at Will

From the issue of one tenement with five acres of arable land adjoining recently in the tenure of Thomas Osbourne, 13s. 4d.

From the issue of one cottage adjoining the said tenement, lately Thomas Osborne's, 6s. 8d.

From the issue of five acres of pasture land on the north side of the Park of our Lord the King, valued at 3/4d the acre, lately in the tenure of Thomas Osborne, 16s. 8d. 36s. 8d.

Woods outside the Park

From the issue of 37 acres and one rood of wood, valued at a yearly average of 20d. the acre 62s. 1d.

Lands and Woods emparked

From the issue of 203 acres of arable land and pasture, the residue of the farm lately in the possession of Thomas Osborne, assignee of Richard Styles, valued at 14d. the acre, £11. 16s. 10d. a year

From the issue of 12 acres of pasture lately in the tenure of Richard Jaquett and deducted and allowed to him above, 60/- a year.

From the issue of 100 acres of wood valued at a yearly average of 20d. the acre £8. 6s. 8d. £23. 3s. 6d.

£39. 18s. 11d. besides 101s. 8d. for the site of the manor and the meadow adjoining.

Divers fields, meadows and pasture lands acquired from various people and now enclosed in the King's Park there.

Lands acquired from the Prior of St. John of Jerusalem in England.
From the issue of 12 acres of pasture at 2/8d the acre 109s. 8d.

From the issue of three acres of meadow lately in the tenure of William Portman valued at 4/- the acre, annually 12/-

From the issue of 14 acres of wood, valued at 20d. the acre, annually 23s. 4d. £7. 4s. 8d.

Land acquired from the Master and Fellows of Eton College
From the issue of six acres of meadow lying on Chawkehill at 4/- the acre, 24/-

From the issue of 14 acres of wood, at 20d. the acre, on a yearly average, annually, 23s. 4d. 47s. 4d.

Land acquired from the Master of the Prebend of Rugmere
From the issue of 23 acres of arable land and pasture, taking one acre with the other, 2/8d. £4. 8s. 0d. annually

From the issue of 40 acres of meadow at 4/- the acre annually £8. 0s. 0d.

From the issue of 66 acres of pasture, valued at 3/4d. the acre, annually £11. 0s. 0d.

From the issue of 16 acres of wood, valued at 20d. the acre, at a yearly average of 16s. 8d. £24. 13s. 8d.

Land acquired from the Master of the Prebend of Tottenham Court.
From the issue of two pieces of meadow containing 55 acres, one rood, valued at 4/- the acre, annually, £11. 0s. 0d.

Land acquired from the Master of St. Giles.
From the issue of ten acres of pasture valued at 3/4d the acre, annually 33s. 4d.

From the issue of 3 acres and a half of pasture, called Barrowes, at the same rate, 11s. 8d. 45s. 0d. £47. 11s. 8d.

The sum total of the valuation of the aforesaid manor £92. 12s. 3d. from which the site of the manor and the adjoining meadows—101s. 8d.; land with woods emparked—£70. 15s. 2d.; rents, farms, and woods outside the Park, £16 15s. 5d.

Whence . . .

Deduct rents from the said manor of Tyburn and lands acquired from Thomas Hopson, as it is said, namely, to the Duke of Norfolk 66s. 8d.; to the Abbess of Barking, 30/-. In all, £4 16s. 8d.

And there remains net . . . [Unfinished]

Endorsement

The manor of Tyburne in the parish of Marylebone : the appearance or condition of the aforesaid.

APPENDIX 2

Public Record Office, E 101/474/21

[Superscription torn and stained] . . . the fourthe yeare of the raigne of o^{r} Soveraigne Lorde kinge Edwarde the vj^{to} untyll the laste daie of June in the ffyfte yere of the raigne of o^{r} saide soveraigne lorde.

In primis paid for carringe xiij lodes of Railes & Pales from Westminstre to Marybone pke. v^{s} iiij^{d}

Item to a Carpinder & his man for xviij daies worke in settinge uppe the saide Railes and Pales at xxd. the daie xxx^{s}

Item per iij thousand of xj peny nailes xj^{s}

Item p^{r} two hundred of doble tennepeny nailes ij^{s} vj^{d}

Item for fyvescore lodes of sandie gravell from Knightsbrydge to Marybone pke for to overspred the brydge and waies that were made the last yere w^{t} clay gravell wch yf yt had not bene nowe donne, wold have cost vj tymes the charge that yt dothe noew at xd pr carting & carying every lode. iiij^{li} iij^{s} iiij^{d}

It. for mendinge of a greate grate of tymbre worke broken in the fflodde, and makinge of Trenche to convey the water from a house that the deere doo feede at the said grate xxvj^{s} viij^{d}

It. paid to foure laborers for spredinge of gravell for vj daies worke at viijd the daie every man. xvj^{s}

It. for two dogges of iron to the said grate iij^{s} iiij^{d}

Summa viij^{li} xviij^{s}

per me Alexander [page torn]

Workys don [in] Marybone Park in the Vth yere of the Reign of o^{r} Soveraign Lorde Kyng Edwarde the VIth ffrom the iij day of September unto the xxiij day of October last past.

ffurste paide ffor trenchinge and water coursynge of a valley in a paddock for the conveyinge the water in to twoo ponds which yf it hadd nott ben don wolde have byn the dethe of mayny deer and also hyndryd the ffedinge that the king sholde have byn dysappoyntid when hys grace sholde have commandyd any Dere to be gotten in and to be made redy for hys grace x^{s}

Item paide for the taking up of a foundation of bryck and for the water cowrse contaynyng by the Roode xj Rode att xs the Rode v^{li} x^{s}

Item paide for the taking up of ffoundacion of bryck and for the laying and mending of the same and for makinge of a ponde to Receyve the Water contaynyng xx Roods and di[midium] at xs the Rood x^{li} v^{s}

Item paide for stockkinge dyvers placys of the cowrse that the king cold not have cowrsid wt hys grayhounds for shrubbs and bushys xxx^{s}

Item paide for setting and varnishynge of xxx Roods of pale at xijd the Rood xxx^{s}

Item paide for ye nailys for the same palynge viij^{s}

Totle xl^{li} xiij^{s}

APPENDIX 3

Extracts from Public Record Office document, E 101/544/29.

A booke of the Receipts and payments ffor the chardge in the repayringe & amedinge of the Lodges cowrses parrocke pales posts and rayles of Marybone Parke in the countye of Mydd. Done by John ffothergill woodward of the same countye by vertue of a warraunte divested unto him in that behalf as followeth. Viz.

xxii^{o} ffebruar 1566	Imprimis Receyved of Mr. Nicholas Holborne gent deputye Receiver of the sayd countye by vertue of a warraunte divested unto hym for the sayde purpose lxvj^{li} xiij^{s} iiij^{d}

xxvj^{o} martii 1567	Also receyved of sundry persons for xl loppes of the tymber trees felled in the saide parke at xd the pece ix^{s} ij^{d}
iij^{o} maii	Receyvid more for xl topps of pollerde trees felled in the sayde pke at viijd the pece vij^{s} iii^{d}
vij^{o} Junij	Also receyved of sundry persons for the topps of lx small tymbre trees felled in Greate St. Johns Wood for pales post and rayles for the Sayde pke viz xxti at viijd the pece and xlti at vj the pece xxxiij^{s} iij^{d}
xij^{o} Junij	Also receyved of a Tanner at Clerkenwell for the barke of the sayde lx trees at liijd the pece one wth another xx^{s}
xj^{o} Julii	Also receyved of sundry persons for the crowns of xxti pollard okes felled wth in the Lordshipp of Stanwell in the sayde countye for the makinge of pales posts & rayles & for tymber for plankes & joysts for the brydge of the saide pke at vjd the pece one wth another x^{s}
xiiij^{o} August	More received of a Tanner at Stanes for the barke of the same xx trees at iiijd the pece vj^{s} viij^{d} Sum of the receipte afforesayde lxx^{li} xix^{s} x^{d}
xxij^{o} ffebr. 1566	ffyrste payed to Mr. Nicholas Holborne the sayde Receyver for the portage of the sayde lxvjli xiijs iiijd after the rate of iiijd in the pownde xxij^{s} ij^{d}
xx^{o} Martij	Payed also to Mr. Edwarde Carye esquier keper of the sayed Parke of Marybone by thand of John Heynes his underkep. there the somes of money here after followinge aboute the necessarye reparacons of the Lodge there, viz. A Carpenter for vij dayes worke at xiiijd by the daye=viijs ijd. To a Labourer for x dayes work at ixd by the day=vijs vid. To a Tyler for viij dayes worke at xijd by the daye=viijs. ffor iij C of nayles=ijs. Item ffor half a hundred of bowds for ffloring the half=ijs vjd. ffor di C off lathe nayles=vjd. ffor C of Lathe=xijd. ffor di C of Tyles=ixd. ffor xxxvij of ruff tyles—ijs viijd. ffor

	tylepins=ijd. ffor Lyme=vs liijd. ffor CC of brycke= ijs ijd. and for the carriage of a Lode of Sande=viijd amountinge in thole to the some of	xlix^{s} viij^{d}
	Item payed to John Stowe paler in earnest of a bargayne	xij^{d}
xxvj^{o} martii 1567	Item payed to the same John Stowe for the clevinge pitchinge and setting of xxiiij rodds di of pales posts and Rayles at one of the Lodge at xvjd the rodde	xxxij^{s} viij^{d}
	Sum pay	Cv^{s} vj^{d}

[The accounts for 26 March to 24 May have been omitted]

xxviij^{o} Maii	Payede to Robert Westefelde smythe for certayne hokes and hengs for gates weyinge xl lb at ijd ob the pound	viij^{s} iiij^{d}
	Item payed to him also for the new makinge and mendinge of certayne hokes and hengs for gates and for the newe yron he put more to them	ij^{s} viij^{d}
	Item to him more for iij C of single xd nayles at viijd the C	ij^{s}
iij^{o} June	Item to Thomas Parke carpenter ffor vj days worke at xiiijd by the day	vij^{s}
	Item payed to Thomas Taylor carpenter for the lyke tyme at xiijd by the day	vj^{s} vj^{d}
	Item to Thomas Fletcher labourer for iij days worke at ixd by day	ij^{s} iij^{d}
vij^{o} Junii	Payed to Henry Hall carter for the carriage of the gates & postes to the place where they be sett beinge ij lodes at viijd the Lode	xvj^{d}
	Item paid to Thomas Parke carpenter for v dayes worke at xiiijd by day	v^{s} x^{d}
	Item to Thomas Taylor for the lyke tyme at xijd by the day	v^{s} v^{d}
	Item payed to Thomas ffletcher labourer for ij dayes worke at ixd by the day	xviij^{d}
	Sum pay	xlij^{s} x^{d}

[The accounts for 8-11 June have been omitted]

xxj^{o} Junii	Item payed to Robert Westefelde Smythe for two plate locks wth their halves for two greate gates there	xij^{s}
xxviij^{o} Junii	Payed to John Drewry for the carriage of xvj lodes of pales posts and rayles out of greate St. Johns Wood to the sayde pke to the course there at ixd the Lode	xij^{s}
	Item payde to Henry Hall for the carriage of xj lodes more of pales &c from St. Johns Wood unto the sayd pke at lyke rate the lode	viij^{s} iij^{d}
	Item to John Stowe paler for the clevinge of xj C of pales posts and rayles at xijd the hundreth	xj^{s}
xix^{o} Julii	Item payed to Robert Carter glassyer for newe glasynge and repayringe of tholde glas of the old lodge as by his bill of pticlers further appeareth	Lj^{s} viij^{d}
	Item payed to John Stowe paler for xij dayes worke in repayringe and newe settinge of thold pale at xiijd by the day	xiij^{s}
xxviij^{o} Julii	Item payed to Humfraye Hankinson for the ffellynge of xxti pollarde okes att Stanwell in the sayde county at iiijd the tree	vj^{s} viij^{d}
	Sum pay	Cxij^{s} vij^{d}
xx Decembr	Payed to Thomas Stafforde sawyer and his fellowe for the sawinge of vj C xxti fete of plancks at xxd the C at the saide Stowes wharfe	x^{s} x^{d}
	Item payed to Henry Hall for the carriage with his carte of the sayde xvj C of pales posts and Rayles and ij lodes di of plancks & ioysts from the sayde Stowes wharf to Marybone parke at xiiijd the lode	xxj^{s} vij^{d}
	Item for the hyer of a sawe pytt at the sayde Stowes wharf	viij^{d}
xxiij^{o} Decembr	Item payed to John Stowe and John Grome for the pitchinge and newe settinge of threscore rodds of palings of the course at vijd the rodde	xxxv^{s}

Item payed to Richard Turkey Thomas Abblett and Rychard Baron for the quick settinge & dytchinge alongest the same course of lxiiij rodds they fyndinge the quycksett at xijd the rodde Lxiiij^{s}

ultimo Decembr Item payed to Robert Carter glasyer for glassynge at John Heyns lodge accordinge to a byll of the particularities thereof xliiij^{s} vj^{d}

Item payed to the sayde John Haynes for the fellynge of xlti trees wthin the sayde pke by his servaunt at iijd the tree x^{s}

Sum pay ix^{li} vj^{s} vij^{d}

1568
xj ffebruarii Payed to Rychard Wylteshire & John Grome for the newe settynge and pytchinge of lxxiiij roddes of the course at vijd the rodde xliij^{s} ij^{d}

xx ffebr Item payed to Thomas Corkman, Thomas Slater and Thomas More for the quycksettynge and dytchinge of fyfty rodds at xjd the rodde xlv^{s} x^{d}

Item payed to Robert Westefelde smythe for mendinge the swepe of one of the gates for lokes & eyes to the same & certain oth worke by him doon aboute ye gates xjs viij^{d}

xxix^{o} fferbr Item payed to Thomas Parke carpenter for xj dayes worke di in makinge an ende of the newe brydge at the sayde parke at xiiijd by the day xiij^{s} v^{d}

Item payed to Richard Morley Toberte Nytholte & Thomas Abblett for quicke settinge & dytchinge of iiij^{xx} v rodds more of the sayd course at xd the rodde xxxvij^{s} xj^{d}

Item payed to Rychard Wylteshire and John Grome for the newe settinge and pytchinge of lxv rodds and pale more of the sayd course at vijd the rodde xxvij^{s} xj^{d}

Item payed to Thomas ffletcher laborer for vij dayes worke aboute the makinge of the sayde brydge at ixd by the day v^{s} iij^{d}

Item to one Parry for casting upp of a ditch out of St. Johns Wood vj^{d}

Sum pay xj^{li} viij^{s} vij^{d}

xv^{o} April	Item payed to Richard Wilteshire and John Grome for iiij dayes worke in the felling of xiij trees & the clevinge of xlti posts and iiij^{xx} rayles that wanted at xijd by the day the pece	viij^{s}
vj^{o} Julii 1568	Item payed to Richard Brayneforthe for the digginge of lviij lodes of gravell for the brydge at id ob the lode	vij^{s} iij^{d}
	Item payed to him more for the diggynge of xxxv lodes of gravell for the sayd brydge at ij the lode	v^{s} x^{d}
ij^{o} August	Item payed to one Jeffry carter for the carriage of fourescore & thirtene lodes of gravell to the sayd brydge at iijd the lode	xxiij^{s}
	Item paid to John Heynes for so muche by him layed oute for the carryage of posts & rayles to the course and of planks & posts to the brydge	v^{s} viij^{d}
ultimo August	Item payed to Richard Wilteshire and John Grome for vij dayes working besyde totnall pke gate at xijd by the day the pece	xiiij^{s}
	Item to them for the ffellynge off vj trees and cleving them into rayles and posts	iij^{s}
	Sum pay	lxvj^{s} ix^{d}
vij^{o} Septemb.	Payed to Richard Wyltshire and John Grome for the kitchinge and new settynge of xxvj rodds of pales at Totnall courte gate at vijd the rodde	xv^{s} ij^{d}
xxj Septemb.	Item payed to Richarde Wyltshire more for xij dayes worke in further amedinge of tholde pale at xijd by the daye	xlj^{s}
	Item payed to John Grome for tenne dayes of wowrkinge lyke worke at xijd by the day	x^{s}
ix Octobr	Item payed to the sayd Richard Wyltshire and John Grome for the pitching & newe setting of xlij rodds of pales more at vijd the rodde	xxiij^{s} vj^{d}
	Sum pay	lxj^{s} viij^{d}
	Sum total of all the afforesayde payments	lxiiij^{li} vij^{s}

Also the afforesayde woodward desyreth to be allowed uppon ye accompte for his charge and paynes about the pmisses for Lxx dayes at ijs by the daye vij[li]

Edwa : Carye
John ffothergill

APPENDIX 4

British Museum, Lansdowne ms. 166, f. 118

A note of the Mesure of the Bridges gates & Postes Lately Erected about Marybone Parke.
Bridges
The fyrst Bridge contayneth 27 foote & a halfe of Tymber.
The second Bridge contayneth 26 foot & 3 quarters of Tymber.
The thirde Bridge contayneth 29 foote of Tymber.
The whelver[1] [?] Bridge contayneth 6 foote & a qrter of Tymber
The whole is 89 foote & a half.
Gates.
Theire is 15 gates, one gate with another contayneth 4 foote and a half of Tymber.
The whole is 67 foote & a half.
Postes.
Nyne postes wth 7 foote of Tymber in a pare is 31 foote & a half.
Nyntene Postes more wth 6 foote of Tymber in a pare is 57 foote.
The whole 88 foote & half.
In all the gates Bridges & Postes I fynde 245 foot and a half of Tymber wch wanteth a foote & a half of 5 lode of Tymber; by the Carpenters estamate wch tooke the mesure of all wch was above the grounde and he

George Benson
Carpenter

Norton had felled 19 loads of timber 17 lib. in ready money.

Tho. Norton gent Surveyor of the kings wayes.

[1] WHELVER. Oxford English Dictionary gives verb "to whelve", meaning to burn a hollow vessel upside down, and gives derivation from Old Norse *hvelfa*, to arch, which suggests that the fourth bridge was a hump-backed one, rather smaller than the other three.

Endorsement.
A note of the charges of certeine gates by Marybone pke. Send for Necton about it. 19 Junii 1608.
For Hampstead Heath Mr. Necton hath 50 loades of timber, and in money.

APPENDIX 5

Public Record Office, E 317/57

Midd. An Addicyonall Survey of a certaine peice way or Tract of ground Lyeinge and being in Marybone Parke in the County of Midd. But now deducted and taken out of the said Parke by way of Repaire by us whose handes are hereunto subscribed in the Moneth of March 1650. Memorand. Accordinge to two Orders the one from the Ho^{ble} Trustees sittinge at Westminster house the other from the Ho^{ble} Committee of Parliamt for Removeinge of Obstructions the one bareinge Date the seconde of January 1650 And directed to us in obedience to wch said orders wee have measured the peice of ground used as Way or Track lyeinge and beinge in Marybone Parke wch leadeth from Marybone Towne gate to Barrowhillgate And wee doe finde the said Way or Track of ground contayneth by admea^{mt} 330 pole in length And two pole and halfe in breadth wch containeth together 5 chains [?] and 25 pole at xxvj^{s} viij^{d} per annum amounteth unto per annum vj^{li} xvij^{s} vj^{d} wch wee make the reprize of as aforesaid
In all 05:25 vi^{li} xvij^{s} vj^{d}

APPENDIX 6

Public Record Office, E. 320/l.31

Com. Midd. Parcell of the possessions of Charles Stuarte late king of England.

All that peice of parcell of Impaled pasture ground wth the Appurtenances comonly called or knowne by the name of Mariebone Parke Scituate, lyeing & being in the severall parishes of Mariebone and Saint Pancras als: Kentish Towne or one of them in the County of Midd. bounded wth the late Deane and Chapters lande on the East and wth a wood called St Johns Wood on the West and on Mariebone Towne on the South and on Primrose Hill on the North, conteyning in the whole by estimacion ffive Hundred Thirty and Foure Acres more or lesse And all woods, underwoods, timber and Timber trees now standing groweing & being in and uppon the premisses or any part thereof. Together wth all waies, passages, waters, watercourses, liberties, priviledges, franchises, Immunityes, Jurisdictions, proffitts, comodityes, advantages and appurtenances in & about the said Parke belonging or usually occupied or enjoyed as part parcill or member thereof. And all that Massuage Tenement dwelling house or lodge wth the appurtenances called the great Lodge scituate standing & being on that side of the Parke next Mariebone Towne and in the parish of Marybone in the county of Midd. aforesaid conteyning by estimacion one Rode more or lesse now or late in the occupation of John Gibbs. And all that Brick House or Tenement wth the Appurtenances lately new built heretofore called the little Lodge scituate lying and being in the parish of Mariebone aforesaid conteyning by estimacion one Roode more or lesse nowe or late in the occupation of Francis Gibbs. And all that small Tenement wth the Appurtenances called the Standing scituate, standing & being in the Middle of the said Parke heretofore in the occupation of a schoolemaster. And all that Messuage Tenement or dwelling house wth the Appurtenances comonly called the old Lodge scituate on the East side of the said Parke in the parish of St Pancras als: Kentish Towne in the county of Midd. aforesaid together wth a Garden bounded wth a Pale at the Courtyard of the house conteyning in the whole by estimacion one Rode more or lesse. And all Barnes, stables and houses, edifaces, buildings, orchards, gardens, Court yards, waies, passages, comodities, and appurtenances whatsoever to the said severall Messuages, Tenements, or Dwellings belonging or in any wise apperteyning or therewth heretofore used occupied or enjoyed as part parcell or member thersof per ann°.

ALL the deere wthin the said Parke being in number 124 of severall sorts are valued to be worth Cxxx li

ALL the Trees remayning in the abovesaid parke being in nomber Thirteene thousand foure hundred Nynety twoo Trees of Oake, Ash, Service,[1] Elme, & Crabtree, white thorne, & Maple trees,

[1] A service tree is a small pear tree.

(besides Twoo thousand eight hundred and five marked out for the use of the Navy) are valued to be worth D vii^{c} lxxiiij^{li} viij^{s}

MEMORANDUM There is standing in the said parke a frame of three Bay of okan ould Timber uncovered wch is valued to be worth iij^{li} vj^{s} viij^{d}

MEMORANDUM the aforesaid premises are Tithefree. John Ipsley (as the Surveyors are informed) is Ranger or keeper of the said parke by order of the Comittee of the Revenue & Roger Gibbs the father, Francis Gibbs and John Gibbs his sonnes are his underkeepers & it is informed that they have killed three brace of Deeres run the Eleaventh day of July last by warrant & Comand from the said Mr. John Ipsley. Mr. Cary claimeth to be keeper of the said parke by pattent but he hath not made the same appeare although it was desired of him.

This particular is grounded uppon a Survey taken by Ralph Baldwin Gent & others in the moneth of December & by an Addicionall Survey returned in the moneth of July 1650 and is made for by order of the Committee the 20th day of March 1649. Examined and signed.

Jno. Wheatley, Dept. Rege.

Contracted for ye 3d of Aprill 1650.

The Parke and premises with the appurtenances above mentioned are contracted for and agreed to be sold unto John Spenser of London Gent. on ye behalf of Three Troopes of Colonell Thomas Harrison's Regemt. viz. ye Colonells Troope, Major Winthorpes & Capt. Bankes Troopes with other originall Creditors.

This Particular is rated in Fee Simple for Capt. John Spenser, Lieut. Tapp and Lieut Wm. Gough att eighteene yeares purchase for ye present yearly value of all that parcell of impaled ground commonly called or knowne by the name of Marybone Park being Six hundred Twenty Eight pounds and foure shillings in possession & ate ye grosse sume of one hundred Thirty pounds for deer of severall sorts upon ye premises & at one other grosse sume of one Thousand seaven hun. seaventy foure pounds, eight shillings for Tymber Trees . . . And att one other grosse sume of Three pounds six shillings and eight pence for A certeine Frame of three bayes of oaken old Tymber standing in the Park uncovered. According to which rates and values ye purchase money made payable and to be paid for ye premisses Amounts to ye sume of Thirteen thousand Two hundred & fifteene pounds six shillings and eight pence.

Whereof

The one Moity of ye Purchase money is to be paid and defalked within eight weekes now next ensueing The other Moity to be paid & defalked within six moneths next after ye first payment or defalk now aforesaid for payment or satisfaction of which latter Moity securitye is to be given to ye Treasury by a Lease for Fourscore and Nyneteene yeares of ye premisses hereby contracted for. And the whole Purchase to be paid or satisfied either in ready money or in originall debentors charged upon ye Creditt of ye Acts of Parliament aforesaid.

Jno. Wheatley Dept. Rege.

In Attestation of ye Contract and agreement above mentioned we the contractors whose names are subscribed have hereunto put our hands ye 10th day of April 1650.

Jo. Humfrey.

APPENDIX 7

Public Record Office, Crest 6, Vol 2, pp 224-226.

Marybone Parke

My Cosin Wandesford being to bring before my L^{o} Trasurer his petition & they being to be satisfied upon his Interest in Mary Bone pke. Pray for the Informacon of my L^{o} Treasurer will you State that businesse, What partes of ye Parke are free, What Clogged & what hee may have the possession of suitable to his Grant, what must be suspended in respect of any Consideration these tymes have made necessary. Or what you may thinke fitt wth Justice to them, & relation to the publick.

Sr. I am yo^{r}Son & Servt
P. Warwick

Tuesday Novr 20 1660
ffor Sr Charles Harbord.

May it please yor. Lo^{p}.

£	s	d	
			In obedience to yor Lo^{ps}. direccions of ye 20th Nov. last I have considered of the severall Interests and pretences of ye purchasors and Tenants in Marybone Parke, & do find that one Edw: Baker claymes to hold 45 acres & two roodes thereof und^{r} Harrison
68	5	0	lately convicted at ye Rent of 68£. 5s. 0d.
100	0	0	And that the same Edw: Baker claimes to hold 58 acres more of the sd. pke. late in Tapps possession at ye yearly Rent of 100^{ls}.
56	0	0	And that Jo: Stanton claimes to hold 20 acres of Land in ye sd. pke under the said Harrison at ye Rent of 56^{ls}.
89	0	0	And that Nich. Cotterell claimes to hold 40 acres of Land in the sd. Parke und^{r} ye sd. Harrison at ye yearly Rent of 89^{ls}.
160	0	0	And y^{t}: Willi: Tompson claimes to hold 120 acres of Land in ye sd Parke und^{r} Wm: Gough & John Barker late Purchasors thereof at ye Rent of 160^{ls}.
82	10	0	And that Mathew Barrett claimes to hold 55 acres late ye sd. Harrisons at ye Rent of 82^{ls}. 10^{s}.
111	14	10	And that Wm. Byard claimeth to hold 72 acres of Land there late ye sd. Harrisons at ye yearly Rent of 111^{ls}. 14^{s}. 10^{d}.
667	09	10	Sum totall of these Rents is 667^{ls}. 9^{s}. 10^{d} per annum, I find besides hold on by Mr. Clerke, Secretary to my Ld Generall 60 acres wth an
120	0	0	howse in the sd. Parke valued at 120^{ls} per annum. annum.
42	0	0	And by Symondson of the Army 28 acres valued at 42^{ls} per annum.
42	0	0	And by Nicholdson, Sutton & others of the Army 28 acres at 42^{ls} per annum.
204	0	0	Sum totall of these three last parcells is—204^{ls} per annum.
			But by ye Parl: Survey 534 acres valued at ye sum—628^{ls} 4^{s} 8^{d} per annum. So the sum totall of these annual values is—871^{ls} 9^{s} 10^{d}. And Mr Secretary Clarks being deducted there will remayn clare per annum—751^{ls} 9^{s} 10^{d}.

In case yor lo^{p} shall thinke fitt to admitt Sr Geo. Stroude & Mr. Wandesford to take ye possession of the sd. Parke & premises by vertue of his Ma^{ts} Letters patents to them granted dated ye 6th of May 21mo nuper Car. apud Oxon, & to enjoy benefitt thereof untill they shalbe satisfied for ye moneyes due unto them by vertue of his Ma^{ts} Contract about ye business of powder & Armes I humbly consider it fitt for yor Lo^{p} yt. Mr. Auditor Phillipps may take notice of ye sd. Letters patents & Contract & ye sd accompt thereupon to be made, & may keepe Copies or make Inrollm^{ts} of the same for his Ma^{ts} security that the said profitts maybe putt in charge by him and that his Ma^{ty} maybe restored to the possession thereof soo soone as the said Accompt shalbe satisffied, or discharged by any other way.

And care is to be taken that the said three last parcells may remaine in ye peasable possession of ye sd. Secretary Clarke and the Souldiers according to his Ma^{ts} Comand & yor Lo^{ps} warrant unto mee in that behalfe, untill they be satisfied, or that his Ma^{ty} shall otherwise detirmine thereof, All wch I humbly submitt to yor Lo^{ps} great. Wisdome, & shallbe ready to obey yor Lo^{ps} further direccion therein.

C. Harbord, Surveyor
5 December 1660

APPENDIX 8

Some valuations of Tyburn and Marylebone Park

1066	At the time of the Conquest, according to Domesday Book, Tyburn was worth	one hundred shillings.
	and Lillestone was worth	forty shillings.
1086	Domesday Book gives the current valuation of Tyburn as	fifty-two shillings.
	and of Lilleston as	sixty shillings.
1279	On the Middlesex Hundred Roll, Tyburn was valued at (probably an annual valuation.)	£3 3s $4\frac{3}{4}$d
1312	In the Inquisition Post Mortem of Alice de Vere, Tyburn was worth	£5 13s 4d

1347	In the Inquisition Post Mortem of John de Warenne, Earl of Surrey, Tyburn was worth	£11 19s 10d
1511	In his will, Thomas Hobson the Elder says that he has spent nearly	£1,000
	in purchasing and improving of land in Tyburn.	
1538	Thomas Hobson the Younger surrendered land to the value of	£203 5s 10d
	The land emparked was worth	£70 15s 2d
1611	The manor of Tyburn, with the exception of the Park, was sold to Forsett for	£829 3s 4d
1649	The Park was given an annual valuation of	£628 4s 0d
	and was sold for	£13,215 6s 8d
1668	The rental of the Park from this date onwards was	£36 14s 6d
	plus fines on the renewal of the lease,	
1708	The Duke of Newcastle bought Marylebone for	£17,500 0s 0d
1730	The income from the farms in the Park was	£1,217 5s 6d

APPENDIX 9

Some population figures for Marylebone

1086	There were eight families in Tyburn and eight in Lilleston (Domesday Book). Assuming there were approximately five persons in each family, there were in all	80 people.
1279	According to the Middlesex Hundred Roll, there was in Tyburn the manor house and nine families, perhaps	70 people.
1552	The Inventory of goods in the church, made by Edward VI's Commissioners, says there were sixty-six families, perhaps	350 people

1664	The Hearth Tax return lists sixty-six households, perhaps	350 people.
1674	The Hearth Tax return lists seventy-eight households, perhaps	400 people.
1750	According to the Rate Book for that year, there were 950 households, perhaps	5,000 people.
1801	Census Return	63,000 people.
1851	Census Return (for Parliamentary Borough of Marylebone, which included St Pancras and Holborn)	157,698 people
1951	Census Return	75,764 people.
1961	Census Return	69,045 people.

BIBLIOGRAPHY

MANUSCRIPT SOURCES

For Chapter 1, a variety of documents, chiefly in the Public Record Office, was used; details are given in the footnotes. Thereafter, the primary sources were :

1 Records of the Crown Estate Office, indicated by the reference *Crest*, and in the keeping of the Public Record Office.
2 St Marylebone rate books, 1683 onwards.
3 St Marylebone vestry minutes, 1725 onwards. Both these series are at present at the Old Town Hall, Marylebone Road, now belonging Westminster City Council.

All documents are in the Public Record Office, unless otherwise stated.

PRINTED SOURCES

The chief printed source is the Reports of the Commissioners which commence in 1787 and are as follows :

1 Reports of the Commissioners appointed to enquire into the state and conditions of the Woods, Forests, and Land Revenues of the Crown, and to sell or alienate fee farms and other unimprovable rents. Nos 1-17, 1787-93.
2 The Surveyor-General's Triennial Reports. Nos 1-4, 1797, 1802, 1806, 1809.
3 Reports of the Commissioners of His Majesty's Woods, Forests and Land Revenues. Nos 1-120, 1812-1942.
4 Reports of the Crown Estate Commissioners. No 1, 1957.

Particular authorities are quoted in the footnotes but the following books have been used throughout :

1 Davis, Terence. *The Architecture of John Nash*, Studio, 1960. 137 pp, plates, illus, plans, folio.

2 Elmes, James. *Metropolitan improvements; or, London in the nineteenth century; being a series of views of the new and most interesting objects in the British metropolis and its vicinity, from original drawings by Mr Thos. H. Shepherd, with historical, topographical and critical illustrations by James Elmes.* Jones & Co, 1827. xlii, 316 pp, plates, map. 8vo.

3 Eyre, Alan Montgomery. *Saint John's Wood: its history, its houses, its haunts and its celebrities.* Chapman & Hall, 1913. xii, 312 pp, plates, ports, maps. 8vo.

4 Fraser, Sir Ronald. *A House in the Park.* Cape, 1937. 456 pp. 8vo. The house is The Holme, the period before and after the First World War. Not a good novel but worth reading for its evocation of a leisured life in idyllic surroundings.

5 Mitchell, P. Chalmers. *Centenary history of the Zoological Society of London.* Zoological Society, 1929. xi, 307 pp, plates, ports, plans. 8vo.

6 St Marylebone—Borough Council. *Handlist to the Ashbridge Collection on the history and topography of St Marylebone.* Compiled by Ann Cox-Johnson. 1959. vi, 215 pp. 8vo. Reproduced from typescript.

7 St Marylebone—Borough Council. *St Marylebone*; a sketch of its historical development [by A. J. D. Stonebridge], 1952. 16 pp, maps. 8vo.

8 Shepard, Ernest Howard. *Drawn from memory.* Methuen, 1957. 190 pp, illus. 8vo. The author illustrated A. A. Milne's 'Christopher Robin' books. His childhood, spent in Kent Terrace, is described in word and line.

9 Sheppard, Francis Henry Wellaston. *Local government in St Marylebone, 1688-1835; a study of the Vestry and Turnpike Trust.* Athlone Press, 1953. 326 pp, plates, port, maps. 8vo. The best modern book on St Marylebone; its scope is far wider than the title suggests.

10 Smith, Thomas. *A topographical and historical account of the parish of St Mary-le-bone, Comprising a copious description of its public buildings, antiquities, schools, charitable endowments, sources of public amusement, &c, with biographical notices of eminent persons.* John Smith, 1833. 319 pp, 6 plates, map. 8vo. Still the standard history.

11 Spencer, Herbert. *London's Canal; the history of the Regent's Canal.* Putnam, 1961. 183 pp, plates, illus, maps. 8vo.

12 Summerson, Sir John. *Georgian London.* Pelican Books, 1962. 348 pp, plates, illus, maps. 8vo.

13 Summerson, Sir John. *John Nash, architect to King George IV.* George Allen & Unwin, 1949, 299 pp, plates, port, illus, maps. 8vo.

14 Webster, A. D. *The Regent's Park and Primrose Hill; history and antiquities.* Greening, 1911. x, 11-112 pp, plates, maps. 8vo. The author was the superintendent of the Gardens.

15 White, John. *Some account of the proposed improvements of the western part of London, by the formation of the Regent's Park, the New Street, the new sewer, &c, &c; illustrated by a variety of plans and accompanied by explanatory and critical observations . . . The second edition, with additions.* Cadell & Davies, 1815, xciv pp, maps, plans. 8vo.

AUTHOR'S NOTES AND ACKNOWLEDGEMENTS

This book began as a Ph D thesis for Leicester University and I would like to thank them for their generosity in granting me a research scholarship from 1963 to 1965. Any merit this volume may have is chiefly due to the invaluable guidance of Professor H. P. R. Finberg; he is in no way to blame for the blemishes that remain.

I am most grateful to Mr Osborne and Mr Shaw of the Crown Estate Office, and to the staffs of the British Museum, the Public Record Office, and the Guildhall Library. I owe more than I can say to Mr A. J. D. Stonebridge and Mrs C. Gee, lately of St Marylebone Public Library, to Dr Helen Wallis of the British Museum, to Dr Patricia Barnes of the Public Records Office, and to Mr and Mrs John Kirby of the History Faculty Library at Oxford. I should also like to thank Mr T. Collins, Mrs Marie Draper, Mrs Mary Heathcote, Mr David Johnson, Dr Gerda Kircher, Miss Alison Reeve, Dr Ian Roy, Dr Alwyn Ruddock, Miss Veronica Stokes and Sir John Summerson, and I am indebted to the late Professor T. F. Reddaway for valued advice. Westminster City Council, of which St Marylebone is now a part, have done much to encourage the work.

My family have helped me with unfailing encouragement and my husband has drawn the maps which appear in the book. I should like to dedicate this book to my mother who first introduced me to the Park, and to my son Matthew with whom I re-explored it.

January, 1969 ANN SAUNDERS

INDEX

Illustrations are indicated by italic figures